IT ONLY TAKES
One

DR. GARY V. WHETSTONE

WHITAKER
HOUSE

IT ONLY TAKES ONE

ISBN: 0-88368-868-9
Printed in the United States of America
© 2003 by Gary V. Whetstone

Whitaker House
30 Hunt Valley Circle
New Kensington, PA 15068
Visit our web site at: www.whitakerhouse.com

Library of Congress Cataloging-in-Publication Data

Whetstone, Gary.
  It only takes one / by Gary V. Whetstone.
      p.   cm.
  ISBN 0-88368-868-9 (trade pbk. : alk. paper)
  1. Christian life.   2. Success—Religious aspects—Christianity.   I. Title.
  BV4598.3 .W48 2003
  248.4—dc21   2002153466

2 3 4 5 6 7 8 9 10 11 12 / 10 09 08 07 06 05 04 03

Endorsements

The level of teaching that Pastor Gary Whetstone brings to the table is absolutely incredible! You need this. It's going to take you to the next level. You are hearing from somebody who's not just been in the boardroom, but has been right there on the field fighting—and he knows what he's talking about.

—Bishop T. D. Jakes
The Potter's House, Dallas, Texas

Gary and Faye Whetstone attended our church in Tulsa before they began the powerful work that they now have in Delaware. We're excited about the new Bible training they have, to put God's Word practically into people's lives. They have a vision to reach the world for Jesus Christ. We recommend highly what Gary and Faye Whetstone are doing.

—Billy Joe Daugherty, Senior Pastor
Victory Christian Center, Tulsa, Oklahoma

I have been in the pulpits of the world with Gary Whetstone and have personally witnessed the anointing and power that God uses through him literally to change lives. The quality and the depth of his teaching, its interdenominational flavor, its anointed power is something that I encourage you to take advantage of.

—Charles E. Blair, Pastor Emeritus
Calvary Temple, Denver, Colorado

Gary Whetstone is an incredible pastor, teacher, and evangelist to the nations of the world, and he is spiritually qualified to head up this marvelous biblical study. I wholeheartedly recommend this biblical study.

—Morris Cerullo, President
Morris Cerullo World Evangelism, San Diego, California

I believe all those who come under the anointed teaching and the ministry of Pastor Whetstone will be thoroughly equipped to gather in the end-time harvest before the imminent return of our Lord and Savior.

—Rod Parsley, Senior Pastor
World Harvest Church, Columbus, Ohio

Stories from New Champions on the Rise

My husband was a pastor who had left the ministry and gone into a lifestyle of homosexuality and drugs. I had been standing for my marriage, but when I heard how God had restored the marriage of Pastors Gary and Faye, my hope was renewed. They agreed with me in prayer for my husband to come back. Less than three months later, he returned home! God reunited us, and my husband was restored. Before he died of AIDS a year and a half later, we began an HIV/AIDS ministry and our daughter was able to spend time with her dad. When I heard that it only took one spouse to stand for a marriage, it ignited my faith to stand on the Word for my marriage. God's Word works! He said it, and He did it!

—Judy Sanders, Associate Pastor

As Dr. Gary Whetstone has taught the Word, God birthed in me the dream that I could break through the barriers of debt and my mind-set of lack. After stepping out in faith and being faithful in giving tithes and offerings, I am receiving God's blessings. A brand-new car was given to me. Credit-card debt no longer holds me captive, and I have no financial debts except my mortgage. Living to give, as Pastor Gary says, is the only way!

—Kathy Jakubowski, Graphic Designer

From the lessons in *It Only Takes One* by Dr. Gary Whetstone, I discovered that God can use people who feel that they are in insignificant positions to affect His kingdom in greater ways than they could ever have imagined!

—Brian Hadley, Video Editor/Producer

Through Dr. Gary Whetstone's instruction, God has changed me from one who lived controlled by the world to one with the divine revelation of right standing and absolute truth. I have developed an awesome fellowship with God the Father, my Savior Jesus Christ, and my Teacher and Comforter the Holy Spirit.

—Andrea Curato, Pastoral Administrative Assistant

Contents

Preface 7

Introduction 9

1. Unlock Your Future with One New Thought 12

2. God Awakens You—His Champion 20

3. Behold His Masterpiece in the Mirror 55

4. Forward Momentum 76

5. Just Step Out 103

6. Break through Every Barrier 128

7. Make Resistance Work for You 161

8. The Driving Force of a Dreamer 187

9. Focus on the Finish 212

10. The Master Multiplier 237

Gary Whetstone Worldwide Ministries 262

About the Author 264

Notes 266

Preface

To my surprise in 1971, I had a personal encounter with God. He began to reveal to me how to break through every limiting barrier in my life. During the next twenty years, I experienced a whirlwind of challenges and a multitude of successes. Then, in 1991, I knew that it was God's plan to unveil in this book the awesome power, authority, and influence that one person possesses. At that time, demand was strong for me to publish *It Only Takes One*, sharing how I broke through the barriers that divided my family, destroyed our finances, and basically left us with a dismal future.

Also in 1991, publishers and producers offered contracts to me to write other books, produce a movie, and teach a nationwide daily television program. To encourage me to make the commitment, one publisher even flew his private jet to give our church a substantial gift. At first glance, all this attention appeared to be God opening doors for me to minister both nationally and internationally to much larger audiences. However, the Spirit of the Lord revealed that this was not His timing. So I did not accept or sign any of these contracts, regardless of how good the opportunities seemed. Instead, I trusted God's clear direction.

Until now—more than thirty years after my initial encounter with God—I have not had a release in my heart to write this book. Throughout these decades, I have seen God change and empower countless thousands of people by the tested and proven truths now revealed in this book. God's mandate is clear: "Move My people from limitation to liberation!"

Now *It Only Takes One* is in your hands. Use it as *your* tool to walk in the fullness of your destiny! This is *your* time to discover how to step into your life's dreams!

Introduction

I hate you! I hate you!" These words rang out in the ears of a young man in the grip of mental torment, confusion, and marital breakup with two small children. A barrage of failure crashed in around him. Life no longer seemed worth living. Suicide appeared to be the only way out. In 1975, that was my—Gary Whetstone's—story.

Rise from Destruction to Victory

The story you are about to read is true. When life's challenges become almost unbearable, the Bible proclaims that God has an answer. He will *"make the way of escape, that you may be able to bear it"* (1 Corinthians 10:13). That is the story of my life. Every time I have faced what seems to be an impossible situation, God has always had a plan of escape for me.

But in 1975, my life had gone from bad to worse: from a terrible time of mental torment beginning in 1968 through 1972; to the pressures of marriage and having two children; to struggling for financial stability; and then ultimately to hearing my wife, Faye, scream at me, "I hate you! I hate you!" Finally, our marriage ended in divorce in 1975. Destruction held me in its death grip at nearly every level of my life: mentally, financially, emotionally, and physically; every area of my life was in jeopardy—my family, my job, and seemingly my relationship with God.

9

Then, one day I saw the answer! I discovered principles in the Bible that changed the course of my life. The truth that God revealed to me completely restored my life. I remarried my wife, Faye, and became the husband and father that God had intended me to be. His power, peace, and fulfilled promises flooded my life. My friend, that's where God wants to take you through this book. Get ready to experience His awesome power, peace, and fulfilled promises as never before!

Don't Be a Casualty of the Conflict

As you read this book, realize that your God-given destiny is within reach! You will learn how to gain the spoils from your greatest battles rather than becoming a casualty of the conflict. Your greatest strengths with God come to light during your greatest days of darkness.

As you read *It Only Takes One*, you will see yourself reflected throughout each chapter. Be honest in identifying yourself. This book will uncover barriers that have held you back and show you how to break through. It will be an incredible journey of power and deliverance.

The story that I briefly shared earlier occurred during the most difficult years of my life. I faced tragedy, disappointment, and disillusionment. Some of my suffering was self-inflicted, some came from my family's past, and some resulted from circumstances outside my control. As the pain culminated, my life became a living hell on earth.

Today, are you or someone you know facing overwhelming circumstances? Are you wondering, *How can I ever get out of this grip of failure and destruction?* Maybe the battle is in your marriage or family. Perhaps your vocation lies in the ashes of disaster. Do you feel as though your future is at stake? Maybe the problems threaten even your very fellowship with God. Take heart! In this book, you will discover how to conquer every conflict with confidence.

Break through to Your Destiny

My friend, the decision is in your hands. Do you want to break through to make a difference? If so, this is a day of supernatural transformation for you! Today is like no other day in your life.

You have in your hands a book that can connect you to your destiny—a destiny that no one else can fulfill except you. The deliverance and breakthroughs are here to catapult you over every obstacle that you face. Don't let your victory slip away. Get started right now on the road to your dreams by simply turning this page!

1
Unlock Your Future with One New Thought

I n the midst of the destruction, ash heaps, and ruins of life's conflicts, failures, and frustrations, God raises up champions. Throughout history, we have seen countless individuals win life's battles against great odds. I am one of those who won, and my life has never been the same!

The reason I was able to rise from destruction to victory, as I will share in detail later, is that I experienced a God-inspired, life-giving new thought. One of the greatest challenges in our generation today is that few people are getting any new thoughts that have the power to change their lives.

Experience God's Champion Thoughts— A New Mind-Set

In this book, you will experience one new thought after another. I call these *champion thoughts*. You will discover principles and God-authored truths that will empower you to bring dreams to reality. This is likely to be a new way of thinking for you because it is not the normal mind-set of most people, including many in the church. These are not natural thoughts but supernatural, God-inspired, proven champion thoughts that will bring you into victory.

In *It Only Takes One*, I am not attempting to establish *new* truths but will bring to light the *power* and *application* of God's timeless truths. In other words, I want to help you operate at a new level. His truths can literally *enable* you to receive their full benefits and cause you to live as the champion that God intended. As you learn how to unleash the power of truth in your life, you will walk in a newfound freedom.

CHAMPION THOUGHT:
Truth Has Authority

Did you know that truth in itself has "the power...[and] right to control, command, or determine" an outcome?[1] Indeed it does. In fact, this is the definition of the word *authority*. In other words, truth has authority. It is so powerful that once truth is discovered, nothing can stop it.

CHAMPION THOUGHT:
Simply Knowing the Truth Liberates You

Notice, I stated that when truth is *discovered*, nothing can stop it. Jesus said, "And you shall **know the truth**, and the truth [that you become intimately aware of] *shall make you free*" (John 8:32, emphasis added). You see, Jesus revealed here that truth in itself is the freeing or liberating agent. Truth will make you free. It is not the individual who believes the truth. It is not the actions of an informed person. Nor is it a rational or logical approach that creates the freedom. No, truth stands on its own. Just by coming to *know* it, Jesus explained, you step into the liberating experience of the truth. Knowing it unleashes the power of truth's authority in your life. As you continue through the pages of *It Only Takes One*, you will begin to understand the power of truth.

What You Don't Know Has Already Hurt You

Knowing the truth is critical. The world says, "What you don't know won't hurt you." The truth is *What you don't know has already hurt you.* All the problems, pain, and disappointments that you have experienced so far are the result of not knowing the truth that will set you free in those areas. That's why God said in His Word, "*My people are destroyed for lack of knowledge*" (Hosea 4:6).

Yes, what you don't know has *already* hurt you, but I have good news for you! The truth that you are *about to know* will change your life. It will give you what is commonly known as a breakthrough. In fact, it will bring one breakthrough after another.

CHAMPION THOUGHT:
The Interjection of Truth Breaks through Limitations

It's time for *your* breakthrough. Let me give you a snapshot of what this word means. I have heard it shared—and now have seen it proven—that a *breakthrough* is "the sudden burst of advanced knowledge that goes through every barrier or line of defense."

It is important to understand that living in your former mind-set with yesterday's experiences keeps you bound in the limitations of your history, only to repeat it. However, a "sudden burst of advanced knowledge" has the power to catapult you through those barriers to new horizons. This advanced knowledge, which is knowing the truth about the future, has the power to break through what you consider to be your past and present reality.

You see, to break through, you must interject advanced knowledge into your circumstances. When you shine its light into an area of your life, truth bears its authority against your defeated mind-sets, frustrations, inabilities, restrictions, and walls of limitation. These barriers then must bow to the power of that truth. Why? It is because the authority of truth is greater than any inhibiting influence you face.

Understand the Authority of Truth

Yes, truth has authority over everything that tries to withstand it. Nothing can stop truth once it is unveiled. For instance, in each case that comes before a court of law, the prosecution presents evidence against the accused, who offers his or her defense. The court may hear believable testimony from eyewitnesses and learn other convincing evidence. However, irrefutable proof of truth, such as DNA, can break through even the strongest, credible evidence. In a court of law, all opinion is silenced when the evidence is proven as the truth. Truth pierces everything that people have seen and testified about because the truth has greater influence than opinions, views, and even agreeing perceptions of the facts. Proven truth silences and mutes all other arguments.

Today, we are seeing media reports about the reevaluation of some criminal cases. After a significant amount of evidence was presented and people were convicted of crimes years ago, many are now being released from prison because of wrong convictions. Years later, new evidence is being introduced that is proving their innocence. Because of new scientific discoveries, it can now be established that some of these individuals did not commit the crimes for which they are serving time. Unfortunately, in these situations, innocent people paid the penalty for our lack of having access to truth.

Maybe there is growing evidence against *your* life—mistakes you have made, sins against God, failures in life, lack of taking appropriate action, or the inability to pursue your dreams. Perhaps you are guilty of not living in the fullness of all that God created for you. If so, the truths that you will experience in this book will break through that mounting evidence to bring you into freedom.

These Principles Work for Everyone

These truths will work for you. In fact, these principles operate for people in all walks of life regardless of whether they are new, growing, or mature believers—and even if they are unbelievers. The truths that cause you to live as a champion work for everyone equally because *"God is no respecter of persons"* (Acts 10:34 KJV). For this reason, you will read stories in this book about believers in the Lord Jesus, as well as those who are not Christians, who have experienced breakthroughs. Regardless of their backgrounds, each discovered how to unleash the authority of God's truths to influence his or her environment.

Not Theory but Practical Application

Many of us are familiar with being taught by people who have never applied the information they teach. For example, it is common to learn business principles from a professor who never owned a business or to receive marriage counseling from someone who has never been married. There is a major difference between theory and real-life experience. This book does not contain man's theory. Instead, it reveals established, eternal biblical truths that have the actual, real-life authority to create a future of fulfillment and success for you! God's Word is established. His truths are unchangeable, and they *do* carry their authority forward into your future.

CHAMPION THOUGHT:
Break the Molds of the Limiting Clichés

A common barrier that will stop many truths from penetrating people's lives occurs when they refuse to know the truth.

Former mind-sets and beliefs about the status quo, or current condition, often stand as defenses against any new thoughts of truth. That's why we hear negative clichés, such as You can't teach an old dog new tricks, or explanations that the younger generation has a different way and will not work together with the older generation. Why? Is age such a resistant factor? Or has the information and application of that information become stagnated in the minds of some? Champion thoughts are often met with resistance because people hold on to past ways of doing things. They counter new thoughts with, "But it's always been done this way."

Have you blamed others for your lack of fulfillment? Have you heard or even found yourself quoting limiting clichés as reasons why you cannot move forward? Are you hiding behind these or similar excuses?

- It takes two to tango.
- It's a 50/50 proposition.
- Life is not one-sided. It's a give-and-take world.
- Everyone expects something in return, i.e., *quid pro quo*.
- You scratch my back, and I'll scratch yours.
- It's not *my* job.
- If I only had _____, I could or would _____.
- When my ship comes in, I'll....
- I was not born with a silver spoon in my mouth.
- I don't have a rich uncle.
- I grew up on the wrong side of the tracks.
- When it rains, it pours.
- Murphy's Law: If something can go wrong, it will.
- *Qué será, será*—What will be, will be.
- Get real. This is how it is.
- You'll just have to learn to live with it.

It is time to break the old molds. Destroy all the wrong beliefs. Remove limiting thoughts from your mind, such as "If I only had...." Get rid of all the hindering perspectives that have turned into excuses.

CHAMPION THOUGHT:
Continuing in Yesterday's Thoughts Will Bring You Only to Where You Have Been

---

You must realize that you are living in the fullness of all that you have known so far. Otherwise, you would not be where you are right now. In fact, if you continue to do and think the same as yesterday, you will go only to where you have been. If you want to live in your past failures, then immediately close this book and put it down! Otherwise, if you keep reading, I will put more than a challenge before you. You will be faced with a mandate of change, and you will experience truths that will empower you to make that change.

Breakthrough Thinking—Your Charge to Change

Are you frustrated? My definition of *frustration* is "knowing the need for change, but not having the ability to bring it about." Are you facing barriers that you can't see your way through? Are your dreams out of reach? If your answer is, "Yes," then you need a real change.

The champion thoughts in this book will cause you to know what you have never known. You will be what you have never been. Then, you can move to where you could never go and do what you were unable to do. *It Only Takes One* will provoke your mind to a new way of thinking. Its truths are not to excite you but to incite you to action. If you want a change, then get ready for your breakthrough.

Truths such as the following will set you free:

• Your history has no authority to forecast your future once you experience a breakthrough.

- Truths you learn will free you to initiate a new tomorrow.
- God gives big dreams to unqualified people in small places to reveal His glory.
- Cancel the harvest of your past by planting new seeds for your future.

You have probably heard it said that graveyards are the greatest deposits of unfulfilled dreams and visions. Don't allow yours to be added to that tragedy. Realize that, yes, your dreams *can* come true. This book will show you how. Consider the pages that you are about to read as a roadmap to a future that has been out of your reach until now.

2
God Awakens You— His Champion

A re you ready to discover one of the most powerful truths in the entire Bible? Your life will never be the same as you grasp the truth about righteousness. This key unlocks all that God has for you. Before you can know how to fulfill your dreams, you must understand your position and purpose. This and the next chapter will lay the foundation in these two areas before we launch into revealing how to walk in your dreams. My friend, I stand in awe of what God is about to do with your life. Get ready!

CHAMPION THOUGHT:
Live Freer than Religion Allows

While throughout time man has recognized the need for a relationship with God, he often has not sought it based upon God's will as revealed in the Bible. Consequently, humanity has created erroneous traditions, rituals, attitudes, doctrines, and theologies all in the name of religion. In this, mankind has accepted a form or structure of religion as a substitute for God Himself.

We must not serve and worship God according to man-made doctrines. We have to do it God's way! Jesus said, *"But seek first the kingdom of God and His righteousness, and all these things shall be added to you"* (Matthew 6:33).

The focus here is on *"His righteousness,"* not our attempts to become righteous! You see, what many call *religion* is really man's attempt to find God or become righteous enough that God will accept him. It is a human interpretation of what people should do or not do to become right with God.

There are many sincere people in the religious world. Being sincere, though, does not mean that what you believe is actually *true*. The danger is that you could be sincerely *wrong!* The Bible, which reveals God's will, is the ultimate guide to all truth.

Man's religion lulls its followers into a lukewarm state and holds them captive with strict religious adherence and rigorous rules. But God wants us to live *freer* than religion allows. In other words, we need to live without more restraint. Life already has many restrictions. We do not need additional limitations from man's self-imposed religion.

CHAMPION THOUGHT:
God and His Word Free You to Live in Righteousness Consciousness

---

Now, if so much of religion is man-made, how can we know the difference between man's misguided attempts to find God and God's true will? The answer is clear. Man's religion, tradition, and wisdom heap upon humanity what I call *sin consciousness*, while God and His Word free us to live in *righteousness consciousness*.

Sin consciousness is the focus on one's sins, shortcomings, failures, inability, and anything that causes insecurity, inferiority, shame, guilt, or condemnation.

Righteousness consciousness is the focus on Jesus' finished work on the cross at Calvary and on His resurrection, which brought man into right standing with God as if sin had never existed.

This awareness frees one to walk in Jesus' victory and authority to accomplish God's purposes.

In the Bible, the word translated as *righteousness* is used to mean "right relationship with God" or "uprightness."[1] The *Amplified Bible* explains it as *"right standing with God"* (Genesis 15:6). Righteousness is the ability to stand in the presence of God without any sense of guilt or inferiority, as if sin had never existed. When we do not understand the effects of God's righteousness, we consequently doom ourselves to walk in sin consciousness.

Jesus Christ is a gift to you. He freely gave you His righteousness and grace. The apostle Paul declared, *"But unto every one of us is given grace according to the measure of the gift of Christ"* (Ephesians 4:7 KJV).

The Bible also clearly teaches that *everyone* who accepts Jesus Christ as Savior is made righteous by His blood, which He shed on the cross: *"For he [the Father] hath made him [the Son, Jesus] to be sin for us, who knew no sin; that we might be made the righteousness of God in him"* (2 Corinthians 5:21 KJV).

Notice here that Jesus *"made"* us righteous. It is a state of being for us, not one we struggle to become. Righteousness is not what man attains but a gift he receives. You already *are* what Jesus has made you. When you repent of your sins and accept His gift of salvation, you don't have to do anything to *become* right with Him.

In this verse that we've just read, we see that Jesus became sin, not by His sin but by ours. The Bible tells us that *"while we were still sinners"* (Romans 5:8), God took everything wrong in mankind and put it upon His sinless Son Jesus. He made Jesus sin for us to bring us into right standing with Himself. This divine action frees us from all religious manipulations and dogmas requiring action on our part to gain God's acceptance. We cannot achieve this righteousness through self-discipline, behavioral changes, or strict religious adherence. Jesus did it all for us. He gave His righteousness to us as a gift in exchange for our unrighteousness. The righteousness of God removes the cover from man's works and reveals us not naked but clothed in God's right standing.

Therefore, as Christians, our past sins should no longer affect us. We might remember them, but they are merely information, unable to impact our lives. We should no longer have emotional scars that attach us to the events. In short, while you might remember your sins, God's objective is for the Cross to set you free from the *effects* or the *condemnation* of those sins.

CHAMPION THOUGHT:
Focus on What Jesus Did Right, Not on What You've Done Wrong

Have you ever noticed that the more you look at sin, the bigger it becomes? On the other hand, the more you focus on God's gift of righteousness, the less sin becomes amplified. Therefore, if you examine anything, it should be your position in His righteousness, not your sinful barriers. The way to escape sin consciousness is not to focus on what you've done wrong but on what Jesus did right.

I suggest that not only during Communion but also throughout every day of your life, you examine what Jesus did for you in and through His death and resurrection. When you do this, you step from the rule of sin into the freedom of fellowship with Christ.

If you don't understand Jesus' righteousness in you, then you have the power to say only how miserable and sin ruled you are. If you focus on your sins, you will live in bondage emotionally, mentally, psychologically, and perceptively. This way of living is not biblical.

Consider how most people perceive life and relate to God and others. Many of us suffer from inferiority, insecurity, shame, guilt, and condemnation. Learn to recognize these symptoms of what I call sin sickness, and you will be well on your way to defeating sin consciousness in your life!

CHAMPION THOUGHT:
You Are God's Champion, Not Inferior

The first symptom of sin sickness that we will discuss is inferiority. The word *inferior* means "to be less....It signifies to be overcome, in the sense of being subdued and enslaved."[2] Inferiority can affect your relationships with God and with others. Man's religion continually tells us how sinful and inferior we are in the presence of a holy God. However, the truth is that Jesus took all our sinfulness, so we are now free to come into God's presence without any fear. We can know that He will accept us as we are because of Jesus' righteousness: *"To the praise of the glory of His grace, by which He has made us accepted in the Beloved"* (Ephesians 1:6).

I have heard it stated that *grace* is "God's **R**iches **A**t **C**hrist's **E**xpense." It is *"God's unmerited favor"* (v. 2 AMP). Because of Jesus, God completely and instantly accepts you as you are when you come to Him.

Therefore, because God has accepted you through Christ's righteousness and grace, you can approach His throne without any sense of inferiority. The book of Hebrews encourages us to *"come boldly to the throne of grace, that we may obtain mercy and find grace to help in time of need"* (Hebrews 4:16).

When are you to go to God? Anytime you need help, He is ready to receive you. No accusations of inferiority can stand against you because the Bible declares: *"Now hath he* [Jesus] *reconciled in the body of his flesh through death, to present you holy and unblameable and unreproveable in his sight"* (Colossians 1:21–22 KJV). Because of Jesus, you are now *"holy and unblameable and unreproveable."*

Can you identify any feelings of inferiority present in your interactions with others? They might be caused by your weight, height, hair color, race, ethnicity, nationality, genetics, age, education, social status, skills, gifts, talents, economic level, or other areas. Many of us are self-conscious, which means that we allow our senses to rule us. This is sin consciousness, which makes us very aware of ourselves and our natural limitations. We walk in this natural perspective instead of remembering our supernatural relationship with God. Righteousness consciousness, on the other hand, causes us to see ourselves as *"more than conquerors,"* with the ability to fellowship with God. The Bible says, *"Yet in all these things we are more than conquerors through Him who loved us"* (Romans 8:37).

You should have the conquering consciousness of a champion. Walking as a champion is righteousness consciousness, while walking in defeat is sin consciousness. Jesus has made you victorious. Remember that you are not *becoming* a champion. If you are a Christian, then you *already are* God's champion.

CHAMPION THOUGHT:
There's No Need to Be Insecure—Perfect Love Casts Out Fear

The next symptom of sin sickness that we will address is insecurity. The *American Heritage Dictionary* defines *insecure* as "not sure or certain; doubtful....Inadequately guarded or protected; unsafe....Lacking self-confidence; plagued by anxiety." An insecure person often lacks boldness and is defensive. This symptom of sin sickness causes him to use natural remedies, rely on natural plans, and resort to natural wisdom. He also usually lacks faith regarding his health, financial stability, and peace of mind.

If you are insecure, you are attempting to operate in your own ability instead of being the fearless believer who stands in the assurance of Jesus' love and acceptance. If you will trust in His love, it will cast out all your fear, enabling you to *"do all things through Christ who strengthens"* you (Philippians 4:13). The Word of God promises: *"There is no fear in love; but perfect love casts out fear, because fear involves torment. But he who fears has not been made perfect in love"* (1 John 4:18).

Insecurity is easy to detect because of the fear and sense of dread that accompanies it. Right now, think about your future. Do you picture something going wrong? Are you apprehensive about what might lie ahead? Do you fear that a cataclysmic event will occur that will require greater ability to handle than you possess? It could be marital dysfunction, economic chaos, some form of physical breakdown, or another challenge. If you think in this fear-filled way, that is insecurity.

God wants to banish these perceptions from you, so that you can begin to move with His Spirit. They hang like heavy weights around your neck. When insecurity affects you, you tend to restrict yourself from certain activities and environments because you perceive that you cannot conquer them relying on Christ alone. That is sin consciousness. Because you do not see yourself in right standing with God, you forget that you are His champion. Remember that, as the Bible teaches, He is greater in you than all your obstacles: *"You are of God, little children, and have overcome them, because He who is in you is greater than he who is in the world"* (v. 4).

CHAMPION THOUGHT:
The Cure of Shame: Let "the Right" in You Dispel "the Wrong"

Another symptom of sin sickness is shame. In the *American Heritage Dictionary,* the word *shame* is defined as "a painful emotion caused by a strong sense of guilt, embarrassment, unworthiness, or disgrace" or "one that brings dishonor, disgrace, or condemnation."

Shame is troubling you if you continually remember and feel the effects of something dishonoring in your life. Perhaps you have had an abortion, engaged in premarital sex, or suffered a breach in a relationship, and shame resulting from any of these experiences repeatedly dogs you. Maybe you are overweight, and you are embarrassed about how you look. Possibly a member of your family has dishonored you or your family name.

How do you defeat shame? The answer is not by doing penance or making amends to God. You defeat shame by becoming righteousness conscious. I am more concerned about putting "the right" into you than removing "the wrong." You see, understanding your right standing in God dispels the wrong attitudes you have adopted.

CHAMPION THOUGHT:
No One on Earth Can Remove Your Guilt, but One in Heaven Already Has

---

Another symptom of sin sickness is *guilt,* which means "the fact or state of having committed an offense, crime, violation, or wrong" or "a feeling of responsibility or remorse for some offense, crime, wrong, etc., whether real or imagined."[3]

This is different from the emotional effect of shame because guilt is the *fact* that you committed an offense or the *sense of responsibility* for a wrong, whereas shame is a painful *emotion* about an event, act, or circumstance. Now, shame and guilt can exist because of real or imagined events, acts, or circumstances. People also can feel shame and guilt because of others' actions and circumstances over which they have no control.

Think about your life. Is there a point in time when you missed the mark and you feel guilty about it? This can be in any area of life. Maybe you had a premarital relationship. Possibly you said something wrong to your supervisor or did a halfhearted job on an assignment. Perhaps you stole money or physically harmed someone. Whatever it is, now you cannot get past that one act. Do you continually dwell on it, thinking, *If only I had never done it, I would be in a different place in life?*

This chapter will show you how to eradicate guilt and the emotional effect of the shame that goes with it. You might be thinking, *Well, how can anyone take away my guilt? It's a proven fact that I am guilty. I cannot go back in time to undo what I did. Nobody can unscramble my scrambled eggs.*

That's partially true. No one on earth can remove your guilt, but I know One in heaven who can! Not only *can* He, but the good news is that He *already* has! When Jesus died on the cross, He took all your sins upon Himself. He buried all your guilt, shame, and penalties. Then, when He rose from the dead, He rewrote your history. He wiped clean the slate of your life and wrote on it, "Not guilty," with His very own blood!

When you accept Jesus as your Savior, you accept what He has already done for you. You become free of all guilt. Although your past record of wrongs no longer exists with Him, you might have to pay some natural penalties because of what you did. However, now you have liberty in Christ. Not only that, but also you will live eternally with Him in heaven!

It is important to understand a common practice that accompanies guilt. Many people make guilt offerings in an effort to ease their consciences. Thinking that they can reduce their guilt, they might even participate in "Christian" activities, such as prayer, giving, church attendance, or singing in the choir. On the outside, Christians and even church leaders might appear to have a strong desire to serve God, but their true motivations can be guilt-ridden. Sadly, they might not recognize it.

We must become less aware of our past failures, focusing instead on God's power to change our lives and circumstances. No religious activity can remove our guilt. Righteousness consciousness must penetrate our sin consciousness. Only this can free us from our sense of guilt. Jesus already paid the price. We simply must receive His free gift.

CHAMPION THOUGHT:
Jesus Has Cancelled Your Penalty

Another symptom of sin sickness is condemnation. The word *condemn* means "to pronounce to be guilty; sentence to punishment."[4] Condemnation is the sentence of future penalty following judgment. It is the sentence passed because of an action that has occurred. In a court of law, for example, a judge may find a person guilty of murder and condemn or sentence him to life in prison.

Condemnation happens not only to people who commit crimes. We also see it in everyday life. If you commit adultery, for example, your sentence, humanly speaking, is that you will never have a healthy marriage. Apart from God, you will never be able to love effectively again because this sin has marred your life. Because of it, your future sentence looks very bleak.

Nothing—not even religious activity—can change your future sentence (condemnation). The reason for this is that you cannot change your past facts (guilt). However, as we discussed earlier, Jesus can change it! In fact, He already has. As He removed your guilt, He canceled your condemnation. That's why the Bible proclaims, *"There is therefore now no condemnation to those who are in Christ Jesus"* (Romans 8:1). Jesus broke all rejection and ended all condemnation.

When you accept Jesus' finished work on the cross, there is no future spiritual penalty for your past offenses. God forgives you of your sins (guilt) and brings you into right relationship with Him as if your sin never existed. He annuls all your future spiritual penalties (condemnation), so you do not have to walk in them. God not only rewrites your history but also your future!

Champion Thought:
When Righteousness Consciousness Overcomes Sin Consciousness, Nothing Can Limit You

Righteousness consciousness makes you constantly aware of your position in Christ. Similarly, sin consciousness makes you constantly aware of your position with the enemy, who has his grip of destruction, death, and inability on your life. Righteousness consciousness acts like a catapult on an aircraft carrier. It immediately thrusts you into the awareness of the Holy Spirit's abilities in you. It releases you from your perceived limitations and the devil's clutch.

If you submit to God's righteousness, then you catapult over all condemnation, accusation, ridicule, inferiority, insignificance, and the sense of inability. You realize that your right standing with God is not because of your ability to handle matters but through Christ who died for you. You therefore recognize that your strength is not of yourself. It is of Him. When you understand this, absolutely *nothing* can limit you!

Champion Thought:
Your Position Changes Your Condition, Not Vice Versa

Because Jesus has already won the fight for you, you are God's champion by position. You are more than a conqueror. Your new right standing with God is because of who Jesus is. You must be completely established in Jesus and identity yourself in this new championship position that He gave you. This is now who you are; this is now your position.

The condition of your life today does not reflect your position. In other words, your past and present circumstances might not reveal that you are God's champion. However, this does not affect your position. Nothing but what Jesus did for you on the cross determines who you are—not your history, education, ethnic origin, IQ, financial status, posture in life, or anything else.

Your position is right standing with God, and this will not change. However, your condition can change. In fact, your position changes your condition, *not* vice versa. This means that when you receive the revelation of your position of righteousness in Christ, no longer will the challenges in your life limit you. Instead, righteousness will change you and your circumstances. You will go from defeat to victory in every area of your life when you focus on the revelation of Jesus' righteousness in you.

After you receive this revelation, you need to establish that in every area of your life, you are righteous in Christ. Look at your position, not your condition. No longer see yourself as being in your condition. Instead, see yourself as being in your new position. Remember, your position will change your condition.

CHAMPION THOUGHT:
Your Best Is Never Enough

Next, we will delve into another conflict with which Christians continually struggle: self-righteousness versus God's righteousness. Let's first examine the difference between these:

Self-righteousness is man's effort to achieve recognition from and acceptance by God. It is man's attempt to fulfill God's Word through his own strength to relieve the effects or penalty of his sin.

God's righteousness is God's gift imputed to man through the death and resurrection of His sinless Son, Jesus Christ, whereby He put man in right standing with Himself as if sin had never existed.

For more information about this subject, please refer to *Your Liberty in Christ*—my book and course in the School of Biblical Studies. Here, we will summarize this topic.

The apostle Paul wrote about Israel:

> *For I bear them witness that they have a zeal for God, but not according to knowledge. For they being ignorant of God's righteousness, and seeking to establish their own righteousness, have not submitted to the righteousness of God.*
>
> (Romans 10:2-3)

Here, we see that, while the Israelites thought they were serving God, actually they were establishing their *own* righteousness. Remember, earlier I explained that we can be sincere but sincerely wrong. Paul wrote the above verses because the Israelites, through legal adherence to the Word of God, were endeavoring to please God through their behavior, religious customs, or the clothing they wore.

This is what man's religion does. It demands our effort to achieve right standing with God. However, this verse shows that such attempts at righteousness are the result of ignorance. The truth is that we must yield ourselves to God for Him to reveal the true gift of His righteousness. We must become so deeply rooted in God's righteousness that we refuse to turn to self-righteousness.

If we do not want to walk in ignorance, it is vital that we recognize these two forms of righteousness. Let's study the difference.

CHAMPION THOUGHT:
Recognize the Symptoms of Self-Righteousness: Holier or Lowlier Than Thou

---

We can guard against self-righteousness by ensuring that we follow God's Word with correct motives. Not only does it matter *what* we do but *why* we do it.

Ironically, the symptoms of self-righteousness can manifest in seemingly opposite ways. Think about the average mentality of a religious person. Generally, a person who operates in self-righteousness exhibits false humility, prideful high-mindedness, religious piety, or unworthiness.

At first glance, humility and unworthiness appear as opposites of pride and high-mindedness. How can they all be indicators of self-righteousness? The answer is that people with any of these attitudes believe that the degree of their right standing with God is based upon the amount of right they do. They also think that they lose points with God when they do wrong. This kind of behavior is relying upon self-righteousness. Whether you feel "*holier* than thou" or "*lowlier* than thou," you are operating in self-righteousness!

CHAMPION THOUGHT:
Through God's Righteousness, Everything Is Finished for You

The full benefits of God's righteousness are too numerous to discuss here, but we will address several.

Remember, righteousness is a gift from God imputed to you by what Jesus did, not by what you do. Therefore, you can do nothing to attain righteousness except to accept Jesus and His finished work at Calvary. God's righteousness removes the pressure of performing, because through Him, everything is finished for you.

CHAMPION THOUGHT:
Good Works and Holiness Are the Results of Righteousness, Not the Cause

---

God does not require us to change first in order to become right with Him. No, when we accept Jesus, we are immediately in right standing with Him. Then, His right standing with us literally changes us. It is the Lord who causes us to do the good works and live in holiness. The Bible tells us that Jesus *"gave Himself for us, that He might redeem us from every lawless deed and purify for Himself His own special people, zealous for good works"* (Titus 2:14).

You see, good works and holiness are the results of righteousness, not the cause. In other words, God's righteousness empowers you to do good works and live a holy life. You don't act right to become righteous. No, you become righteous, then live right. When you are in right standing with God, you emanate the life of Jesus, who is now in heaven. No longer are you a sinner saved by grace and still destined to sin, but you are clothed with the righteousness of God Himself, empowered to live a holy life.

Let's carry this point a little further. Since you cannot *gain* righteousness by good works and holiness, you cannot *retain* righteousness by good works and holiness. If you can grasp this truth, it will change your entire life!

CHAMPION THOUGHT:
Walking in the Spirit Causes You Not to Walk in the Flesh

Let's look at this from a different perspective. The Bible says,

But I say, walk and live [habitually] in the [Holy] Spirit [responsive to and controlled and guided by the Spirit]; then you will certainly not gratify the cravings and desires of the flesh (of human nature without God). For the desires of the flesh are opposed to the [Holy] Spirit, and the [desires of the] Spirit are opposed to the flesh (godless human nature); for these are antagonistic to each other [continually withstanding and in conflict with each other], so that you are not free but are prevented from doing what you desire to do. But if you are guided (led) by the [Holy] Spirit, you are not subject to the Law. (Galatians 5:16–18 AMP)

You see, great willpower does not keep us from indulging our flesh. We no longer walk in the flesh or *"gratify the cravings and desires of the flesh (of human nature without God)"* because we now walk in the Holy Spirit. The way to rise above our fleshly desires is not to focus on what we have done or will do wrong but on what Jesus did right. In other words, the revelation of righteousness catapults us through temptation. With Jesus, we will overcome!

We either walk in the flesh or in the Spirit. If we are not experiencing the results of a Spirit-led walk, then we are living according to the dictates of our physical bodies. Obeying the flesh causes sin to twist, augment, distort, and pervert our perceptions. It drives us into sin consciousness. This evil taskmaster then heaps inferiority, insecurity, shame, guilt, and condemnation upon us. Mental anguish torments us, and we have no power over the flesh.

If we only understood God's righteousness and obeyed Him, we would see that our authority in Christ is awesome. Never forget:

> *God raised us up with Christ and seated us with him in the heavenly realms in Christ Jesus, in order that in the coming ages he might show the incomparable riches of his grace, expressed in his kindness to us in Christ Jesus.*
> (Ephesians 2:6–7 NIV)

CHAMPION THOUGHT:
Receive Righteousness by Believing and Speaking

The only way you can experience right standing with God is through Jesus' death and resurrection. He paid the price for you to have His righteousness. God's Word tells us how to accept Jesus' gift:

> *If you confess with your mouth the Lord Jesus and believe in your heart that God has raised Him from the dead, you*

35

*will be saved. For with the heart one believes unto righteous-
ness, and with the mouth confession is made unto salvation.*
(Romans 10:9–10)

Speaking Jesus' lordship over your life and believing that God
raised Him from the dead puts you in right standing with God. It
really is that simple!

Settle the issue of salvation and His righteousness once and
for all. If you have not already done this, I urge you to do it now. I
invite you to pray this simple prayer to anchor your salvation and
righteousness in Jesus:

> Father, thank You for loving me. Thank You for giving
> Your Son Jesus to die and to be raised from the dead for me.
>
> Jesus Christ, Son of God, I believe that You rose from
> the dead. Come into my heart, forgive me of my sins, and
> be my Lord and Savior. Jesus, I declare that You are Lord,
> and that You are Lord of my life. God, thank You for for-
> giving me and washing me by the power of Jesus' blood
> without any effort on my part.
>
> Jesus, You were made sin that I might be made the righ-
> teousness of God in You. By Your death and resurrection,
> I am in right standing with God. Now, I live without any
> inferiority, insecurity, shame, guilt, or condemnation.
>
> Thank You, Father, that I live as if sin had never
> existed. Through Jesus' resurrection, I stand before You
> holy, blameless, and above reproach.
>
> Right now, I submit to Your will. I believe the truth of
> Your Word. Teach me Your ways, Lord, that I might walk
> in them only. I believe and decree that now I am in right
> standing with You, God, and nothing can change this. In
> Jesus' name, Amen.

That's how easy it is to be in right standing with God![5]

The Revelation of Righteousness Is the Key to Walking in God's Freedom in Every Area

Now that you are righteous, you must receive the *revelation* of righteousness, or you will not walk in all that God has designed for you. This is *extremely* important! I cannot emphasize it enough. If you have prayed and believed the prayer stated earlier or something similar, then you are righteous. However, you will not walk in all the benefits that Jesus has for you unless you receive the *revelation* of righteousness.

Because your natural mind processes earthly information, it cannot understand righteousness. God deals in the unseen supernatural realm. So to grasp His truth, you must understand supernaturally, not with your natural mind. To do this, you need a new perspective, a new way of seeing. You need revelation knowledge.

What is revelation knowledge? It is truth and information revealed, unveiled, or disclosed only by a direct encounter with the Holy Spirit. It is a *spiritual* impartation of knowledge as opposed to the normal way we obtain information. It is a receiving instead of a learning. The Holy Spirit discloses truth beyond our natural senses and human minds.

Have you ever read the Bible or a book like *It Only Takes One* and felt as if the words literally jumped off the page to touch you? Suddenly, the words became much more than print on a page. You might have even read them before, but something unique happened this time. The words struck your spirit with wisdom, so you could see something new to you. It was as if blinders had been ripped from your eyes. That is the Holy Spirit unveiling and revealing His truth to your spirit, not to your natural mind. Throughout life, you must look for this uncovering of knowledge that originates from God, not man. Otherwise, you will live far beneath God's best!

When the revelation of righteousness unveils Christ within you and your position in Him at the right hand of the Father, everything in the natural realm will pale in His presence. You see, righteousness is a shock wave to your system. It completely transforms your comprehension of how to live. You start seeing and thinking differently. It will hit you like a sledgehammer when you realize its awesome truth.

My Wife

After my wife, Faye, received the revelation of righteousness, she was never the same. In 1982, she and I were attending Bible school in Tulsa, Oklahoma, where we were studying righteousness. For years Faye had been struggling to understand this truth, because she had not heard of righteousness before she met me.

Then, from 1975, when I received the revelation of God's righteousness, I never ceased telling her about it! She was trying to be a good Christian woman, but all this talk of righteousness did not make sense to her.

During the Bible school course one day, I said to Faye, "Ahhhhh! Glory! Yes! This is what I've been telling you. This is it!"

She became angry, saying, "I don't understand it. I am sick and tired of hearing this stuff. It doesn't make any sense to me. I'll just go to church, be a good Christian, and do what's right. Then, God will be happy with me."

"No," I urged, "it's not that way! It's not that way! It's not that way! It's not that way!" However, no matter what I said, Faye could not understand righteousness.

Continually, I prayed, "God, show it to her. Show her. Please liberate her from this consciousness of sin and being a 'goody two-shoes.' Loose her from the bondage of trying to be somebody else."

Then, one day we came home from class for lunch. Afterward, Faye went to the living room and began reading a book on obedience. She thought being obedient would put her in good standing with God.

Suddenly, Faye set the book down and started screaming, "Ha! Ha! Haaaaaa!"

I ran from the kitchen, greatly concerned. A screaming wife is very unsettling!

"I got it! I got it! Haaaaaa!" she squealed, as she jumped back and forth from one sofa to the other without touching the floor!

Remembering that the windows were open, I thought, *The neighbors will think I'm beating her. They'll think I'm throwing my kids against the wall or something. What if they call the police?* Immediately, I ran around the apartment, closing all the windows and shutting the blinds. I turned on the air conditioner to cover the sound of her piercing cries.

Where do we go from here? I wondered, still unsure of why Faye was yelling.

"I got it! I got it!"

What should I do next—call 911? Is it a disease? Is it infectious?

"I got it! I got it!"

I shouted above her, so she could hear, "What is it that you've got?"

Faye eventually calmed down enough to answer me. She had finally received the revelation of God's righteousness in her! It was as if a fog had lifted, and the entire concept made sense to her. Faye was free at last! Because the rule of sin consciousness broke from her life that day, she has been a completely different person ever since!

Have you had a direct encounter with God to understand His righteousness yet? If not, you *will* receive it if you ask Him for it! This is a thrilling journey that you don't want to miss! The revelation of God's righteousness in you will absolutely transform you. It will pierce every inferior mind-set and break all repetitive behavior patterns and other influences that have dominated you. This is the key to walking in God's freedom for every area of your life.

CHAMPION THOUGHT:
You Are God's Child

God created man to be free. Yet we often run away from Him only to become free men living as slaves, and God grieves. I want to share a powerful story about how to escape slavery and return to your liberty in Christ.

Before we begin, it is important to recognize the difference between *relationship* and *fellowship* with God.

> *Relationship:* When you receive God's gift of righteousness, you enter into a relationship with Him as a son. Sonship is your relationship with God as His child. Righteousness is your connection with Him, as a branch connects to the vine. You are in relationship with God as His child because of righteousness.
>
> *Fellowship:* Communion with God through the Holy Spirit is fellowship. It also is joint participation with Jesus in a shared direction and purpose. Fellowship is how you cooperate with Him to carry out His will in your life.

Therefore, your relationship with God is as a child. Righteousness is your connection. Fellowship is the flow through that connection. God and you are connected, and the life of Christ flows through you to the world.

CHAMPION THOUGHT:
You Can Lose Fellowship, Not Relationship

Sometimes as Christians we find ourselves distant from God because of sin. When this happens, we feel that we have lost His righteousness. However, the truth is that the sins of the believer attack *fellowship* with God, not *relationship*. If we sin, we don't lose our sonship. We don't lose His righteousness. We lose communion and cooperation with God—fellowship—but we are still His children. Righteousness is free, but fellowship must be maintained. This is an awesome understanding.

Now, please don't confuse this with the doctrine of "eternal security," which says, "once saved, always saved." People *can* purposely turn from God and lose their relationship with Him. However, my point here is that we do not lose our salvation every time we sin. God is married to the backslider and relentlessly pursues us, even when we sin. (See Jeremiah 3:14.) A great example of this is seen in the story of the Prodigal Son.

The Prodigal Son

Many have heard the story of the Prodigal Son before, as well as wrong conclusions that have been drawn from it. This is not a parable of a lost person who became saved. Nor is it about a person who was saved but then lost his salvation.

This story is the Bible's clearest example of a person who lost the understanding of *whose* he was and *who* he was. In this story, the son lost *fellowship*, not *relationship*. He was still a child of his father, but they lost fellowship. The son no longer communed with and jointly participated with his father, but the man was still his father.

In your life, if you sin after receiving God's righteousness, He will not say, "You are no longer My child." No, sin simply produces a breach in your fellowship with Him. Similarly, if your child disobeys you, your fellowship suffers, but you are definitely still a parent to that child.

Now, let's examine Jesus' parable of the Prodigal Son, which is recorded in Luke 15:11–32. A father had two sons. When the younger one asked for his portion of the family estate, the man divided his wealth and gave that son his part. Traveling to a distant country, the young man *"squandered his estate with loose living"* (Luke 15:13 NAS).

After the son had nothing left, a famine came to that land. Needing money, he began to work in the fields of a citizen there, feeding pigs. He became so hungry that even the pigs' food looked good. Yet no one gave the son anything.

Do you find yourself away from God in a wrong place, feeling miserable and tormented? If so, remember, this is not communion. You are not cooperating with Christ. If this description fits you, it's time to rise to a new level of communion and fellowship, hearing His voice and doing His will. God is still in His house, waiting for your return. He hasn't left.

Now, Jesus said that the Prodigal Son *"came to his senses, [and] he said, 'How many of my father's hired men have more than enough bread, but I am dying here with hunger!'"* (Luke 15:17 NAS). The son finally came to the point of breaking his self-will. Then, the awakening process began. This exposed the lie about *whose* and *who* he was, and what was available to him, so he said,

> *I will get up and go to my father, and will say to him, "Father, I have sinned against heaven, and in your sight; I am no longer worthy to be called your son; make me as one of your hired men."*　　　　　　　　　　　(vv. 18–19 NAS)

Some people think that this is a positive attitude, spoken in humility. No, it is false humility. You see, when we say to God that we are no longer worthy to be called His sons or daughters, we are declaring that we have lost our *relationship* or righteousness with Him. This is not true. No one can take away what Jesus gave to us. Instead, we have lost only our *fellowship.* Likewise, the Prodigal lost only his fellowship, yet his statement indicates that he sensed a loss of his relationship (righteousness).

You see, a son's relationship with his father is not based on what he does but on *who* he is. Remember, we studied earlier that you are not righteous because of what you can do. No, you are righteous because of *whose* and *who* you are—a child of the Father.

The Prodigal Son lost that sense of sonship. He saw himself from his own standpoint, not his father's. Instead, he should have said, "I will go back to my father to ask for forgiveness. Because I am his son, he will re-empower me. I will not look for a job in Dad's house. I will simply act like the child of the house that I am."

Do you see the difference between losing fellowship and relationship? You cannot get to sonship from servanthood. You are either a son by birthright or not a son at all. A father does not make his son a servant. No, his son is his heir; therefore, the servants serve the son.

Now, let's read what happened when the young man went home: *"He got up and came to his father. But while he was still a long way off, his father saw him, and felt compassion for him, and ran and embraced him, and kissed him"* (Luke 15:20 NAS).

This is what happens when people repent, turning back to God. If they make even a partial turn toward Him, God rushes to them. He longs to hear His wayward children ask, "Dad, are you still there?" If you have fallen away from God, I urge you to run toward Him. Do not wait.

The son's next statement clearly exposes his misconception, but his father pays no attention to his boy's notion:

> And the son said to him, "Father, I have sinned against heaven and in your sight; I am no longer worthy to be called your son." But the father said to his slaves, "Quickly bring out the best robe and put it on him, and put a ring on his hand and sandals on his feet."
> (vv. 21–22 NAS)

Now, *"the best robe"* is the robe of right standing, depicting his relationship as a son. Shoes in that era were a sign of freedom because slaves did not wear them. Here, the father saw that his boy was not living as a free man, so he put shoes on his feet to restore his freedom as a son.

"*A ring on his hand*" means that the father restored sonship privileges. It was a signet ring, which was a sign of honor and authority. In those days, a person used a signet to stamp documents with his legal seal of authority. Therefore, the Prodigal Son's ring symbolized that he had the same authority as his father. Now, he had the full ability to use his father's name because he had returned to submit to his father's direction. The right to his family's estate was restored to the Prodigal.

Afterward, the father threw a party! Understand that when you restore your righteousness consciousness and fellowship with your heavenly Father, He celebrates.

Now, what would have happened if the Prodigal Son had not returned home to ask for forgiveness? He would not have enjoyed the benefits of the right standing that he already had with his father. Returning to the father restored his use of all that was his the entire time: righteousness, sonship, forgiveness, prosperity, abundance, health, and family identity.

No matter how far you might stray, God looks to restore your loss of fellowship with Him. Like the Prodigal Son, turn from your sin, confess it to your heavenly Father, and He will receive you back into His house. The Bible promises: "*If we confess our sins, He is faithful and just to forgive us our sins and to cleanse us from all unrighteousness*" (1 John 1:9).

CHAMPION THOUGHT:
It's Time to Remove Your Fig Leaf

When we sin, we have a tendency toward covering up instead of running to God for forgiveness. This has happened from man's beginning. In fact, covering up sin started in the Garden of Eden. After Adam and Eve had disobeyed God by eating of the Tree of the Knowledge of Good and Evil, the Bible explains: *"Then the eyes of both of them were opened, and they knew that they were naked; and they sewed fig leaves together and made themselves coverings"* (Genesis 3:7).

When God came walking in the garden, Adam and Eve hid themselves. The Lord called to Adam, *"Where are you?"* (v. 9). He knew where Adam was, but He wanted Adam to discover where he was. Instead of truthfully uncovering his error and acknowledging that he had violated God's commands, Adam accused Eve. (See verse 12.) They each put on fig leaves.

I call this the fig-leaf syndrome, and it is still being used today. It is the pattern of accusing others for one's position and condition in life and excusing oneself. It is refusing to accept the responsibility for one's own actions that caused the problem initially.

You see, when you "wear a fig leaf," you deny yourself the relationship of being in the position of God's child, walking in the authority of righteousness. You are sin conscious instead of righteousness conscious. This causes you to cower, hide, and cover up sin. You must realize that we cannot cover up or run from sin. To remove the stain of sin, we must receive God's forgiveness and the cleansing of Jesus' blood. The fig-leaf syndrome says that you are still in sin. Righteousness consciousness says that you are free of it.

Do you have *your* fig leaf on? Do you need to take it off before we continue? It's time to relieve every person from the responsibility of your sins and challenges. If someone has hurt you or fails to meet your expectations and support you, don't become angry, bitter, frustrated, or disappointed. Instead, release that person in prayer. Rid yourself of all excuses. See yourself as righteous in Jesus, and soar with His ability within you. Other people cannot do for you what Jesus has already done, so let their shortcomings go. (I have found that this is a powerful revelation, especially when I counsel married couples.)

CHAMPION THOUGHT:
Wanted—Dead and Alive in Christ

As I sought the Lord for the revelation of righteousness, I studied and studied the Bible for six months. I read and reread the verses on righteousness, but for a long time they were simply words on a page. I could not understand what God wanted me to see. That all changed one day when He gave me one of the most profound open visions in my life. This might sound unusual, but this experience forever changed my life.

At the time, I was sitting up in bed when the walls of the bedroom disappeared before my eyes! Although I was still physically at home, I saw myself in a completely different setting and time in history.

Suddenly, I was walking up the hill of Golgotha 2,000 years ago as Jesus carried His cross! I watched another fellow pick up the cross and carry it for Him. As I tasted dirt in my mouth from the dusty roads, I thought, *This is wild! I am actually here, watching Jesus going to the cross!*

The crowd screamed and cheered when the soldiers nailed Jesus to the cross. What happened next changed my life forever! I was at the foot of the cross with Jesus, crucified, above me. Then, His blood began to wash me. It was not a couple of drops, but His blood *poured* over me. I then saw myself in Jesus, hanging on the cross. Then, as He died, I died!

Immediately, the vision closed. I was back in my apartment. Utter silence permeated that room.

Instantly I realized, *I am dead.* I had received the revelation of righteousness that in Christ I am dead. *Gary is no longer a problem. What a relief! I am dead, and now Jesus lives through me. It's not me, but Jesus, doing the living!* When I discovered that I am no longer a problem, it transformed my life!

That day, all the Scriptures I had read on righteousness suddenly became alive. My heart cries out for you to receive His full revelation, too.

Your position in Christ means that you are dead in Christ and raised together with Him to live in new life. When Jesus died and rose from the dead, you died and rose in Him. The same power that raised Him from the dead dwells in you! Now, He lives in and through you to touch the world with His life-changing power. From this identity of being in Jesus' resurrection, established by the truths of God's Word, you are to live a life that proves you are what God has made you—His champion.

CHAMPION THOUGHT:
Your Life Is Not Your Own

Christians often accept that Jesus has come to live in our hearts by faith. Realize that He was not ashamed to do this. The Bible asserts: *"Both the one who makes men holy and those who are made holy are of the same family. So Jesus is not ashamed to call them brothers"* (Hebrews 2:11 NIV).

If Jesus is not ashamed to call us His brothers, then likewise we must see that without limiting Himself, He has *"seated us with him in the heavenly realms in Christ Jesus"* (Ephesians 2:6 NIV). By identifying with us, He does not limit Himself, but empowers us.

He became sin, taking upon Himself the iniquity of us all, so that *"we might become the righteousness of God in Him"* (2 Corinthians 5:21). He died for us, so that we could live in Him. He became cursed, so we are now blessed.

Your righteousness is not based on your ability to believe. It is based on the reality that Jesus identified with you so that you might identify with Him.

While we were sinners—under the enemy's control—Jesus substituted Himself for us. He paid the penalty for our sin. In so doing, He made us righteous. Jesus did not distance Himself from us. No, He became a sin offering for us. Therefore, His death is our death. His resurrection is our resurrection.

Your life as God's champion does not come from an act or an initiative of your own. It is the result of what God did for you through Jesus' death and resurrection.

The Bible declares:

> *It will become a sign and a witness to the Lord of hosts in the land of Egypt; for they will cry to the Lord because of oppressors, and He will send them a Savior and a Champion, and He will deliver them.* (Isaiah 19:20 NAS)

Jesus is God's first Champion. Your position of being a champion is based entirely on the fact that Jesus, The Champion of God—The Champion of champions—identified with you to free you of sin, making you God's champion. He came to live not only *in* you, but also *through* you. He purchased you, so that He can achieve His will through your life. Now, your life is not your own. It is a vessel for Jesus to minister through. It's time to release The Champion within you, so that He can touch this world through your life. It is for this reason that God has made you His champion to the world.

Man with Abusive Hands

On a recent Sunday morning, I taught this simple but profound truth that Jesus substituted Himself for us and became our perfect sacrifice. I stated that He is not shocked by anything that you have done. Jesus knows you. He bore your life of sin, I explained. He paid the penalties of your life of abuse and everything that you have done.

During the evening service on that same Sunday, the Spirit of God led me to pray for people with pain or challenges in their hands. As I obeyed, miracles happened, and God healed many people.

As I returned to the platform, the Spirit of the Lord revealed to me that He wanted to heal a man in the service who had used his hands abusively—fighting, beating women, and causing pain and destruction in other people's lives through his hands. So I announced, "There is someone here whose hands have been used in abuse. God has inhabited your life, and He wants your hands never to be used again in an abusive action."

A man stood up, broken and crying. Tears streaming from his eyes, he came to the altar with his hands stretched out in front of him. That night, this man presented his hands to Jesus, confessing that he had beaten his wife and continually fought aggressively. A breaking took place within his heart as he received the revelation that his hands are not his own.

This man realized that his hands and all his actions were actually in Jesus' death as He paid the penalty for the sin of humanity. That revelation broke the influence of using his body for any destructive purposes. The man saw that Jesus bore those hands, so they would be used for God's glory. He understood that he had had no right to use what belongs to God for any purpose other than what God had intended.

Realizing that Jesus inhabits his life, this man discovered that his hands literally are no longer abusive but belong to the living Lord Jesus—the One who now lives through him. From that day forth, this man's hands would be used for healing, grace, mercy, and the outreach of God's love.

The revelation of righteousness was a very powerful breakthrough for this man. It will be for you also. Once you receive the revelation of being dead in Jesus' death, free from the nature of sin, and alive in Christ with Him living through you, you will understand as never before the meaning of the apostle Paul's words:

For I through the law died to the law that I might live to God. I have been crucified with Christ; it is no longer I who live, but Christ lives in me; and the life which I now live in the flesh I live by faith in the Son of God, who loved me and gave Himself for me. I do not set aside the grace of God; for if righteousness comes through the law, then Christ died in vain.
(Galatians 2:19–21)

And if Christ is in you, the body is dead because of sin, but the Spirit is life because of righteousness. But if the Spirit of Him who raised Jesus from the dead dwells in you, He who raised Christ from the dead will also give life to your mortal bodies through His Spirit who dwells in you. (Romans 8:10–11)

You must see that a new species of mankind has risen in the righteousness of Christ. This new man is not captivated and beaten down by sin. No, he is released in Jesus' fullness of grace, power, and authority. Champion, now you are one of this new species of man!

CHAMPION THOUGHT:
The Limits Are Gone—
You Can Reign as a King in Life

Now, how are you to live as a new species of man? The Bible is very clear about this:

For if by the one man's offense death reigned through the one, much more those who receive abundance of grace and of the gift of righteousness will reign in life through the One, Jesus Christ. (Romans 5:17)

In this new life, righteousness enables you to reign as a king! Your reigning authority is through Jesus. So it does not originate from what *you* do but from the recognition of what *He* has done.

You are to function in a limitless capacity over your environment and every circumstance. Instead of operating in sin's effect, you operate in the effect of Jesus' finished work on your behalf. So the objective of righteousness is for you to reign. In Christ, you have dominion, because He has delegated His supreme authority to you. *"And He put all things under His* [Jesus'] *feet, and gave Him to be head* [to rule] *over all things to the church, which is His body, the fullness of Him who fills all in all"* (Ephesians 1:22–23).

What does verse 23 say Jesus fills? He fills *"all in all."* He even fills everything that is not submitted to or occupied by the government of God.

Here, the fullness of Jesus is His body, the church. You see, we are His fullness—the full expression of who He is *in* us, *to* us, and *through* us. He then fills *"all in all"* through us. Because the church fills *"all in all,"* we are to be the voice of His authority in our generation, penetrating every environment. As Christians, God has called us to exercise His authority in every level, including government, education, science, family, social groups, the corporate world, and everything that exists. The church is the awesome presence of God's Spirit, ruling and influencing the world.

Do you have an area of your life where you are not reigning? If so, you are not allowing the revelation of righteousness to have its proper authority in that territory. Sin consciousness still dominates you there.

Once you receive this revelation of righteousness, the limitations of natural circumstances end. The ability of God's intervention engages. Don't ever restrain Him because of your unbelief or the apparent finality of your negative circumstances. God speaks from His eternity and authority, not from your ability or circumstances. His Word has far greater authority than any situation. Are you ready to walk beyond the limitations of the natural realm to reign in life? Nothing can limit you any longer!

God Seeks One to Stand in the Gap

Noah

Throughout history, God has looked for people who would walk in righteousness to carry out His authority in their generation. Consider Noah, for example. Chapters six through eight in Genesis record the account of Noah and the ark. Here, we read that God was so displeased with human perversion, corruption, and violence that He sought to destroy the earth. However, a lone man stood out in the crowd of wickedness: Noah. God said to Noah, *"I have seen that you are righteous before Me in this generation"* (Genesis 7:1). The Bible says, *"But Noah found grace in the eyes of the LORD....Noah was a just man, perfect in his generations. Noah walked with God"* (Genesis 6:8–9).

Because of this *one* person named Noah, God could execute His strategy to save humanity and the wildlife. He planned to preserve Noah, his seven family members, and a portion of the animals on the earth. Through this remnant, God would repopulate the world.

To launch this plan of salvation, God told Noah to build an ark because He was about to flood the earth. This was Noah's advanced knowledge. It empowered him to break through every barrier to create that life-saving ark. The Word of God says,

> *By faith Noah, being divinely warned of things not yet seen, moved with godly fear, prepared an ark for the saving of his household, by which he condemned the world and became heir of the righteousness which is according to faith.*
> (Hebrews 11:7)

The Bible is filled with examples of God looking for individuals, one at a time, to execute His authority. In another scenario, the prophet Ezekiel declared God's message to his generation:

The people of the land have used oppression, and exercised robbery, and have vexed the poor and needy: yea, they have oppressed the stranger wrongfully. And I sought for a man among them, that should make up the hedge, and stand in the gap before me for the land, that I should not destroy it: but I found none. (Ezekiel 22:29–30 KJV)

Here, the people had operated in an abusive mind-set. God's response was to use one man to *"stand in the gap"* and turn the tide of evil. In this passage, God does not say, "I sought for a group," or, "I sought for a lot of people." He looked for only one. In the midst of the evil strongholds that needed to be torn down, God wanted to see if anyone would *"stand in the gap"* on behalf of hurting people. He was looking for only one.

CHAMPION THOUGHT:
You Are God's Champion

God is always looking for one individual to stand for righteousness in an evil environment to execute His authority. In Noah's time, God searched for one righteous man to champion His cause. Today, God continues to look for one to champion His cause. My friend, because Jesus identified with you, you are now that one! It only takes one, and you are God's champion of the hour! Now that you know *whose* and *who* you are, reign! Be the champion that you are. Speak like it. Think like it. Move like it.

CHAMPION THOUGHT:
You Have a New Name

Abraham was God's champion to his generation and for many to come. When God promised to create nations from Abraham, the Bible says, *"Abraham believed God, and it was accounted to him for righteousness*" (Romans 4:3). After Abraham had shown himself faithful, God announced,

> *No longer shall your name be called Abram, but your name shall be Abraham; for I have made you a father of many nations. I will make you exceedingly fruitful; and I will make nations of you, and kings shall come from you. And I will establish My covenant between Me and you and your descendants after you in their generations, for an everlasting covenant, to be God to you and your descendants after you.*
> (Genesis 17:5–7)

Here, we see that God changed this man's name from *Abram,* which means "father is exalted," to Abraham, which means "father of a multitude."[6] Throughout the Bible, the Lord has changed people's names to declare their new identity in Him along with His personal promises to them.

My friend, if you prayed, dedicating your life to Jesus and becoming a child of God, you have a new identity. No longer are you defeated, destined to eke out an existence in your own strength. You have been adopted into the family of the King! You are now identified with Christ and are a Christian. You are identified with *the* Champion. Therefore, your name is now *Champion.*

For the remainder of this book, I will call you by your new name, *Champion,* to declare your new identity and life of promises in Him. Champion, you have stepped into an awesome experience with God!

You have discovered that you are God's champion by position, which is righteousness. You know *whose* and *who* you are. Now, we need to determine specifically *why* you are that and *what* you should do about it. In the next chapter, you will learn God's reason for making you His champion! He has a personal purpose for you.

3
Behold His Masterpiece in the Mirror

Champion, you now have discovered *who* you are. You are a child of God, walking in the power and righteousness of Jesus Christ Himself. He died and rose again for you so that you can live in Him, and He in you, on this earth.

Two important questions remain: *Why* are you God's champion today, and *what* should you do about it? Multitudes live their entire lives without ever knowing these answers about themselves. Living life without purpose results in feelings of insignificance, meaninglessness, depression, and even worthlessness. This chapter will shed light on the power of purpose.

You are about to learn that God created you—enabled you with ability and authority—as a champion for a reason. He designed you with an awesome power called *purpose*. The following truths will clarify why you were born and show you how to live larger than your current existence.

CHAMPION THOUGHT:
Purpose Is the Highest Motivator

Knowing the purpose or reason for living is the most significant form of motivation on the earth. It has been said that the people with the greatest commitments are those who have identified the most worthy causes. You see, as humans, we must know that the cause—or *the why*—of an objective is worthwhile. Otherwise, our motivation can easily become thwarted. Like a candle in the wind, our enthusiasm can have its light snuffed out. If we lose sight of our purpose—*the why* of our existence—we will surely drift off course.

CHAMPION THOUGHT:
"The Why" Always Precedes "The What"

The cause—or *the why*—is critical. But how can we find *the why* for our lives, when it seems that everyone is scurrying about, trying to figure out *what* to do next? Books, seminars, courses, and entire schools abound to show us *what* to do and how to do it, but few teach us *why*. However, to get *the what* right, we must first know *the why*. We cannot know what to do next in our lives if we first don't know why we are here. Let's consider several examples from others' lives.

Alexander Graham Bell

Alexander Graham Bell (1847-1922) is known as the inventor of the telephone. However, did you know that both his mother and his wife were hearing impaired and that Bell's main interest in life was to help the deaf to hear and speak? He taught deaf pupils and opened a school to train teachers of the deaf. Along with his efforts to create devices to help the deaf, he began to work on sending multiple telegraph messages over a single wire. Then, in 1876, Bell successfully spoke the first words ever on a telephone. He later used the prize money awarded to him for his new invention to establish an association to help the deaf.[1] Bell also invented the audiometer, an early hearing aid, and improved the phonograph.

Inspired by his compassion to help the deaf, Alexander Graham Bell invented a device that has transformed the world. It is difficult to imagine life without the telephone. Yes, we use telephones to keep in touch with family, friends, and business associates, but there are many other uses now. The telephone has revolutionized how the world operates in business. Going online on the Internet and using faxes are now possible through the telephone. We use answering machines, voice mail, and electronic mail because of this apparatus. Callers can bank, shop, arrange travel reservations, and engage in many other activities by telephone. Life has never been the same since this invention.

It is obvious that Alexander Graham Bell's motivation was not fame or wealth; it wasn't even to invent the telephone. The purpose of his work was to help the deaf. This dream propelled him on a quest that resulted in several significant inventions that changed the course of history. The cause of helping people with hearing challenges motivated him to persevere and break through the barriers before him. Do you see how *the why* preceded *the what!* Bell discovered what to do after he had a reason to do it.

Christopher Columbus

As another example of *the why* preceding *the what*, consider Christopher Columbus (1451–1506), the European explorer who discovered America. His name literally means "Christ Member."[2] Notably, this was also his position in Christ! Because of his Christ-centered faith, Columbus knew his purpose, *the why*, and then *what* to do about it.

The way he signed his name revealed Columbus's destiny. His signature included "Christopher Ferens," which means "Christ Bearer," because he believed he was called of God to take Christ to the world.[3] His purpose was to carry out his very namesake. Then, to fulfill this purpose, Columbus set sail around the world. Focused on serving God in this manner despite enormous hardships, the Christian explorer explained, "The fact that the Gospel must still be preached to so many lands in such a short time—this is what convinces me."[4] Because of this great cause, Columbus was able to break through the barriers of the entire known world to take the Gospel to people in uncharted lands. He revolutionized the world, as we will discuss further in a later chapter.

David and Goliath

Next, consider the story of David and Goliath, found in 1 Samuel 17. You probably know that David took down the giant Goliath with a simple slingshot and stone. However, maybe you have not seen some of the powerful truths about purpose and cause in this biblical account.

You may recall that Jesse sent his son, David, to check on and take food to his three older brothers. They were away at battle for the nation of Israel under King Saul. As commanded, David left his father's sheep, which he tended, and came to his brothers to see how they were faring in the war against the Philistines. While David talked with them, *"the champion, the Philistine of Gath, Goliath by name"* (1 Samuel 17:23) stood in defiance of the Israelite armies. The giant threatened to enslave the nation of Israel if he won the fight. Cowering in fear, neither King Saul nor the Israelite soldiers could see any way to prevail in this battle.

The men informed David, *"The man who kills him [Goliath] the king will enrich with great riches, will give him his daughter, and give his father's house exemption from taxes in Israel"* (1 Samuel 17:25). As David spoke to them about this, a personal conflict arose with his oldest brother, Eliab, who overheard the conversation.

> And Eliab's anger was aroused against David, and he said, "Why did you come down here? And with whom have you left those few sheep in the wilderness? I know your pride and the insolence of your heart, for you have come down to see the battle." (v. 28)

In other words, Eliab accused his youngest brother, saying, "David, I know your pride. I know your heart. I know that you have a wrong motive and purpose. The only reason you are here is to see the fight."

"And David said, 'What have I done now? Is there not a cause?'" (v. 29). This is a very important question. Earlier, as David had listened to the negativity of his countrymen, he rose with another profound statement. Speaking about the need for someone to kill Goliath to remove *"the reproach from Israel,"* David had declared, *"For who is this uncircumcised Philistine, that he should defy the armies of the living God?"* (v. 26). By this, David meant, "Goliath is not a covenant person. Why is he standing here? Let me at him!"

David's words reveal that he saw the cause of the battle. He knew that the people of Israel were in covenant with a mighty God as their Covenant Keeper. This uncircumcised enemy was assaulting their covenant and defying the living God Himself. Goliath was attacking Israel's very purpose. You see, God had selected Israel to be His covenant people for a reason. Their purpose was to demonstrate that the God of Israel is truly the God of the entire earth. We could say that they were in right standing with Him. Therefore, nothing in all this earth had the right to stand against Israel or enslave them because God—our Father, the Father of Israel, Jehovah—had already set them apart for Himself. David understood Israel's covenant purpose and tied it to this battle with Goliath.

CHAMPION THOUGHT:
The Reason for Conflict Is to Abort Purpose

You must remember that a champion looks for *the why* of the conflict. It is always tied to purpose because the enemy wants to abort the purpose of God's people. He will fight to destroy your purpose. Therefore, Champion, whenever you are in a conflict, look for the cause. Look at it as an assault against your purpose. This will help you not to give up before your victory comes.

David's personal purpose was also at stake, not just the nation's purpose. Before this conflict with Goliath, God had anointed David, despite his youthful age, as Israel's next king after Saul. Then, *"the Spirit of the LORD came upon David from that day forward"* (1 Samuel 16:13).

David not only understood the covenant purpose of Israel, but also knew that his personal purpose was to lead the nation as king someday. He realized that now was the time to begin walking in his God-ordained purpose. Saul and his men were in fear. No one would take a stand to fight this enemy of God. David, therefore, boldly decided to step into the conflict, and he knew just how to do it—with a mere slingshot and stone.

CHAMPION THOUGHT:
Right Standing and Purpose Qualify You to Act

Notice that David recognized *who* he was: a covenant man in right standing with God. He also understood *why* he was on the earth: His purpose was to lead Israel in making their God known as the God of the entire earth. Because he knew *who* he was and *why* he was here, David knew *what* to do. Being in right standing or righteous before God (as we learned in the previous chapter) and knowing your divine purpose (as we are discovering in this chapter) are all you need to determine what you should do. These two components—both of which originate only from God—qualify you to act in agreement with His will. Everything else then falls into place when you know these two truths for your life.

CHAMPION THOUGHT:
When Purpose Is Known, Nothing Has the Authority to Withstand It

After clearly identifying the purpose for this battle, David went to King Saul to explain his desire to kill Goliath. As David told Saul,

> *Your servant used to keep his father's sheep, and when a lion or a bear came and took a lamb out of the flock, I went out after it and struck it, and delivered the lamb from its mouth; and when it arose against me, I caught it by its beard, and struck and killed it. Your servant has killed both lion and bear; and this uncircumcised Philistine will be like one of them, seeing he has defied the armies of the living God.*
> (1 Samuel 17:34–36)

As a shepherd for his father, David had diligently carried out his delegated responsibility. He protected the sheep, provided nourishment for them, and worked to grow his father's household financially as the sheep multiplied. When the lion and bear came to destroy what was under David's charge, he had seen the cause of the conflict and fought to save the sheep. Then, as David saw Goliath threatening Israel, he realized that this was also the same cause. In both cases, David's purpose was under attack. An enemy was threatening his charges—those for whom David was responsible. He knew that just as God had empowered him to destroy the lion and bear, so also God would strengthen him to kill Goliath. There was no difference.

In the battle against Goliath, David did not compare his own abilities, strategies, or weapons with the giant's. Instead, he knew that regardless of how capable and armed Goliath was or how inadequate and ill-equipped he himself appeared, this enemy champion did not stand a chance against God's champion operating according to His divine purpose.

You see, David realized that once God's purpose is known, nothing has the power to withstand it. For this reason, you should never equate your purpose with a plan or with the lack of provision.

As a champion, your purpose stems from your relationship with the Author of that purpose. Regardless of circumstances, you must walk in your divine purpose.

CHAMPION THOUGHT:
God Has Purposed It, and He Will Also Do It

Let me take you on a short journey in the Bible for a few moments to explain further. Isaiah prophesied from the voice of God, saying,

> Remember the former things long past, for I am God, and there is no other; I am God, and there is no one like Me, declaring the end from the beginning, and from ancient times things which have not been done, saying, "My purpose will be established, and I will accomplish all My good pleasure"; calling a bird of prey from the east, the man of My purpose from a far country. Truly I have spoken; truly I will bring it to pass. I have planned it, surely I will do it.   (Isaiah 46:9–11 NAS)

Another version of the Bible states the last part of verse 11 this way: "I have spoken it, I will also bring it to pass; I have purposed it, I will also do it" (KJV). In the book of Jeremiah, God said, "I am watching over My word to perform it" (Jeremiah 1:12 NAS). In these verses, we see that God is backing His purpose, which He has spoken, with action. In other words, God said, "From whom do I need to get permission? Who can stop Me? I am God. I have purposed and spoken it. I will perform it. I will do what I said. Nothing can stop My purpose."

Do you realize that Jesus is "upholding all things by the word of His power" (Hebrews 1:3)? The very Word that He has spoken is the reason you exist. (See John 1:1–13.) Because of this final and absolute authority, I believe that you will experience the manifestation of truth as you continue reading It Only Takes One.

CHAMPION THOUGHT:
God Spoke His Purpose for You before Creation

With that thought in mind, consider 2 Timothy 1:9, which says,

> *Who has saved us and called us with a holy calling, not according to our works, but according to His own purpose and grace which was given to us in Christ Jesus before time began.*
> (2 Timothy 1:9)

Notice here that God did not call us *"according to our works, but according to His own purpose and grace,"* which He gave to us in Jesus before Creation (emphasis added). We are not to carry out *our* purpose, but His.

That word *"called"* is *kaleo* in the Greek.[5] It is "akin to the base of *keleuo*; to incite by word, i.e., order:—bid, (at, give) command."[6] In other words, 2 Timothy 1:9 states that before the foundation of the world God called each of us and spoke His purpose for us. He knew you before time began. God saved you, called you, purposed you, and gave grace to you. He set you on a course so you arrived in a specific time frame, empowered by Him to do what He purposed. He created you for a specific reason that no one else could fulfill. Purpose is God's reason that He created you as a champion.

CHAMPION THOUGHT:
Creation Must Bow to Fulfill Your Divine Purpose

Now, since God spoke your purpose before Creation, how can anything that is created have the ability to stop His purpose in you? If creation could stop God's purpose in you, then it would be higher and more influential than the Creator.

Realize that your position and purpose were not established because of a need in this earth. No, God established you in your position to carry forth His purpose as He called you. Once you know your position and purpose, nothing can stop it. In fact, creation actually serves God's purpose in you. David had this mindset. That's why he boldly attacked the giant warrior with a simple slingshot.

The book of Ephesians explains that creation serves God's purposes. Discussing the forgiveness of our sins, the Bible says, *"Having made known to us the mystery of His will, according to His good pleasure which He purposed in Himself"* (Ephesians 1:9).

God purposed in Himself to have a good, pleasurable will for your life. Your purpose is not by happenstance or chance. No, He specifically and uniquely designed you to carry out the good pleasure of His will and purpose.

The passage continues, saying, *"In Him also we have obtained an inheritance, being predestined according to the purpose of Him who works all things according to the counsel of His will"* (v. 11). Notice that God works *"all things"* according to His purpose. Another version of the Bible relates this verse as follows: *"In him we were also chosen, having been predestined according to the plan of him who works out everything in conformity with the purpose of his will"* (NIV). In addition, the Bible tells us, *"And we know that **all things** work together for good to those who love God, to those who are the called according to His purpose"* (Romans 8:28, emphasis added).

When did God call you? Before Creation. When did God purpose you? Before Creation. Therefore, once you see the purpose of your life, God Himself, who created everything, mandates that it all work together in tandem or in cooperation to bring that purpose to manifestation. Therefore, everything in creation is designed to follow God's purpose—including why He made you!

Let's briefly summarize what we have learned here. Resistance to purpose has no authority because God backs His purpose with

action. He has, by divine selection, created man for His own pleasure to manifest His purpose on the earth. Therefore, God is working all things according to His good pleasure and will to fulfill His
purpose. This is why creation cannot withstand God's purpose but
instead must bow to fulfill it.

In a later chapter, we will discuss this point in further detail.
For now, simply realize, Champion, that God has given *you* a
divine purpose. You are not the originator of that purpose; you
simply discover it. Then, God will use all creation and everything
within His power to cause you to fulfill your divine purpose! Nothing can stop it.

CHAMPION THOUGHT:
Until Purpose Is Known,
Only Abuse Will Result

Many people—perhaps even you—think that knowing a person's purpose is out of reach. You might be thinking, *Well, this is
just too simple. Sure, David killed Goliath with a stone and a slingshot,
but it was just a lucky shot. Yes, a few people have had some breaks
in life and stumbled onto good fortune. Now, they jump up on their
soapboxes, declaring, "We've found a reason for living," but this can't
be true for everyone.* My friend, God's promises are not idle words.
Neither are they for a select few. We all can know and walk in our
purpose—including you!

The tragedy of not understanding our purpose is very common
today. As a result, abuse has become prevalent. Abuse can be
described as using something without the consideration or knowledge of the purpose for which it was created. Until the purpose of
a thing is known, abuse is most likely to result.

For example, consider this common scenario. You needed to
tighten a screw. Instead of locating a screwdriver, which is designed
or purposed to do the job, you grabbed a table knife from the

kitchen drawer. What happened? You put the table knife into the screw head and twisted. Sure, the screw began to tighten, but because you used the knife out of its intended purpose, you abused it.

Most of us know what an abused knife looks like. When you go back to the drawer, days later, to reach for a table knife to spread your butter, don't you pass over all the knives that have what I call "the twisted tip"? Why? The twisted tip, which is the proof of abuse, mars the knife and makes it no longer good for its original purpose. That knife is then overlooked for the next task at hand.

This is where humanity finds itself today. Because people have not known their God-given purpose, they have misused their lives. Many have even been abused by others or have fallen into negative circumstances instead of being used for God's intended purpose. Also, when they did not know the purpose of the things in their lives, they have misused them. As this pattern continues, we become all too familiar with abuse. This further dwindles the ability to understand purpose. Eventually, not only does it appear impossible to know the purpose, but people don't even realize that there is a right purpose.

Today, abuse is rampant. There is spousal abuse, verbal abuse, child abuse, sexual abuse, drug abuse, animal abuse, spiritual abuse, abuse of authority, and more. You can find it at every level and aspect of life. In each case, the victim carries the scars of abuse, just as the twisted table knife does.

People who have been abused often begin to distrust the dreams of their hearts. They have difficulty trusting themselves, the people around them, and even God. They may not believe that He is *for* them or that He is willing or able to make their lives count for anything. Seeing themselves as "used goods" and worthless, their hearts break. At times, the pain seems unbearable.

That's the bad news. But there is good news!

CHAMPION THOUGHT:
God Can Use the Broken and Abused

Unlike the marred table knife—destined to be overlooked for the next meal—a person who has been abused *can* be restored to his or her intended purpose. In fact, this is why Jesus came to earth. He said,

> *The Spirit of the LORD is upon Me, because He has anointed Me to preach the gospel to the poor; He has sent Me to heal the brokenhearted, to proclaim liberty to the captives and recovery of sight to the blind, to set at liberty those who are oppressed.* (Luke 4:18)

Jesus came to heal those who have been abused and liberate them from their prisons of purposelessness. However, until they allow Him to heal their broken hearts, they will continue to question, *Will my life amount to anything?* Without Jesus, they will search for significance and strive for fulfillment in other venues. However, they will never find it, because significance and fulfillment can be found only by recognizing *who* they are in Christ (position) and that God has created them for a reason (purpose).

My friend, do you have a broken heart? Or have you thought that knowing your purpose is impossible? It's time to realize that the One who inhabits eternity has set your destiny before you were ever created. God did not put you here by mistake. No! He appointed you to be on the earth now, and He knows what He's doing.

Don't ever think that you are an accident. Even if your birth into this world was unplanned by your earthly parents—possibly out of wedlock or because of rape—you have a God-ordained purpose. The enemy may have tried to keep you from getting here, but you made it! Your existence is proof that you are not a mistake, because all human beings are created by God. Even in the midst of destruction, the Bible promises: *"The LORD will perfect that which concerns me; Your mercy, O LORD, endures forever"* (Psalm 138:8). Therefore, you can be *"confident...that He who has begun a good work in you will complete it"* (Philippians 1:6). Remember that God, who has purposed it, will do it.

In the past you may not have known God's purpose for your life, but your future does not have to be purposeless. Your history is not relevant to your future. It does not matter once you discover your purpose. Regardless of all the failures, faults, and frustrations in your life, you are God's champion. Start rejoicing! All the earth is eagerly awaiting the revealing of His purpose in your life.

CHAMPION THOUGHT:
You Are Uniquely Designed to Do the Extraordinary

God has deposited within you the seeds of every gifting and quality necessary to bring forth the dream that He has planted in your heart to fulfill His purpose. These are not natural strengths but abilities that come by grace. Remember that God purposed and gave you grace before the world began. At your creation, He divinely equipped you in line with your extraordinary purpose.

It is critical for you not to leave your gifts dormant or allow them to stagnate. Our generation needs what God has designed you to contribute, and God desires for you to fulfill it. Now is the time to acknowledge and bring out the gifts within you, so the Holy Spirit can develop, empower, strengthen, and enhance them. They will grow as you begin to walk in them.

Focus on the areas that you are gifted in instead of those you are not. Tap into your positive points, not the negatives. It is important that you do not educate your weaknesses. This is a common distraction. Many people waste precious time and resources doing this. For example, if we were applying these truths to business, I would advise you that it's better to hire the strengths of another than to strengthen your weaknesses. You see, if you don't have a gift, someone who *does* have it can do it better. Regardless of how much you educate yourself in the areas of your weaknesses, you will never develop yourself to the level of a person who does have those gifts.

You need to recognize what you are designed for and do that, or you will operate in the flesh. If you don't follow your purpose, then stress, frustration, lost time, wasted resources, and abuse will result. Also, you will miss what God originally called you to do. Acknowledge that you are not gifted in everything. Be the one God created you to be. It only takes one to fulfill your unique purpose. You are that one. You cannot be something else. Get a vision—a clear, uncluttered view—of why God created you. Then, when you "know that you know" what your purpose is, you will not be distracted from it.

CHAMPION THOUGHT:
Follow God's Purpose, Not Opportunity

Another common distraction is following opportunity. Most people look for opportunity, but God sets our destiny. There is a significant difference between these two. Knowing this truth will help you to make the right decisions.

God guides us by supernatural leadership—not by opportunity! His leadership is contrary to man's promotion. When someone perceives or recognizes a special gift, calling, or anointing in your life and wants to bring you into the limelight, it does not necessarily mean that God is directing you. His direction must come from within you as the Holy Spirit reveals the will of God to your heart. Even if many doors open at once, and opportunities seem to overtake you, first check to be sure that these doors are in line with your God-designed purpose and His will for your life.

Never forget the passage in Acts, which says about God and man,

> And He...has determined their preappointed times and the boundaries of their dwellings, so that they should seek the Lord, in the hope that they might grope for Him and find Him, though He is not far from each one of us; for in Him we live and move and have our being. (Acts 17:26–28)

As a Christian, you should never allow external circumstances to lead you. Do not let the "door of opportunity" or "human promotion" guide you. Instead, you can know the voice of the Lord. He is the Door. Let Him lead you. Speaking of Himself as the Door and the Good Shepherd, Jesus said,

> The sheep hear his voice; and he calls his own sheep by name and leads them out. And when he brings out his own sheep, he goes before them; and the sheep follow him, for they know his voice. Yet they will by no means follow a stranger, but will flee from him, for they do not know the voice of strangers....Most assuredly, I say to you, I am the door of the sheep....If anyone enters by Me, he will be saved, and will go in and out and find pasture. (John 10:3–5, 7, 9)

It pays to obey the Lord "from the inside out" instead of responding to opportunity, which appears "from the outside in." Your life will be blessed when you have His witness—the absolute assurance in your spirit that you are following the Lord's purpose. Hear His voice and follow it, regardless of any circumstances. Don't ask your checkbook if you can obey God's will! Following your purpose and obeying God do not require permission from anyone or anything—including money!

Good opportunities—which may even appear to be in alignment with your purpose—will come, but you need to take only God's divine appointments. For example, as I mentioned earlier, publishers approached me more than a decade ago to write this and other books. Yes, I knew that I was to write these books, and the financial arrangement was very enticing at that time. However, the Lord revealed to me that this was not His timing for me to walk in that aspect of my purpose. These opportunities were not His divine appointments. Therefore, I turned down the contracts.

CHAMPION THOUGHT:
To Every Purpose, There Is a Time for Execution

You see, not only do you have a divine purpose, but there is also a time that God has for you to walk in it. The Bible reveals a startling truth about purpose: *"A wise man's heart discerneth both time and judgment. Because to every purpose there is time and judgment, therefore the misery of man is great upon him"* (Ecclesiastes 8:5-6 KJV). The *New International Version* substitutes *"procedure"* for the word *"judgment"* here. Judgment is executing a matter. It is using governing authority to carry out a legal sentence with the ability to bring it to bear. Therefore, *"to every purpose there is time and judgment"* means that every purpose has a special time span in which it is to be executed according to a specific procedure.

Notice, verse six here says, *"Therefore the misery of man is great upon him."* In other words, God has placed purpose in the boundary of time. He has ordained a specific time for its execution, and if a person does not know this, his misery is great. Why? It is because he does not understand why he exists. He doesn't know his purpose. Therefore, he does not recognize the timing or understand the way to execute God's plans.

Remember what happens when someone doesn't know an object's purpose. He is likely to abuse or misuse it. Consequently, a man who does not understand these truths will do what God intended him *not* to do. The man will disobey God's purpose.

In the process, he will miss God's appointments for his life. This man, like each of us in the past, walks *"according to the course of this world, according to the prince of the power of the air, the spirit who now works in the sons of disobedience"* (Ephesians 2:2). Why does the enemy want man to follow him? It is because he wants us to miss God's purpose, timing, judgment, and provision. He wants you to miss why God created you.

Champion, it's time to know your purpose!

CHAMPION THOUGHT:
You Can Discover God's Purpose and Will for Your Life

Are you ready to discover your specific God-ordained purpose, vision, dream, and gifts? This is *not* impossible to determine. God desires for you to know your purpose. Otherwise, how can you ever fulfill it? He did not create you and leave it to chance that you would stumble upon it one day. He has shown each of us how to find it.

I have been able to discover purpose. You can, too. Here's how: First, read the Bible to identify the areas of purpose that you do not understand. As you do, ask God to reveal these to you. Then, when He enlightens you, study the Scriptures in those specific areas to gain the revelation of purpose that you lack.

For example, early in my marriage, I spent seven years studying God's Word and praying to identify and clarify the areas of purpose that I did not understand. During that time, the Holy Spirit showed me that I did not know God's purpose for a man, a husband, a father, marriage, work, providing for my family, or even money. I realized that I needed to know why God's purposes existed, so that I would no longer abuse the reason God had them in my life. That is when I learned that once purpose is known, *nothing* can stop it.

Second, during your Bible-study pursuit, it is critical to pray in line with the Bible. We are to pray God's Word back to Him. In doing this, we pray *His* will and purposes, not ours. Remember that David said, *"The LORD is my shepherd; I shall not want"* (Psalm 23:1). Instead of being dominated by human need and want, we should be praying the very Word of God. Thus, we will become dominated by His will and purposes. Here is an example of how to pray the Scriptures in order to reveal your specific divine purpose.

Pray the first chapter of Ephesians. Thank God, in verses four and five, that He has chosen *"us in Him* [Christ Jesus] *before the foundation of the world, that we should be holy and without blame before Him in love,"* being *"predestined...to adoption as sons by Jesus Christ to Himself, according to the good pleasure of His will."*

Then, in verse six, also thank Him that *"He made us accepted in the Beloved,"* so that all rejection is gone from you.

Tell God that you receive His promise of knowing His will and purposes, according to verse nine. It says He has *"made known to us the mystery of His will, according to His good pleasure which He purposed in Himself."*

Again thank God, in verse 11, because, *"In Him also we have obtained an inheritance, being predestined according to the purpose of Him who works all things according to the counsel of His will."*

Pray for God to enlighten you, so that you don't simply exist or act without clear purpose. According to verse 17, ask Him to open the eyes of your understanding and *"give to you the spirit of wisdom and revelation in the knowledge of Him."*

Ephesians 1:15–23 contains the apostle Paul's personal prayer for the New Testament church. Use it as your roadmap for daily prayer. In the School of Biblical Studies, we instruct our students to pray this passage ten times each day for the Holy Spirit to unveil the person of Jesus and His purpose for their lives. The power of the Word in these verses has revolutionized countless lives. Pray it. Read it. It's yours!

Next, as you pray, remember that God did not speak your purpose *after* you were born. No, He spoke it *before* He created the entire world. Pray 2 Timothy 1:9, thanking God that He *"has saved us and called us with a holy calling, not according to our works, but according to His own purpose and grace which was given to us in Christ Jesus before time began."* Realize that your purpose operates by grace, which He gave to you before the world began. Pray, "Father, I thank You that the divine purpose for my existence originated in You before Creation. *You* decided that I was to live in this era and generation, be from this family in this nation, be of this race with this sex at this time and in this posture of life. Thank You that I *will* accomplish Your purpose for my life."

Also pray Romans 8:28, thanking God that all creation obeys His purpose: *"We know that all things work together for good to those who love God, to those who are the called according to His purpose."*

Let God Accomplish His Purpose through You

Are you beginning to grasp the awesome reality of these truths? You are in right relationship with God by *His* design—not yours. The purpose of your life is not simply to eke out an existence and have a few nice things to make you feel significant. No, Champion, you are here to carry out a dream that has been locked up in the very heart and mind of God since before Creation! This is the reason that you exist.

Your purpose is not to be a mystery. You are to know what God has purposed you for in the earth—*the why* preceding *the what.* Then, you are to walk in that purpose by awakening to the reality that God mandates all creation to complete and bring into manifestation His purpose for you.

In closing this chapter, I encourage you to pursue the preordained call of God that has sent you into this generation to fulfill His purpose. Don't ever think that your purpose is insignificant. No, no, no! It is the most powerful truth to know other than your position in Christ. Once you discover your purpose, *you* will be a force to be reckoned with. Creation will bow to obey, and the enemy must remove his hands from God's purpose in you. When you know your purpose, you can radically transform your entire environment.

Champion, when you act upon your purpose *with* God—not just *for* Him—you have the ability to break barriers, remove restraints, do the impossible, see the unseen, speak what creates, pray what manifests, and receive God's will. We will discuss these topics further in the chapters that follow.

4
Forward Momentum

Champion, you now know what a breakthrough is and understand that truth has the authority to liberate you. Because of your position in Christ, you realize that nothing can remove you from the place to which God has lifted you. You have learned how to discover your unique purpose, recognizing that nothing can stop what God has spoken about you before Creation. Knowing these truths places you in a position of readiness. Let me explain.

CHAMPION THOUGHT:
As a Man Thinks in His Heart, So Is He

You have probably heard it said, "Your attitude determines your altitude." It is true that what you think of yourself, your circumstances, and other areas impacts how high you can go in life. This is another way of explaining a biblical truth that says, as a man *"thinks in his heart, so is he"* (Proverbs 23:7). If you have renewed your mind to the truth of what God has already made you and you know the power of your purpose, then you can soar in life. In other words, if you see yourself as God's champion, then you will be able to overcome every obstacle before you to achieve His purpose. However, if you think that you are defeated, powerless, limited by your abilities, and without purpose, then you will be content to sit on the sidelines of life, watching others succeed and find fulfillment.

Realize that this is a paradigm shift in your thinking. It is a move from an old pattern of thoughts to God's mind-set. If you can make this leap to accepting God's truths—moving from what you thought was true to actual reality—then you are ready to walk as God's champion. In fact, by simply accepting these champion thoughts—knowing the truth—you have forward momentum. You are light-years ahead of others with no understanding of these truths. It is critical for you to establish in your thinking that God's way is truth. Do not simply *entertain* it. In other words, don't think of these truths as a *possibility*, but realize that they are *reality*. If you have accepted this new mind-set, then you are ready to move forward!

CHAMPION THOUGHT:
You Were Born for Such a Time as This

Do you remember what Jonas Salk contributed to society? What did Alfred Bernhard Nobel invent? How did the words of a Sunday school teacher named Mr. Kimball affect eternity in 1855? As you continue reading *It Only Takes One,* you will discover how these individuals single-handedly revolutionized their generations. Yet they—and other individuals like them—still affect our lives today.

Have you ever realized that most major transformations of history were not forged through corporate decisions made by *groups*? Instead, history records names of *individuals* who have changed life as people knew it. We can find repeated occurrences in which one daring person with conviction set the stage to shape human history, penetrating barriers and establishing a new path for all to follow. Some have set good standards, while others have had evil effects on the world.

For example, individual believers, such as the apostle Paul, recorded many of the key principles in the Bible. For centuries, Christians have built their lives, families, and futures upon these truths. Today, this is still the theology by which we live. As we have discussed, Alexander Graham Bell and Christopher Columbus revolutionized the world. Other examples abound of individuals who changed the world.

Literally, it only takes one to bring a huge transformation to humanity. Regardless of our circumstances and backgrounds, God has designed each of us to have a profound impact on our generation. By acting on our purpose, we each have the potential to change nations, governments, states, cities, businesses, schools, and families, as well as many other areas.

Queen Esther

The book of Esther describes the account of a Jewish orphan's rise to queen in Persia. Through God's blessing, Esther found favor with King Ahasuerus and impacted an entire nation. The Bible says,

> *The king loved Esther more than all the other women, and she obtained grace and favor in his sight more than all the virgins; so he set the royal crown upon her head and made her queen instead of Vashti.* (Esther 2:17)

Meanwhile, Haman, the wicked prime minister under King Ahasuerus, plotted to massacre the Jews. He began by building a gallows to hang Mordecai, Esther's cousin and adoptive father. When Esther sought Mordecai's advice, he replied, "*Who knows whether you have come to the kingdom for such a time as this?*" (Esther 4:14).

Risking death because she was uninvited, Queen Esther approached the king's court. She pleaded for mercy on behalf of her people. Again, God blessed Esther, and the king greatly favored her, granting her desire to spare the lives of her people.

Then, he commanded his servants to have Haman hanged on the gallows, which Haman had built for Mordecai.

Esther risked her life to deliver her people from annihilation. Not only did the king spare the Jews, but he also blessed them and promoted Mordecai to the powerful position of second in command. The brave actions of this one woman changed the course of history for the Jews. You see, God had placed Esther into that kingdom in the position of queen for such a crucial time. Had she not been sensitive to God's call upon her life, she would not have been ready to move as God directed. The enemy would have destroyed her and the entire Jewish population in Persia.

Realize that *you* also were born for such a time as *this*! God has a specific purpose for you. Yes, it only takes one, and *you* are that one. If you know these truths, get ready for your adventure with God.

Ready, Set,...Now What?

All right, you might be thinking, *I understand it! I am the one. I am ready. I am all set to move. But what should I do next?* There is one thing you must do before stepping out.

CHAMPION THOUGHT:
Prepare for Your Destiny

You must prepare to walk in God's purpose for your life. This is a critical step. You need to get into position for Him to use you and move through you. Although you might be tempted to skip this step because you are eager to launch out into what God has planned for you, don't miss this crucial element. Otherwise, you will likely get ahead of God's timing and be unprepared to fulfill your purpose.

CHAMPION THOUGHT:
Preparation Is Not Wasted Time

Many people who have accomplished great breakthroughs in the world spent considerable time preparing to walk in their destinies. Because they had set aside time to prepare themselves, they were in position to break through their barriers. Don't ever think that preparation is a waste of time. It is necessary for you to complete your God-ordained mission in life.

To illustrate this point, let's consider several champions who prepared in order to fulfill their missions in life.

Roger Bannister

A medical student from England, Roger Bannister was the first person to run the mile in less than four minutes. After suffering defeat at the Olympics in 1952, Bannister stopped competing for the next year to work on building his endurance. This time of preparation paid off because in 1954, after nearly withdrawing from the race due to the weather, he finished "the so-called 'miracle mile'" in under four minutes.[1] Overcoming every obstacle, Bannister broke through all his barriers to excel at his God-given gift. He succeeded in his dream, however, only after he had devoted himself to a necessary time of preparation.

Upon discovering that he had the gift of "sudden and abnormal athletic effort," Bannister had begun his training for track. As a student physician, he had thoroughly studied the human body—"a running machine"—and the physical mechanics of his sport. He then adopted training methods to increase his speed.[2]

This young man caught a glimpse of his destiny. Recall the definition of breakthrough: "a sudden burst of advanced knowledge that goes through every barrier or line of defense." With his gift of sudden bursts of physical effort, coupled with advanced knowledge—a vision—of his future, Bannister prepared himself to defeat every barrier. Then, victory was his. However, preparation was paramount to his success.

Queen Esther

Earlier, we discussed the Jewish orphan, Esther, who became queen in Persia. Before the king selected her as queen from among the beautiful virgins in the entire kingdom, Esther had spent twelve months in preparation. According to the custom, for one year she underwent a regimen of special cosmetics and food. Only then did she enter the king's presence for his scrutiny, and he chose her over all the other women as queen. (See Esther 2:1–18.) Her time of preparation paid off.

On another occasion, Esther prepared herself before entering the king's presence. When Haman had planned to kill the Jews, Queen Esther commanded that Mordecai and all the Jews fast for three days for her. *"My maids and I will fast likewise,"* she said. *"And so I will go to the king, which is against the law; and if I perish, I perish!"* (Esther 4:16). After her time of preparation and fasting, Esther entered the king's inner court, risking her life for this important cause. She again found favor with him and afterward interceded on the Jews' behalf, exposing Haman's wicked plot. Thus, Esther thwarted the scheme to kill her people.

Preparation is crucial to fulfilling your purpose.

John the Baptist

The life of Jesus' cousin, John the Baptist, is also an excellent illustration of preparing for one's purpose. This unique prophet actually moved to the wilderness for his purpose to be manifested.

Prior to the birth of John the Baptist, the angel Gabriel appeared to Zechariah to explain his future son's mission. Declaring that Elizabeth, Zechariah's wife, would bear a son named John, the angel announced,

> Many of the people of Israel will he [John] bring back to the
> Lord their God. And he will go on before the Lord, in the
> spirit and power of Elijah, to turn the hearts of the fathers

81

*to their children and the disobedient to the wisdom of the
righteous—to make ready a people prepared for the Lord.*
(Luke 1:16–17 NIV)

Because it was foretold in the Scriptures, the Jews knew that
their Messiah would eventually arrive to deliver them. However,
John the Baptist had advanced knowledge about the Savior. This
separated him from the status quo of the crowds, many of whom
eventually followed his ministry. Let's examine how John received
this advanced knowledge.

Elizabeth had a cousin named Mary, who would become the
mother of Jesus. Now, when both of these women were pregnant,
Mary came to visit Elizabeth.

*And it happened, when Elizabeth heard the greeting of Mary,
that the babe [John the Baptist] leaped in her womb; and
Elizabeth was filled with the Holy Spirit. Then she spoke out
with a loud voice and said, "Blessed are you among women,
and blessed is the fruit of your womb [Jesus]! But why is this
granted to me, that the mother of my Lord should come to me?
For indeed, as soon as the voice of your greeting sounded in my
ears, the babe [John the Baptist] leaped in my womb for joy."*
(Luke 1:41–44)

Remarkably, Elizabeth recognized that Mary's unborn baby
was her Redeemer. Then, an even greater miracle occurred. John
the Baptist, *while still in his mother's womb,* leaped for joy at the
sound of his Lord's mother's voice! John recognized the promised Messiah, his cousin! Here, we see that even before he was
born, John had advanced knowledge of his purpose, which was
to prepare his people for the coming of Jesus. This knowledge
empowered John to break through every barrier to fulfill his purpose.

As John grew up, he moved to the desert wilderness to prepare
himself for his ministry. The Bible explains: *"So the child grew and*

became strong in spirit, and was in the deserts till the day of his mani-festation to Israel" (Luke 1:80).

Once when asked who he was, John clearly explained his purpose: *"John replied in the words of Isaiah the prophet, 'I am the voice of one calling in the desert, "Make straight the way for the Lord"'"* (John 1:23 NIV). Notice that his mission in life was no secret to John.

Jesus also confirmed John's purpose, saying, *"He is the Elijah who was to come"* (Matthew 11:14 NIV). By this, He revealed that John the Baptist had fulfilled the angel Gabriel's prophecy regarding Elijah's coming before Jesus. You see, to the Jews, the coming of Elijah had been a major indicator that their Messiah was at hand. Jesus explained that John was the one for whom they had been waiting, the one who would point to the Lord.

Breaking through all the religious norms—every part of the status quo—John's voice had prepared the world for a fresh move of God's Spirit. However, this was not an easy message to hear. It is interesting to note that John did not preach in the local synagogue. Nor did he knock on people's doors, asking if they wanted to believe. While there is nothing wrong with these forms of ministry, John understood that they were not part of his purpose. No, the people had to travel to the desert wilderness to hear John. After all, he was *"the voice of one crying in the wilderness: 'Prepare the way of the LORD'"* (Mark 1:3). Now, this was a laborious trip, which took time. However, it was the price the people had to pay to hear God's message of that hour.

How much are you willing to go through to hear God today? Are you willing to break free from wrong allegiances, alliances, belief systems, cycles, and understandings that obstruct your path to Him? That's what John the Baptist did. He did not live in the environment where most people did. Instead, he worked in the wilderness away from everything that could hinder his purpose. Consequently, people had to exert the same extra effort to hear his message.

Those who wanted to listen to John also could not stay in the multitudes, where most people were in agreement about life without the Messiah. No, they had to break free from the status quo. They had to go into a quiet and remote place, away from the crowds and bustle of life. There, without any hindrances, they could recognize that *"still small voice"* of God (1 Kings 19:12) within the prophet's message.

What did John mean as he compelled the people to prepare for the Lord? What was his mind-set as he mandated this change in their lives? The answers to these questions lie in John's very life. Remember what we read earlier about him: *"So the child grew and became strong in spirit, and was in the deserts till the day of his manifestation to Israel"* (Luke 1:80)? Before his public ministry began, John lived in the wilderness. This is how he prepared himself for the day in which he would begin crying out, *"Prepare the way of the LORD"* (Matthew 3:3; Mark 1:3; Luke 3:4). Think about it: In the wilderness John prepared himself to prepare others to prepare themselves! God had called him to be a forerunner to prepare the world for Jesus.

John asked people to stop their daily activities to recognize that God was about to move in a new way. He boldly urged them to prepare for that life-changing experience, which was accepting Jesus as their Messiah and living according to His will.

Right now, I encourage you to examine your life. Have you spent the necessary time to prepare for the move of God in *your* life? Most people think it will happen by itself. Their perspective of God is, "God will move if He wants to. Whatever He wants to do will happen." They leave their lives to fate, saying, *"Qué será, será.* What will be, will be." This is a grave error. Instead of accepting this mind-set, you need to prepare for the entrance of God in the area of your life where He desires to move. You must prepare yourself for change, for the move of God.

God's *"still small voice"* speaks to you like John the Baptist crying out in the wilderness, *"Prepare the way of the LORD."* If you serve God and listen to His Holy Spirit, He will show you which way to go and how to prepare yourself for it. His Word tells us, "*Your ears shall hear a word behind you, saying, 'This is the way, walk in it,' whenever you turn to the right hand or whenever you turn to the left*" (Isaiah 30:21).

Is It Time for Revival?

For thousands of years, God's people have prepared to fulfill His purposes. Repeatedly, great miracles have followed when His believers have pressed in to pursue Him at all costs and taken the time to prepare themselves for His move. To understand how this works in modern times, let's briefly turn back the pages of history to approximately one hundred years ago.

Modern church history records January 1, 1901, as the obscure beginning of a new move of the Holy Spirit in the United States, the effects of which we are still experiencing today. However, most Christians do not know who the forerunners were or how it began.

Charles F. Parham (1873–1929) is known as the founder of the movement called Pentecostalism in America. One church-history expert reports:

> Parham's focus was world evangelism, but in his opinion, the church of his day lacked the power necessary to fulfill the mandate of the Great Commission. He yearned for that outpouring from heaven that would make the church a dynamic force in the earth, both in word and in deed.[3]

Here, we see that Parham recognized the need to prepare for God's next great move.

In the summer of 1900, Charles Parham discovered isolated reports of missionaries speaking in tongues, which were actual languages unknown to themselves. Parham became convinced that God was about to pour out His Spirit, causing a worldwide revival that would usher in the return of Jesus. Therefore, in the fall of that year, Parham opened Bethel Bible College in Topeka, Kansas, to prepare his pupils to receive personally the coming outpouring of the Holy Spirit and then take it to the world.[4] The school focused on prayer along with biblical studies. In fact, each student participated in a prayer vigil during the twenty-four hours of daily prayer at the school.[5]

After the students completed their courses in late December 1900,[6] Parham directed them to study Acts 2, where believers first spoke in tongues.[7] Several days later, on New Year's Eve, they held a "Watchnight Service." As Parham fulfilled a request to pray for one of his students, Agnes Ozman (1870–1937), she received the expected baptism and spoke in tongues! Within days, Parham and others of his students also received "their personal *Pentecost*."[8]

In 1906, when Parham started a similar short-term Bible school in Houston, Texas, William J. Seymour (1870–1922), a local African-American holiness pastor, wanted to enroll. However, due to "southern segregation laws and customs, his application posed a problem. Parham, nonetheless, skirted the legal restrictions by arranging for Seymour to sit in an adjoining room where, through an open door, he was able to listen to the lectures."[9] Do you see how Parham and Seymour did not allow resistance to stop them from preparing themselves to receive from the Holy Spirit?

Seymour then went on to carry Parham's teachings from Houston to Los Angeles. There, in 1906, the Azusa Street Revival, which lasted several years, broke out under Seymour's leadership and prayer. "The revival spread nationally with the establishment of new congregations and the transformation of existing ones."[10] "From Los Angeles, news of the 'outpouring' of the Holy Spirit spread across the nation and around the world by word of mouth and the printed page. Before long, Pentecostal revivals could be found in Canada, England, Scandinavia, Germany, India, China, Africa, and South America."[11]

As believers have rediscovered the history of the Azusa Street Revival, they have seen how this great move of God can be traced back to William J. Seymour, who attended Charles Parham's Bible school. Do you see how God uses individual people to change the face of the world? What would have happened if Parham and Seymour had allowed the segregationist policies and other setbacks to prevent them from teaching and learning about the Holy Spirit? Do you see how important every person is in the kingdom of God?

Parham's message and the ensuing Pentecostal movement was only the beginning. An outgrowth of it was the charismatic movement, which officially began in 1960, when Dennis Bennett (1917–1992) announced to his Episcopal church in Van Nuys, California, that he spoke with other tongues.[12] The charismatic movement then spread to other Protestant denominations, the Roman Catholic Church, and Orthodox churches.[13] Also, "new independent Charismatic churches and fellowships"[14] and worldwide denominations[15] sprang up.

God used Parham and then Seymour to begin a great, new move of His Spirit. However, it was not only for themselves. No, God used these individuals to spread revival to America and around the world. Church-history experts wrote about the Azusa Street Revival, "The gifts of the Holy Spirit (1 Corinthians 12), understood by most denominations as having ceased at the end of the first century, had been restored."[16]

These people believed the truth about the baptism in the Holy Spirit. Then, only after preparing themselves by studying the Word, praying, and waiting on the Lord, they received the desired gift.

CHAMPION THOUGHT:
Preparation Creates a Safe Haven for Your Purpose

It is critical that you prepare yourself, so God can use you and move in your life. Yes, this will involve effort. The move of

God in your life does not happen by itself. You need to know certain truths before you can be in position for His move. It is that simple. If you are out of position, then what God wants to do will not happen through your life. He desires to use you, but if you are unprepared, then He will not. Therefore, you will not experience the sudden burst of advanced knowledge; you will not be able to resist the enemy; or you will be distracted by other issues. Consequently, you will not pave a pathway for people to move through, as God had intended. You see, when you prepare to walk in your destiny, you create a safe haven for yourself and your purpose.

Now is the time to prepare yourself so that you are in the position to receive from God. First, you must determine whether you are in the proper position.

CHAMPION THOUGHT:
Dead Reckon Your Life

Take time to locate where you are today in God's plan. In every journey on the seas—whether in charted or uncharted waters—a navigator must dead reckon the ship. In this process, a sailor calculates a vessel's position, based upon the last known position, taking into account wind, currents, the ship's speed, and other factors. Similarly, you need to dead reckon your life. This critical task identifies your current position as best as possible. From there, you can plot a course to your new destination. If you have no estimation of where you are today, how can you know the next steps to take? How can you even see the end of the course? How will you ever know if you have arrived there?

CHAMPION THOUGHT:
Measure How Far You Are in God's Plan

It's time to check how you have been living. Imagine now that we could pull back the curtains of your life to reveal what the Spirit of God had spoken about you before Creation. What would we learn if we read line upon line and chapter after chapter everything God had purposed for you to be and do? How would you line up at this moment? What would your position be compared with His plan?

Also, what would we discover if we could use a measuring tool to reveal your level of conviction and effort to line up with God's plan? Would we see that you have accepted barriers with no hope of ever breaking through them? Would we discover that you have stifled or silenced God's voice in your spirit because it required effort and faith to follow? Or, instead, would we learn that you have had a burning desire to fellowship with God in such a supernatural way that you have broken through barriers that others counted as impenetrable?

Realize that your purpose, which God reveals in your spirit, will not be made clear unless you have commitment, conviction, and faith to follow Him despite all resistance and walls of defense. If you do not have these in your life today, then you need to prepare yourself.

CHAMPION THOUGHT:
Your Highest Level Today Will Be Your Lowest Tomorrow

As you determine your current position and measure yourself against God's plan, don't be discouraged if you find yourself falling short. Acknowledge that the highest level in life that you experience today will be your lowest level tomorrow. Here is where you need to set what I call your "base acceptable bottom." Determine that you will go only up from here with God, and that you will fall no lower. Encourage yourself because life will get only better from today forward.

Once you begin following God's plan for your life, you will find fulfillment. Please don't misunderstand. God does not promise an easy life without conflict and difficult circumstances. However, when you walk according to His course, He commits to fill you with peace, joy, and fulfillment. Life will be an exciting adventure instead of a grueling, nightmarish game of survival.

It's time to capture in your spirit the plans God has for you. Then, prepare yourself. God promises that He will reveal the path to fulfill His purpose in your life. It doesn't matter where you are when you begin! You simply need to start. The Bible explains that His road will be clear. You will not get lost.

> *A highway shall be there, and a road, and it shall be called the Highway of Holiness. The unclean shall not pass over it, but it shall be for others. Whoever walks the road, although a fool, shall not go astray. No lion shall be there, nor shall any ravenous beast go up on it....But the redeemed shall walk there....They shall obtain joy and gladness, and sorrow and sighing shall flee away.* (Isaiah 35:8–10)

CHAMPION THOUGHT:
Free Yourself from Everything outside Your Divine Purpose

As part of your preparation, you need to set yourself apart for your divine design. Remove everything from your life that does not honor God. The Bible instructs:

> *But the firm foundation (laid by) God stands, sure and unshaken, bearing this seal (inscription): The Lord knows those who are His, and, Let every one who names [himself by] the name of the Lord give up all iniquity and stand aloof from it. But in a great house there are not only vessels of gold*

and silver, but also [utensils] of wood and earthenware, and some for honorable and noble [use] and some for menial and ignoble [use]. So whoever cleanses ["purge," KJV] himself [from what is ignoble and unclean, who separates himself from contact with contaminating and corrupting influences] will [then himself] be a vessel set apart ["sanctified," KJV] and useful for honorable and noble purposes, consecrated and profitable to the Master, fit and ready ["prepared," KJV] for any good work.

(2 Timothy 2:19–21 AMP)

According to this passage, two categories of people exist:

• Vessels of gold and silver that are set apart for honorable and noble purposes, consecrated and profitable to God, and prepared for His work

• Utensils of wood and earthenware for menial, unclean, and ignoble use, which are in contact with contaminating and corrupting influences

In which category do you fit? God wants you to be a vessel of gold or silver in His great kingdom. Therefore, if anything in your life dishonors Him, purge yourself of its influence. Remove the hindrances and distractions in your life that are insignificant, invaluable, unnecessary, and have no bearing on eternity and the fulfillment of God's purposes. Free yourself from everything that is outside your divine purpose.

CHAMPION THOUGHT:
Determine Which of the Four Sources of Wisdom Are in Operation

---

In your preparations, it is critical that you break away from all corruption. You must do this to protect your purpose. Declare, "I will not be bound by anything that dishonors God. I refuse to allow any intimidation to hold me under the gun spiritually. I refuse to submit to corruption. Instead, I now acknowledge that my spirit hears from God, so I am effective in His kingdom and will fulfill His purpose for my life."

Discover the sources of the influences around you to determine whether they are corrupting. You see, everything has a source. Evaluate what you see, hear, and sense. You must know the source of the wisdom that is trying to direct your life. Analyze your conversations with others, the television programs you watch, the books and magazines you read, and all your surroundings. Ask yourself about each, *Is this from man, the world, the enemy, or God?* This question will help you to pinpoint which of the four sources of wisdom are operating in your life:

- Man—earthly reason and logic
- The world—*"the lust of the flesh, the lust of the eyes, and the pride of life"* (1 John 2:16)
- Demons
- God

I could write an entire chapter on these types of wisdom. However, to stay on course with the purpose of this book, I will simply list several passages from the Bible that further explain this principle:

> *Who is wise and understanding among you? Let him show by good conduct that his works are done in the meekness of wisdom. But if you have bitter envy and self-seeking ["strife," KJV] in your hearts, do not boast and lie against the truth. This wisdom does not descend from above, but is* **earthly, sensual, demonic.** *For where envy and self-seeking ["strife," KJV] exist, confusion and every evil thing are there. But the wisdom that is* **from above** *[God] is first pure, then peaceable, gentle, willing to yield, full of mercy and good fruits, without partiality and without hypocrisy.* (James 3:13–17, emphasis added)

For all that is in the world—the lust of the flesh, the lust of the eyes, and the pride of life—is not of the Father but is of the world. (1 John 2:16, emphasis added)

That your faith should not stand in the wisdom of men, but in the power of God. Howbeit we speak wisdom among them that are perfect: yet not the wisdom of this world, nor of the princes of this world, that come to nought: But we speak the wisdom of God in a mystery, even the hidden wisdom, which God ordained before the world unto our glory. (1 Corinthians 2:5-7 KJV, emphasis added)

Realize that you live in a corrupt world that is hostile and contrary to the wisdom of God. Take responsibility for what you see, hear, think, and say. As God's champion, you are not to be an open pit for anything that flies by. Your enemy will use everything he can to try to corrupt your divine purpose. Remember that his goal is to abort your purpose. To do so, he will try to bind you to anything but the wisdom of God.

Sever yourself from the effects of all corrupting influences and ungodly wisdom. You might need to break some unholy alliances with friends or coworkers. Maybe you need to turn off negative television programs. Perhaps you need to stop reading certain materials. Pray and be sensitive, allowing the Holy Spirit to direct you.

When you are set apart for God, you are a joy to Him. This is part of your preparation for walking in His plans. Then, when it's time to step out according to your divine purpose, you will be ready because you have focused in prayer and broken the yokes over your life. You will be free to move as God directs.

CHAMPION THOUGHT:
Cut off the Bad Root, Not the Bad Fruit

If, after examining your life today, you find some areas that do not line up with God's Word and purpose, determine what is causing these negative results. Remember that for every effect, there is a cause. The way to change a result or effect is to change the cause. In other words, you need to find the root of the error and remove it. Until you do this, it is useless to cut off the bad fruit in your life. The negative root will continue to poison your life until you destroy that bad root.

Before the end of this chapter, you will learn how to identify the root of every negative fruit, and then add the knowledge of the truth to cut out that root. The result will be godly fruit in your life.

CHAMPION THOUGHT:
Use God's Process to Change Course—Meditation, Revelation, Motivation, Action, Fruit

---

As you find areas in your life that do not line up with God's plan, the need to change course will be clear. How can you effect the necessary change? In our School of Biblical Studies, we teach a principle that I call Meditation, Revelation, Motivation, Action, Fruit. This is what I personally use to understand and implement the course changes that God desires for my life. This system for change works for everyone because it is based upon God's Word.

Remember, though, that if after learning this truth you don't engage in it, this principle will become useless to you. Continue to use this system throughout your life for divine direction, for the power to change, and to release the authority of truth into your life. Then, you will not have to settle for living less than God's best.

The Bible school course contains more details, but here we will summarize this truth. This principle states:

- *Meditation* produces *revelation*
- *Revelation* produces *motivation*

- *Motivation* produces *action*
- *Action* produces *fruit*

Meditation Produces Revelation

The Bible commands us to meditate on the Word of God. We find the biblical standard for the principle of meditation in the book of Joshua:

This Book of the Law shall not depart from your mouth, but you shall meditate in it day and night, that you may observe to do according to all that is written in it. For then you will make your way prosperous, and then you will have good success. (Joshua 1:8)

The last part of this verse promises that biblical meditation will work for you. However, you must do it as God directs in this passage. Here, the Bible instructs that you must meditate on God's Word continually so you can obey it.

In applying this principle to changing courses in your life, you need to meditate on the Word of God until He reveals His truth to you for the particular area in which you need direction. Meditate until you have the revelation of truth, which means that the cover is removed and you can see the matter as He does.

How do you meditate? The word *meditate* means to mutter and speak His Word over and over again. Therefore, you are to read the Bible and listen to yourself speak portions of it over and over and over and over again until it affects you. If you continue this process, you will capture the insight, understanding, wisdom, and revelation of God. Why? It is because He desires to show you how to obey His Word and fulfill His plan for your life.

CHAMPION THOUGHT:
The Quality of Your Biblical Meditation Determines the Quality of Your Life

---

If you will meditate on the Word of God for just one day, your conscience will begin to soften so you can recognize the areas in your life that do not line up with the Bible. If you meditate on God's Word for a week, you will begin to know the parameters of His direction for your life. If you meditate on His Word for a year, you will see the narrow road of His plan. If you meditate in the Scriptures for a lifetime, you will cause your every step, one step after another, to be ordered by God.

You see, the quality of your biblical meditation determines the quality of your life. The reason for this is that the more revelation of the Word you receive through meditation, the more truth you know, and the freer you will become. This directly causes your quality of life to rise.

The longer you meditate on God's Word, the more areas of your life you affect, such as relationships, finances, business, and school. This principle works the same way in every area. Earlier, we discussed praying passages in the Bible to discover your divine purpose. This truth will help you to do that.

I cannot emphasize enough how critical meditation—rolling God's truths over and over again in your mind—is in your preparation. It is the beginning of your change in course! From this significant first step in the process comes revelation, motivation, action, and fruit.

Revelation Produces Motivation

When God reveals a truth to you, it produces the motivation to press forward. It encourages you to move toward the area of revelation. One reason we are not ready to act is that we have not received the revelation of God's truth in an area. If we lack this aspect, we don't have the faith to move forward because we don't see a firm foundation to step out on. Fear can easily grip us since we don't know what to do.

On the other hand, many people prematurely step out. They begin projects but are not spiritually developed enough to finish them. They have not properly prepared themselves to move into their divine purpose. Consequently, they do not have the required experiences of faith or truth to break through all the barriers. Unfortunately, many become shipwrecked and sidelined in their walk with God. Often, when this happens, they don't want to think about their purpose again. They believe it should have worked but didn't, so their purpose becomes a source of frustration.

Remember that frustration is nothing more than a desire for change but the inability to bring it about. You need not be frustrated any longer because now, through this truth, you *will* have the ability to change!

Motivation Produces Action

Implementing God's revelation in your life is critical. You must act on it. When His revelation motivates you, it is the greatest impetus and produces the most momentum for activity. That's why a person with divine revelation in an area will do far more than others without His revealed truth.

After meditating on the Word, you will see truths revealed that you have never known before. You can then act on this divine revelation with confidence because you are sure that this is God's direction for your life. Not only will you know what to do but God will give you the motivation to do it. The Bible tells us, *"Work out your salvation with fear and trembling, for it is God who works in you to will and to act according to his good purpose"* (Philippians 2:12–13 NIV). God works with your will to help you fulfill His purpose for your life. He motivates you to accomplish His plan.

Action Produces Fruit

Fruit is the visible expression of power; it's the product or end result. I like to define *fruit* as "the outward expression of the inward work." The Bible describes *"the fruit of the Spirit"* as *"love, joy, peace, patience, kindness, goodness, faithfulness"* (Galatians 5:22 NIV).

Acting on God's revelation, after meditating on His Word, produces results. Many of us look to bear fruit *before* action. No, fruit is the *result* of acting. It follows afterward and is not for us alone but also for those around us. Therefore, if we are bearing fruit for God, it is because we have been acting on His Word and are in right standing with Christ. We are exercising the Word of God, which is producing fruit or outwardly expressing the inward life of His Spirit.

As you walk in this truth, there will be evidence. The fruit of God's truth in your life will speak volumes. You will not need to convince anyone that you know it. They will see the manifested fruit of truth in your life. This is part of God's plan. As His truth is revealed in your life, it brings glory to Him—not you—and draws others to Him. We will discuss this further in later chapters.

Using the principle of Meditation, Revelation, Motivation, Action, Fruit will produce the successful results that you are looking for. When you take the time to prepare for your purpose by meditating on the Word of God, receiving His revelation of truth, and stepping out on it as He motivates you, then you will not be shipwrecked. You will see the fruit of the fulfillment of God's purpose for your life. His truth works!

CHAMPION THOUGHT:
Your Current State of Conflict Locates You

Today, if you find yourself in the midst of conflict, use that situation to locate your position. The Bible explains:

> *If you have raced with men on foot and they have worn you out, how can you compete with horses? If you stumble in safe country, how will you manage in the thickets by the Jordan?*
> (Jeremiah 12:5 NIV)

In other words, wherever you are having difficulty keeping up, that is your starting place to prepare for victory. For example, if you are having trouble in your marriage or with your children, then that is the area where you should begin your course correction to get back on God's plan for your life.

CHAMPION THOUGHT:
Change the Inside before You Look for Change Outside

It's time to evaluate yourself. If your life is not satisfying, then something is wrong. Don't become frustrated. Recognize the need to change inside before you look for change outside. If you change your inward life, you will have the outward change (fruit) that you desire. Look for the inward part of your life that needs changing. Then, change it through the principle of Meditation, Revelation, Motivation, Action, and Fruit.

Right now, I encourage you to list the areas of your life that are not working and are causing conflict. Then, begin the process of change. As you do, stay committed to your breakthrough!

CHAMPION THOUGHT:
Take the Fruit Test Today

If you are facing challenges with any area of life, begin tracing that area backward through the process of Meditation, Revelation, Motivation, Action, and Fruit, starting with Fruit. Determine the level that you have not mastered and correct that level before expecting to progress further. Let your current conflict help locate the level that you need to strengthen. Here's how.

Do a fruit test. Check your life by honestly answering each of the following questions:

Fruit

Question: Are there any areas of your life in which you are not experiencing the fruit of the Spirit: *"love, joy, peace, patience, kindness, goodness, faithfulness"* (Galatians 5:22 NIV), or other godly, successful results?

Answer: If you don't have any godly fruit in a particular area, go back to check your actions.

Action

Question: Are you acting on God's truths in that area?
Answer: If not, go back to see if you are motivated to act.

Motivation

Question: Are you motivated to step out in truth in that area?
Answer: If not, go back to see if you have God's revelation.

Revelation

Question: Do you have divine revelation of truth in that area?
Answer: If not, go back to the level of meditation.

Meditation

Question: Are you meditating on God's Word day and night in that area?

Answer: If not, find passages in the Bible regarding that area and begin meditating on them continually until you see the truth revealed.

You can trace your every failure and success through this principle. It works in every case.

CHAMPION THOUGHT:
Cut Your Excess Baggage

As you have read the previous pages, perhaps you have discovered some areas that you need to revisit. Do whatever the Holy Spirit shows you in order to become free of any yokes that have bound you and held you back from living God's best. Don't waste another moment. Just do it.

Do you need to remove some excess baggage from your life? If so, get rid of it. Maybe you need to forgive someone who has wronged you or is involved in the challenges facing you. If so, cut this person loose. Don't hold the wrong against him any longer because, as you hold it against him, you bind it to yourself. Thus, you jeopardize or defeat your divine purpose.

CHAMPION THOUGHT:
Freedom without Subsequent Action Results in Reoccurring Bondage

---

In closing this chapter of *It Only Takes One* and opening the next, you are closing a chapter in your life and opening a new one. You are stepping into your divine purpose. Once you know that you are a champion for God, have a vision of His purpose, and have prepared yourself for His move by becoming free of all encumbrances, then, you are ready to step out. This new champion position requires champion actions. You need to act because freedom without action results only in future reoccurrence of the bondage. In other words, if you do not walk in the truth that God has revealed to you in this book, you are destined to fall back to your former state of ignorance of that truth. Along with that backward retreat returns the bondage and challenges you have struggled against.

CHAMPION THOUGHT:
God Is Mobilizing You for Victory

At this very moment, a finger points at you. It is not the finger of accusation, but the finger of mobilization. Recall the U.S. Army recruiting posters in World War II of Uncle Sam pointing, declaring,

"I want you...." This is the kind of finger I mean here. Champion, you are the one. God wants *you* in His army. He is pointing at you right now, urging you to activate your faith to release the gifts and purpose that He has deposited within you.

God will help you to rise above every conflict, so you can conquer the enemies who attempt to withstand you. First, you must step out in faith. You have trained and prepared. Now, it's time to pick up your weapons and step into the action! You are God's champion. He has already given you the victory. You cannot be defeated. Go for it!

5
Just Step Out

After discovering and properly preparing for God's purpose, Champion, you can begin the journey of fulfilling your divine destiny. It is time to step out on the Word you have heard from God. In this chapter, we will discuss how to take this first step. You will learn how the Word of God literally empowers you to fulfill your divine purpose. Also, you will better understand your authority to speak God's victorious Word against any obstacles that threaten to limit His will in your life.

Neil Armstrong

"LUNAR CONTACT," the lights on the instrument panel glowed.

"Tranquility Base here. The *Eagle* has landed," radioed astronaut Neil Armstrong.

It was mid-1969. The U.S. space program had successfully landed a space craft on the moon as an estimated 528 million people watched via television!

The hatch of the lunar module, *Eagle*, opened and Armstrong began his short but spectacular descent to the surface.[1]

As he carefully placed his size 9½B boot on the gritty soil, Armstrong uttered words heard round the world: "That's one small step for a man." Then, swinging his right foot from the landing gear pad, he said, "One giant leap for mankind."[2]

This historic moonwalk began with one single step. What was once believed to be impossible had just become reality, and it changed the world.

As God's champion, one God-inspired step can likewise transform *your* world. It can break through impossible circumstances to fulfill your greatest dreams. The key is to hear from God, and then step out on His Word in faith. Throughout time, God's champions have proven that it only takes one small step to begin a historic journey with Him. Peter in the Bible is a good example.

Peter

As recorded in the book of Matthew, the disciples witnessed the miracle of Jesus feeding five thousand men (plus women and children) with only five loaves of bread and two fish. Immediately following the miracle, *"Jesus made His disciples get into the boat and go before Him to the other side, while He sent the multitudes away"* (Matthew 14:22). Jesus then went up the mountainside to pray alone until evening, as the apostles sailed across the sea.

By this time, the disciples had seen on many occasions Jesus accomplish everything He had set out to do, including the "impossible." It should have been enough that He had instructed them to go to the other side. However, a terrible storm came upon them in the midst of the sea, and they thought they would die before reaching the other side.

What was Jesus' response? The Bible says, *"Now in the fourth watch of the night Jesus went to them, walking on the sea"* (v. 25). Unconcerned about the storm, He started across the water on foot without a boat or ship!

Seeing a figure approach them on the water in the storm, the disciples cried out in fear, thinking it was a ghost. *"But Jesus immediately said to them: 'Take courage! It is I. Don't be afraid'"* (v. 27 NIV). As the Lord had instructed, Peter broke through the fear surrounding him.

Notice what happened next:

And Peter answered Him and said, "Lord, if it is You, com-
mand me to come to You on the water." So He said, "Come."
And when Peter had come down out of the boat, he walked on
the water to go to Jesus. (Matthew 14:28–29)

Here, Peter heard and understood what Jesus had spoken
to him personally. *"Come"* is a simple word, yet it was powerful
enough to cause Peter to walk on water!

Now, why was Peter the only disciple out of the ship? Perhaps
it was because only he had questioned the Lord. What about you?
If you were in Peter's shoes, would you have asked the Lord to tell
you to come? Would you have stepped out onto the water?

Imagine Peter stepping out of the ship. I can see him now,
with the other disciples hollering, "Get back in here, Peter! Die
with us! Don't believe that ghost, Peter!" The disciples were very
fearful. Convinced their ship would sink, they lost sight of their
faith as they focused on their approaching death.

Peter, on the other hand, did not believe this was an evil appa-
rition coming to them before their death. Instead, he recognized
Jesus. He had seen the authority of this Man. With his own eyes,
Peter had witnessed the miracles that had occurred when Jesus
spoke. Once he had even seen some people tear up the roof tiles of
a crowded home to lower their paralyzed friend to Jesus for healing.
He had heard Jesus speak a simple command to that paralytic, *"I*
tell you, get up, take your mat and go home" (Mark 2:11 NIV). Instantly
healed, the man had been able to obey!

On many occasions, Peter had seen the power of Jesus' words.
Lives suddenly changed, and impossibilities became realities when
people obeyed this Man's commands. Therefore, Peter overcame
his fear and stepped out in faith on Jesus' word, *"Come."* With that
one small step, Peter began his historic "water walk," which no
mere human had ever done before.

CHAMPION THOUGHT:
One Step Brings the Invisible Dream
to a Visible Reality

From this account of Peter walking on the water, you can learn several important keys to fulfilling your personal destiny. First, as we discussed earlier, you must recognize that God is speaking to you. Next, you need to obey what He says regardless of the circumstances. The spoken Word of God will enable you to perform His Word.

When Peter recognized and heard Jesus, this disciple was able to do what Jesus had told him to do. The power to fulfill Christ's commands is contained in His words because He is the Word. For example, let's say Jesus was two hundred yards away from Peter and He commanded, "Jump into My arms." Peter would have been able to jump and land in Jesus' arms simply because Jesus had spoken the command.

In this case, Jesus said, "*Come*"! That was enough for Peter. He did not sit there wondering, *How do I get there? Where's a little boat? How do I make this work?* No, all he needed was to verify that this was Jesus, and then he could do what his Lord had said.

The Bible records that Jesus said, "*Whatever I say is just what the Father has told me to say*" (John 12:50 NIV). If this truly was Jesus, then what Jesus had said was the Father's words, and they simply would be done. Peter knew that if Jesus walked on water and commanded him to do likewise, then Peter could do it, too.

Champion, you must discover what God is saying to you personally. If it *is* from Him, then you *can* do it! One step of faith will bring the invisible dream to a visible reality. Overcoming your fear and stepping out obediently in faith as God directs will cause you to fulfill your divine purpose. The believer's decision path for life is fully obeying God's instructions each step of the way.

That's what Jesus did, and He wants us to do the same! Remember, Jesus said, *"But the world must learn that I love the Father and that I do exactly what my Father has commanded me"* (John 14:31 NIV). He also said, *"I tell you the truth, the Son can do nothing by himself; he can do only what he sees his Father doing, because whatever the Father does the Son also does"* (John 5:19 NIV).

What Jesus heard and saw in His Father's presence, He therefore did. The Father was Jesus' example, and Jesus was Peter's example. Peter knew the power of God rested within Jesus, enabling Him to fulfill God's plan. Therefore, as Peter followed Jesus' example, God's power enabled Peter to perform the Word. Today, as you follow this example of obeying the Word of the Lord, God's power also will surge through *your* life, enabling you to fulfill your divine destiny!

Israelites Crossing the Jordan River

The book of Joshua records an exciting story that further illustrates this truth: One step of faith can bring the invisible dream to a visible reality.

As the nation of Israel prepared to enter the land that God had promised them, they came upon a great barrier: the overflowing Jordan River. Joshua, Israel's leader, heard a Word from God about how to overcome this obstacle:

> *And it shall come to pass, as soon as the soles of the feet of the priests who bear the ark of the LORD, the Lord of all the earth, shall rest in the waters of the Jordan, that the waters of the Jordan shall be cut off, the waters that come down from upstream, and they shall stand as a heap.* (Joshua 3:13)

Notice that the waters would part only *after* the priests stepped out in faith. When the Israelites obeyed the Word from God, they received their breakthrough and crossed over the riverbed onto dry ground. With one step of faith, their invisible dream became their visible reality, and they entered the Promised Land.

CHAMPION THOUGHT:
You Can Walk on the Word

In Peter's case, the word that Jesus spoke was *"Come."* Walking on the water was Peter's example. *"Come"* did not mean, "Get a row-boat." It did not mean, "Sit there in the ship awhile. Then, you will arrive on the other side, and everything will be all right." *"Come"* did not mean, "I am coming." No, to Peter, *"Come"* meant, "Do what I am doing. Walk on My Word and come to Me."

Do you realize that what Peter stepped out on was not the water, although the water was there? He literally walked on a Word from Jesus, which had the power to keep him on top of the water!

CHAMPION THOUGHT:
Anchor Your Faith in the Word, Not in Your Faith

What Word from God will keep *you* on top of things that try to sink *you?* Capture that life-saving Word from God personally. Then, begin to meditate on it biblically, as we discussed earlier.

Tell God, "If You said to do this, then I will step out. However, it is not because I believe, but because *You* instructed me to do this."

Realize that if you pressure yourself, thinking that your prayers will be answered because you believe, then you place all demand upon your belief. On the other hand, if you understand that your prayers and personal destiny hinge upon God's Word, then all demand is on His saying so. Wouldn't you rather trust what God says than what you believe?

Now, please do not misunderstand me. Belief is a very impor-tant part of our walk with God, but it is not the most important aspect. After all, the Bible declares: *"You believe that there is one*

God. You do well. Even the demons believe; and tremble!" (James 2:19). Belief is good and even essential, but it is not enough. The key is not to anchor your faith in your belief but in the power of God. Look at what the Word of God says:

> And my speech and my preaching were not with persuasive words of human wisdom, but in demonstration of the Spirit and of power, that your faith should not be in the wisdom of men but in the power of God.   (1 Corinthians 2:4-5)

Your faith is to be in the power of God.

Remember the biblical definition of faith: "*Now faith is the substance of things hoped for, the evidence of things not seen*" (Hebrews 11:1). Another version of the Bible says, "*Now faith is being sure of what we hope for and certain of what we do not see*" (NIV). We need to place our faith not in our own faith, but in the power of God that will produce what we do not see or have not experienced yet.

We step into the power of God not with logic, thoughts from the enemy, or any attributes of the flesh. No, we step into the power of God through faith because we perceive that His Word is working. After renewing our minds to this truth, we can step out in confidence that we shall succeed in fulfilling God's Word. After all, He said it, He will do it, and that settles it.

CHAMPION THOUGHT:
When You Step Out on a Word from God, You Lose Your Choice

Now, before you step out on a Word from God—whether it is a Word to change jobs, become involved in an area of your church, or anything else—you have a choice in that environment. However, once you commit to stepping out on a Word from God, you lose your power of choice. From that point on, no longer can you choose to follow your own plans if you want to obey His purpose.

For example, once Peter stepped out from the boat onto the water, he could not change course because he was not doing the work. Jesus was. Walking on water is not a rational act. It appears very foolish, especially if the sea is choppy and everyone in your boat is screaming, "We are about to die!" However, after Peter's first step, it was too late to change his mind.

Let's say that you are in Peter's shoes. Your friends believe you will drown if you leave the vessel. However, you decide to do it anyway. You step out on what Jesus said, not on someone else's fear or negative words, such as, "I wouldn't do that, if I were you."

"Well, I noticed that you are not doing it," you might reply. "Obviously you're not me, and you don't see it the way I do. I heard a Word from Jesus, and I see Him doing it. Nothing will stop me now—not even your fear."

Remember that when you commit to obeying God's plan for your life, your only need is to know God's instructions each step of the way. If you recognize what God is telling you to do, and you do it, then surrounding circumstances mean nothing to you. No longer can you choose what to do or ask yourself, *What should I do? Should I do this or that?* Instead, you simply seek God for direction, and then obey His voice.

An illustration here should clarify this point. Let's say a man takes his young daughter to an amusement park. There, he tells her that he wants to ride a roller coaster with her. She thinks about the offer and agrees to go. The father then helps his little girl into a roller-coaster car, makes sure she's safely locked in place, and prepares her for what's ahead. Now, she has made her choice. She will ride this roller coaster. From here to the end of the ride, she has no more choices about what to do. She is strapped into her seat for the duration. All the twists and turns, inclines and descents, rolls and loops, and screams and cries of the other riders might scare her. However, these circumstances cannot influence her choice to be on that ride. Standing up to cry in fear, "Please, let me get off this roller coaster," is no longer an option for her. Her best course of action is to stay in her seat, hold on to her father, rest in his power and judgment, and finish the course.

When you commit to fulfilling God's purpose for your life, that's the extent of your choice. God makes all your choices from there. You choose to go along for the ride—wherever it takes you—obeying and trusting in Him each step of the way.

CHAMPION THOUGHT:
The Power of the Word Enables You to Obey It

Now, let's examine how the power of the Word works. When Peter had his eyes on Jesus and stepped out on the word "*Come,*" he did what Jesus spoke. The spoken Word of God literally *enabled* him to do it. Think about that. How did he do it? The answer is that Peter needed to hear only one Word from Jesus. You might be thinking, *There has to be more to it.* Oh, no, there really isn't. It's that simple. You see, people often think the Gospel is complex, but it really is not. Whenever we complicate simple decisions of obedience to Christ, we muddy our spiritual environment. This clouds our ability to perceive clearly how to accomplish the will of God for our lives. Then, it appears impossible to understand and do what God desires.

There's power in the Word of God. As long as Peter looked at Jesus, kept his faith focused on the power of Jesus' spoken Word, stayed in that environment, and obeyed the Lord, he accomplished God's will.

How is this possible? Why do words have such great power?

CHAMPION THOUGHT:
Jesus Is the Word and Is God

The answer lies in one of the great mysteries of God. This profound revelation, which we are about to examine, will change your life. Knowing this truth will move the conception of God's Word in your spirit to the manifestation of it in your life.

When Jesus spoke, His words were not just expressions of thought. No, in the book of John, the Bible explains that Jesus Christ *was* the Word of God in the flesh, and He *was* God.

> *In the beginning was the Word, and the Word was with God, and the Word was God. He was in the beginning with God. All things were made through Him, and without Him nothing was made that was made.* (John 1:1–3)

Notice that the Word was actually God. Then, later in the chapter, John further explained the identity of *"the Word"* when he wrote: *"And the Word became flesh and dwelt among us, and we beheld His glory, the glory as of the only begotten of the Father, full of grace and truth"* (v. 14).

This verse clearly describes Jesus, because He was God's *"only begotten"* Child. These verses reveal that Jesus is *the Word of God* and *is God.*

The third verse, here, says that *"all things were made through Him,"* which is Jesus, the Word. Therefore, everything that exists came by the Word. Without the releasing of the Word, we cannot experience what He has said, because God is the only One who can cause anything to manifest.

Not one sentence in the Bible says, "Go ahead. Launch out on what you believe." No, it declares that all things existing came from Him who was in the beginning. We are to step out on what *He* said since His Word has the power to make His will happen.

The next verse continues, saying, *"In Him was life, and the life was the light of men"* (v. 4). Here, we recognize that this Word, which created everything, is living. This Word is not simply something God said. It's alive. It is the very essence of who God is.

Finally, the next verse states: *"And the light shines in the darkness, and the darkness did not comprehend [overcome] it"* (v. 5). An emanating power from that Word pierces the darkness, which cannot stop the Word.

You see, everything God says—even today—contains all the power, authority, and creative energy of God. Remember that it is God's job to bring what He said into being. You don't have to strive to do it or prove anything because you are not the one causing His Word to work. It works only by Him. Although the power of the Word is a mystery to the human mind, it is a powerful revelation that can revolutionize our lives.

Now, let's apply this truth to Peter's experience. When he was on the ship, the other disciples feared for their lives. However, in effect, Peter said to Jesus, "If You say, *'Come,'* I know I can walk on Your Word because the Word I've watched is God."

Of course, Jesus said, *"Come,"* and that's all Peter needed. He needed only the *Word,* which *was* God. Yes, that word *"Come"* was actually God! Think about it. Because Jesus is the Word of God personified and is God, then the Word of God *is* God. For clarity, let's look at this statement another way:

Statement	Reason
Jesus = The Word of God	John 1:14
Jesus = God	John 1:1, 14
The Word of God = God	Conclusion (John 1:1)
"Come" = The Word of God to Peter	Matthew 14:28–29
"Come" = God to Peter	Conclusion

Do you think God can cause someone to walk on water? Since He *is* His Word, then His Word has the very same power of God! It carries His full authority and nature; it is God Himself.

Therefore, when Peter stepped out on the word *"Come,"* he did not step out on the letters in that simple word. It was the comprehension that this Man Jesus was the Incarnate Word of God, who is the Word embodied in the flesh, walking in the earth. Peter stepped out on God Himself!

Now, the Bible also tells us that Jesus never changes. *"Jesus Christ is the same yesterday, today, and forever"* (Hebrews 13:8). Today, Jesus is still the Word of God and God Himself. When you read a promise in God's Word or Jesus speaks a dream into your heart, don't think it's impossible. Don't fear the outcome. Remember, when you obey the Lord, His Word empowers you to accomplish His will!

The Bible declares:

> *So shall My word be that goes forth from My mouth; it shall not return to Me void, but it shall accomplish what I please, and it shall prosper in the thing for which I sent it.*
> (Isaiah 55:11)

When God speaks a dream into your heart, He provides all the power and resources to accomplish it. You just need to obey Him and launch out when He tells you the time is right.

CHAMPION THOUGHT:

Unless God Initiates the Dream, Your Highest Aspirations Will End in the Perspiration of Human Effort

---

Consider your greatest dream or desire. You can put all your effort toward it, influence multitudes of people to help you, and invest millions of dollars in it. However, despite all this human effort and resources, your dream will go nowhere unless it came from God. Unless it is a Word that you have received from God, it will not happen. The Bible teaches: *"Unless the LORD builds the house, they labor in vain who build it; unless the LORD guards the city, the watchman stays awake in vain"* (Psalm 127:1–2).

If your dream is not from God, you will wonder later in your life, *What on earth is God doing? My dream is not manifesting. I have been doing my part, believing that He would do His part.* The likely answer is that He has been speaking a different dream to you, but you have not listened.

But this particular area needs a breakthrough, you might be thinking. *It's a worthy cause, and I want to do it.* Go ahead. Change everything you think you can, but how long will it last? If you will instead step out on one Word from God, you can watch Him make it last a lifetime. It will never stop bearing fruit because His Word accomplishes His will. Before taking the first step toward your dream, answer two important questions: *Did you hear it from God?* and *Is this His timing to begin?*

You see, we live on the time line of human history. We should not begin any project or launch out with any dream until we answer this question, What did God say? We cannot run on our own pathway and expect to find fulfillment. No, God's path is the only way to accomplish our divine purpose.

Therefore, before stepping out, you must establish who initiated the dream. If it was not God, then your highest aspirations will end in the perspiration of human effort. You will have invested a portion of your life and resources in something that was destined to fail. I encourage you not to make this mistake. Before you move, find out what God said, then step out only on His Word as He instructs you!

When Peter said, *"Lord, if it is You, command me to come to You,"* that word *"Come"* did not originate from any human natural thought. God initiated it. That word *"Come"* defied the elements, controlled the power of gravity, stopped the process of death, and overcame the power of every negative circumstance. That word *"Come"* caused the reality of walking on water. Peter acted on the authority of this one God-initiated Word, which was the advanced knowledge that he needed to obey Jesus and defy the storm.

CHAMPION THOUGHT:
There Is Power in Agreement

Stepping out on a God-initiated Word engages the very powerful principle of agreement. The Bible is very clear that there is power in agreement. For example, Jesus promised:

> *Again I say to you that if two of you agree on earth concerning anything that they ask, it will be done for them by My Father in heaven. For where two or three are gathered together in My name, I am there in the midst of them.*
> *(Matthew 18:19–20)*

Together, Christians can accomplish great feats for the kingdom of God when they pray in agreement with God's Word. There is no doubt about this. However, we should not spend too much time waiting for others "to get with the program" or join us in agreement. We don't need to feel helpless if we cannot find anyone to agree with us in prayer.

For many situations in your life, no one will be in agreement with you. Often, when a family, company, ministry, nation, or person desperately needs a breakthrough, tragically, few people will stand in agreement long enough for the answer! You see, most people are not willing to do what is necessary to break through. Often, we find ourselves facing many major challenges alone. Thank God, however, that the prayer of agreement with another person is not the *only* way to answered prayer.

CHAMPION THOUGHT:
The One in Agreement with God Unleashes Awesome Power

Always remember that with God, you are the majority, and you have the advantage in every circumstance or conflict. You truly are never alone. The Bible declares: *"What then shall we say to these things? If God is for us, who can be against us?"* (Romans 8:31).

God is on your side when you agree with His Word for your breakthrough. For example, if you have a family conflict or need a financial breakthrough, and you cannot find anyone to pray with you, agree with God. By agreeing with the promises in the Bible—His Word—you can see your circumstances transformed. When a person stands on the Word, God Himself backs that person's stand and fulfills what He has said. God is waiting for you to agree with His Word, so He can perform it in your life!

Keep Philippians 4:13 on your lips at all times: *"I can do all things through Christ who strengthens me."* You *can* accomplish great feats with God by yourself through the authority of His Word. While there is power when individuals agree, one person alone in agreement with God's Word can also change the world.

CHAMPION THOUGHT:
Signs Follow the Spoken Word

Remember that as you step out on the Word of God, Jesus is there with you as He was with the first believers. Let's read some passages that record what occurred after Jesus had risen from the dead and had shown Himself alive to His followers with infallible proofs of power:

> *And Jesus came and spoke to them, saying, "All authority has been given to Me in heaven and on earth. Go therefore and make disciples of all the nations, baptizing them in the name of the Father and of the Son and of the Holy Spirit, teaching them to observe all things that I have commanded you; and lo, I am with you always, even to the end of the age." Amen.*
> (Matthew 28:18–20)

So then, after the Lord had spoken to them, He was received up into heaven, and sat down at the right hand of God. And they went out and preached everywhere, the Lord working with them and confirming the word through the accompanying signs. Amen. (Mark 16:19-20)

Champion, not only are you to obey Jesus' Word, but you are to speak it forth. As *you* declare the Word of God, His very power confirms it with signs following. You can expect breakthroughs to occur by the authority of God's Word when you speak it. Your actions do count. That's why God wants you to declare His Word into impossible, incurable, hopeless, powerless, and dire circumstances. The power of His Word will create breakthroughs!

CHAMPION THOUGHT:
The Word Is Limitless in the Present and Future

We have learned that the Word of God can do much more than lead you to become a Christian. While it is like fire insurance that keeps you from hell, the Word is not limited to your future. The Word is also limitless in your present. Realize that, as a believer, you are a vessel that God wants to use to release His Word into this hurting world. Within you is the Word of Life from God that is to function *through* you in your life and in the lives of others!

Jesus is our Example. Remember that Jesus spoke what His Father told Him to say and did what God instructed. This is our blueprint for fulfilling God's call on our lives.

CHAMPION THOUGHT:
Herald the Word to Cancel Your Challenges

Now, let's investigate other examples of how the Word of God changes your circumstances, so you can fulfill your destiny. Just as

118

the Word parted the Jordan and caused Peter to walk on life-threatening waves, you, too, can stay above your everyday challenges. You can launch out to fulfill your divine purpose.

Debt. Are you affected by it? Are you concerned about it? If so, this could hinder you from achieving everything that God has planned for you. The Word of God is above this fearsome word called *debt*. Yes, there is a name above every name—even the name of Debt. The Bible says, *"At the name of Jesus every knee should bow"* (Philippians 2:10). Debt has to bow its knee to the name of Jesus.

The Word also declares:

> *He raised Him [Jesus] from the dead and seated Him at His right hand in the heavenly places, far above all principality and power and might and dominion, and every name that is named, not only in this age but also in that which is to come.*
>   (Ephesians 1:20–21)

You can herald the Word of God into your financial life to cancel debt! Yes, *cancel* it! This is what my wife, Faye, and I did.

The Cancellation of Our $20,000 Debt

Decades ago, a business venture of mine produced a debt of more than $20,000. I had to postpone paying it at the time because I did not know where to get the money.

In 1977, my wife, Faye, and I were considering how to be free from all debt. We did not want to be under any type of oppression. Yet this $20,000 debt still hung over us. "Let's let the Word of God rule our finances," we agreed, "and our mental well-being, home, family, children, and every part of our lives." Faye and I began to pray, speaking what the Word of God said regarding everything concerning us.

That's when God miraculously healed our small children. Eric's face had been paralyzed, and Laurie's eyes had been crossed. As we spoke the Word over our children, God healed Laurie instantly and Eric within about a month! Next, we needed a miracle regarding our debt.

Around this time, the person to whom we owed the $20,000 called. "Gary, I don't know why I'm doing this," he began, "but we made so much money that it will benefit *me* if you'll let me write off this debt as a loss."

Here was our answer to prayer!

"Don't worry," I stammered. "I'll help you by letting you write off my debt!"

Then, oddly enough, he said, "Thank you." This man had thanked *me*, yet it seemed that *I* had received the biggest blessing. Picture this creditor being grateful to write off my debt and not collect it!

CHAMPION THOUGHT:
God Positions Us in His Authority to Benefit Others

That story of our debt cancellation might seem unusual, but this is an example of God's constant interventions. He positions us and gives His authority to us, so the people around us can benefit from His nature within us. Then, as we speak forth His Word, we become instruments of blessing to those in need. At the same time, God meets our needs, too. This is a different perspective, isn't it? As Jesus promised, *"But seek first the kingdom of God and His righteousness, and all these things shall be added to you"* (Matthew 6:33).

Champion, when you and I work in God's kingdom, we are vessels for His power to pour out to others. In the process, we also get blessed!

CHAMPION THOUGHT:
Just One Word from God Will Rule Your Environment

You don't need a thousand words or a thesis from God. You simply need one Word. When you receive that Word, you can speak it, and it will rule your environment. It will rule your home. It will settle family disputes. It will create order in your finances. It will solve your challenges. The power of just one Word from God is awesome.

CHAMPION THOUGHT:

The Authority of God's Word Flowing through You Has the Same Creative Power Today as When He Produced the World

Now, you might be wondering, *Okay, how does the power of God flow through me?* First, you must recognize that God—who has all authority in heaven and earth—has given His authority to you. Therefore, the Word in you is not the word of a man. It is the living Word of God with all the authority of God Himself. The Word in you is all powerful.

Recall that when God created the world, He spoke, and light, sky, land, and animals came into existence. The book of Genesis contains many verses about how God's words produced new creations. (See Genesis 1:1–28.) His spoken Word literally created the entire world. It had such influence and power that it produced form and life from the void. Remember that God is still the same today as He was then. Therefore, His Word is omnipotent even today. Now, when *you* speak it, His Word still contains all the creative power today that it had when He produced the world!

Well, you might be thinking, *That's nice, but I don't know if it will work for me. I'm no one special.* The following verse proves that Jesus gave His authority to His believers, and now *every* believer can speak His Word with all Jesus' authority. That includes you, Champion!

Jesus told Peter and the rest of His disciples, *"I will give you the keys of the kingdom of heaven, and whatever you bind on earth will* be bound in heaven, and whatever you loose on earth will be loosed in heaven" (Matthew 16:19).

If you are a true disciple of Jesus, all His authority lies within you! Now, you have His awesome power residing in you to use for the furtherance of His kingdom on earth.[3] What are you doing with this life-giving, creative ability?

CHAMPION THOUGHT:

Step Beyond Existing Phenomenon to God's Limitless Reality

Here, we are discussing what I call breakthrough thinking. Operating according to this kind of thinking causes you to go beyond things as they appear. This new mind-set captures the very essence of God's Word, which has the power to create. When you know the creative power of His truth, you can step beyond all existing facts and circumstances into the limitless reality that God desires for you.

CHAMPION THOUGHT:

You Can Go to the Other Side of the Storm

Has God given you a glimpse of some things for you to accomplish? Has He spoken a Word to you about your purpose? What did He say? What is He doing, and how will He bring it about?

The Word He has spoken might seem so big that you have trouble believing it is really from Him. Are you trying to trust God, but finding it difficult to do so? As you examine yourself, you might realize that you are not confident. Maybe you are not walking on the Word that you heard from God. Perhaps fear and confusion are plaguing you.

Right now, I encourage you to open your heart to the Lord. Let Him reveal to you the other side of the storms and circumstances you face. There *is* another side, and Jesus wants you to arrive there safely. He does not want you to be shipwrecked along the way. No, He has a divine destiny in mind for you, and He is there to help you reach it for His glory! Listen as He gently speaks to your heart, "Let's go to the other side now." Then, agree with His Word, and take that first step as He leads.

It is time to uncover the Word of the Lord for your life. Dust off those dreams, and study what the Lord has shown to you. Remove the limits that you have placed on God regarding your dreams. Seek Him with an open heart about your future. Then, listen for Him to confirm that those dreams are from Him, so you can step out on His Word to you.

CHAMPION THOUGHT:
Take Extraordinary Steps to Unleash God's Deposit within You

The steps that you will take to walk in your purpose will be extraordinary. As you discover and begin to move into what God has deposited within you, you will find yourself making stands in unfamiliar territory. Peter found himself standing on top of the water! The Israelite priests found themselves standing on dry ground in the middle of an overflowing river! You will find yourself in a place that you have never been before.

No longer will you live an ordinary, natural life. God has works planned for you that are so supernatural that you cannot even imagine them. The Bible says that *"we are His workmanship, created in Christ Jesus for good works, which God prepared beforehand that we should walk in them"* (Ephesians 2:10).

Champion, God has prepared supernatural works for you. However, to do them, you need to take extraordinary steps of faith. When God speaks to you, and you walk in His preordained steps, the works you do will undeniably be His works. That's why it will require faith to step out. You won't be able to do these works in your own strength. How will you respond when God leads you to prove what He has deposited within you? Will you step into it? Will you act and obey Him?

CHAMPION THOUGHT:
Faith without Works Is Dead

Once you understand what God has deposited within you, and you begin to believe that He has a plan for you, immediately you will find yourself in a test. Will you act on it?

You see, you cannot have real faith without corresponding actions. The Bible explains that *"faith without works is dead"* (James 2:26). You must act on your faith. This is not a passive existence. When you act on your faith in His Word, the results will be thrilling!

Mr. Edward Kimball

A couple of years ago, one of my staff members received an E-mail message from a friend. It contained some interesting facts, which we verified. This story clearly illustrates the phenomenal fruit from one man's step of obedience.

In 1855, Mr. Edward Kimball, a Sunday school teacher was used by God to lead Dwight L. Moody, a Boston shoe clerk, to give his life to Christ. D. L. Moody went on to become an evangelist.

During one of his ministry trips, Moody met F. B. Meyer, a pastor in England, whom Moody invited to preach in America in 1891. This launched Meyer's extensive outreach to the U.S. While preaching on an American campus, F. B. Meyer touched the heart of J. Wilbur Chapman, who made a life-changing commitment to God.

"J. Wilbur Chapman...employed a former baseball player, Billy Sunday, to do evangelistic work" with him. "Bill Sunday held a revival in Charlotte, N.C. A group of local men were so enthusiastic afterward that they planned another evangelistic campaign, bringing Mordecai Ham to town to preach.

"During Mordecai Ham's revival, a young man named Billy Graham heard the Gospel and yielded his life to Christ."[4]

Now, here's the rest of the story. To date, Billy Graham "has preached the Gospel to...over 210 million people in more than 185 countries and territories," including heads of state.[5]

While George H. W. Bush was Vice President of the United States and well before his son George W. Bush became the governor of Texas or the U.S. president, Billy Graham spent a weekend with the Bush family. "That weekend my faith took on new meaning," the younger Bush explained. "It was the beginning of a new walk where I would recommit my heart to Jesus Christ." George W. Bush described it as "the beginning of a change in my life."[6]

That weekend with the future U.S. presidents was approximately 130 years after Mr. Kimball had led Dwight L. Moody to Christ! Mr. Kimball's step of faith began a series of events that eventually caused millions to hear the Gospel, including U.S. presidents. Do you see how one Sunday school teacher affected countless lives? Yes, it only takes one.

Never underestimate your purpose in the kingdom of God! Step out in faith, knowing that God has an awesome plan that you cannot begin to fathom.

Ray Weaverling

Ray Weaverling, a man in our church, dreamed for years of working full-time in the ministry. He faithfully worked at his job in the U.S. Postal Service, yet daily dreamed of the day when he would be free to work for God full-time. Ray had known that this was God's plan for his life, so he had attended and graduated from our Bible school. He had wonderful plans of serving the Lord, which he often spoke about.

One day, my wife, Faye, asked, "Ray, how old are you?"

"Fifty-five," he replied. "The Lord has promised me that I will live to be seventy," he added.

"So how many years do you have before you're seventy?" she asked.

After quickly calculating, Ray's face revealed his alarm. "Fifteen," he replied, suddenly realizing that his time was very short.

"That's not much time to do all that you have planned, is it?"

"No," Ray answered, recognizing the need to make some drastic changes in his life.

Not long after that conversation, we learned that Ray had quit his job and launched out into the full-time ministry that he had dreamed of for years. Now, he lives by faith, since he no longer receives his salary. However, his needs are always met, and he is thrilled with his new life. He is fulfilled beyond measure, doing the Lord's work.

Ray's story is a good example of what we have been discussing in this book. He knew who he was in Christ. He understood his divine purpose and had a God-inspired, clear vision for his life. He had taken the time to prepare himself. He had heard a Word from God regarding what to do. He believed the Word and knew that God would use him. However, Ray lacked one thing: action. Once he realized this, he stepped out in faith according to God's leading and began to fulfill his purpose. Now, every day is more fulfilling than the day before.

Are you realizing that it could be time for you—as it was for Ray—to move toward your dream? Are you ready to activate God's ability through His connection with man? Remember, Champion, you have important, specific contributions to make to your generation. Creation is waiting for you to fulfill your destiny. Will you start stepping into it, today? You *can* do it despite all the obstacles that withstand you. Now is the time to use your faith.

In the next chapter, we will examine how to break through all your barriers!

6

Break through Every Barrier

Every one of us faces barriers in life; therefore, the truths contained in this chapter can significantly affect your future. You will discover how to penetrate all that stands in the way of your divine purpose. While others criticize your dreams, you will learn how to rise above their defensive mind-sets, fear, bitterness, hostility, and resistance. You will understand how to press on in the face of adversity. You will find out how to transition from a difficult past to a thrilling future. This chapter will unveil the secrets to breaking through your barriers and show you what to do afterward!

CHAMPION THOUGHT:
Barriers and Conflicts Are Common, Not Necessarily Indications of Error

---

Throughout this book, we are examining the lives of many individuals who broke through the defenses of resistance in various arenas to contribute greatly to society. History records multitudes of champions whose decision paths pierced barriers in their environments, such as race, gender, medicine, communication, sports, and even the known world. All these people had at least one element in common: barriers and conflicts. You see, those who walk in their purpose as champions fulfill their calling by overcoming obstacles.

That's what makes them extraordinary. Without the presence of resistance in their lives and the ability to break through it, they would not change their environments.

Realize, therefore, that as you step into God's purpose for your life, you *will* face barriers, conflicts, obstacles, and resistance. This is not necessarily an indication of something wrong with you, nor the sign of missing God's will and being on the wrong path.

CHAMPION THOUGHT:
The Enemy Attempts to Steal God's Word from You

Remember that the enemy struggles against you to abort God's call on your life. One of the devil's most important weapons against you is erecting barriers to trick you into giving up on your divine purpose. He is trying to steal God's Word from you, especially the truth regarding your purpose.

In a parable about a sower sowing seed, Jesus exposed the enemy's strategy of stealing the Word. He said,

The sower sows the word. And these are the ones by the wayside where the word is sown. When they hear, Satan comes immediately and takes away the word that was sown in their hearts. (Mark 4:14–15)

As a thief, Satan is watching for the most opportune time to steal from you. Be alert to guard your divine purpose and the Word of God in your heart. Do not relinquish it to the enemy.

CHAMPION THOUGHT:
Never Let a Confidence-Conflict Defeat You

Although you trust God and stand strong, the devil will attack. He will try to deceive you into thinking that he is stronger than you.

In this conflict, the enemy's plan is for you to shift your confidence from God's power to the devil's abilities. Jesus explained,

> When a strong man, fully armed, guards his own palace, his goods are in peace. But when a stronger than he comes upon him and overcomes him, he takes from him all his armor in which he trusted, and divides his spoils. (Luke 11:21–22)

You see, Satan trusts in his armor! You are in a confidence-conflict with the devil and his kingdom of Darkness. The enemy counterfeits the confidence system of faith that God has established. Satan does this by trying to pervert your faith in God, tempting you to believe that the enemy's power can stop you. The truth is that no barriers or weapons are stronger than God and His Word in your life. Champion, don't ever let a confidence-conflict defeat you!

CHAMPION THOUGHT:
Turn Your Conflicts into Conquests

Nothing can defeat you, for you have the conquering consciousness of a champion. God has made all His children *"more than conquerors"* (Romans 8:37), and that includes you! The Bible teaches:

> For whatever is born of God overcomes the world. And this is the victory that has overcome the world—our faith. Who is he who overcomes the world, but he who believes that Jesus is the Son of God? (1 John 5:4–5)

God has already given the victory to you. Therefore, through Christ, you have the power to turn your conflicts into conquests!

CHAMPION THOUGHT:
Break Internal Barriers from the Outside In and the Inside Out

---

As you pursue your God-given purpose, you will face barriers, such as adversity, other's defensive mind-sets, hostility, bitterness, fear, your past failures, physical limitations, lack of knowledge, financial restrictions, and excuses. Some obstacles will be external, while others will be internal.

External hindrances include those that are man-made as well as those that are found in creation. Some examples of man-made hurdles are systems, actions, and mind-sets of people. Obstacles in creation are such elements as nature, natural laws, weather, and natural disasters.

You will also discover internal barriers. These are areas of your life that are out of alignment with God's will and purpose. They consist of your physical, mental, and spiritual challenges.

God's Word commands us:

Present your bodies a living sacrifice, holy, acceptable to God, which is your reasonable service. And do not be conformed to this world, but be transformed by the renewing of your mind, that you may prove what is that good and acceptable and perfect will of God. (Romans 12:1–2)

Internal barriers exist when you allow your unrenewed mind to rule your life through sin consciousness. Recall that sin consciousness is focusing on your sins and human shortcomings. This is why you need to meditate on God's Word continually. As your mind is renewed, you also strip away the former ways of your old man or flesh. In the next chapter, we will discuss in detail how renewing your mind works. For now, realize that the Bible teaches:

You have stripped off the old (unregenerate) self with its evil practices, and have clothed yourselves with the new [spiritual self], which is [ever in the process of being] renewed and remolded into [fuller and more perfect knowledge upon] knowledge after the image (the likeness) of Him Who created it. (Colossians 3:9–10 AMP)

You need to break through these human barriers within you from the outside in. Like an onion, you must strip off or peel away your *"outer man"* to reveal your *"inner man"*—your born-again or regenerated human spirit. God's Word also encourages us: *"Therefore we do not lose heart, but though our outer man is decaying, yet our inner man is being renewed day by day"* (2 Corinthians 4:16 NAS).

As you walk in the Spirit, you will not fulfill the desires of your flesh. Layer after layer of your outer man comes off, revealing more of your regenerated inner man. In this process, you release your spirit from human restraints. Like the onion, as you unveil the center of it, the smell is much more pungent, and you release the very essence or nature of the onion. You see, according to the Bible, if you are a Christian, God lives in your spirit: *"If anyone acknowledges that Jesus is the Son of God, God lives in him and he in God"* (1 John 4:15 NIV).

As you break away your outer man, you are actually revealing and unleashing the Spirit of God within you. This is what I call breaking internal barriers from the *outside in*.

Now, you also have internal barriers that need to be broken from the *inside out*. Since God's Seed remains in you, the nature of Christ within you breaks through the limitation, inhibitions, restrictions, and the human consciousness of your outer man. This happens as you submit yourself to God. The more you yield your will to Him, the more barriers He breaks within you.

As you grow in Christ, you will continually discover barriers that need to be broken. These are not necessarily new attacks. You are simply taking ground that your *outer* man could never give up but your *inner* man has the right to claim. In the process, you develop more and more into the image of Christ and become freer and freer. God gives you an awesome, ongoing freedom *"from glory to glory"*:

Where the Spirit of the Lord is, there is liberty. But we all, with unveiled face, beholding as in a mirror the glory of the

Lord, are being transformed into the same image from glory to glory, just as by the Spirit of the Lord.

(2 Corinthians 3:17–18)

Champion, you will become freer than you thought possible, which, in turn, will empower you to fulfill your divine purpose.

Along the way, each external and internal restriction you face might appear to be a valid reason for giving up. However, you must not quit. Remember that while every barrier is an "obstacle" to you, it is nothing to God. Before you were born, He had a purpose for you and saw all the resistance that you would face. He already has a plan for you to break through. His Word promises: *"And let us not grow weary while doing good, for in due season we shall reap if we do not lose heart"* (Galatians 6:9).

CHAMPION THOUGHT:
Champions Have Advanced Knowledge to Enable Them to Break Through

In *It Only Takes One*, we are looking at the lives of many individuals who have forged history. With great convictions and significant actions, these champions have produced permanent changes for mankind, overcoming great adversities. Often, these individuals have endured public ridicule and even risked their lives to achieve their breakthroughs.

One of the secrets to the success of champions is that they have a clear vision in a specific arena for the future. Their glimpses of advanced knowledge inspire them to press on through every barrier and defense. This intense motivation and focus propels them to discover, invent, create, achieve, and lead mankind on previously uncharted paths. These breakthroughs require passing through every line of defense. Meanwhile, many other people, on the other hand, accept the status quo as the way it always will be.

Is it *your* turn to step through the barriers of human norms that can easily dominate you and those around you? As you read the following section, think about the dreams in your heart or yet undefined glimpses of your destiny that God is revealing. Is He igniting a vision in your spirit for your future, which will then launch you through every barrier?

CHAMPION THOUGHT:
Advanced Knowledge Forever Breaks through Barriers

Before achieving a breakthrough, an individual suddenly has a theory or insight about the other side of a barrier. However, because of accepted behavioral patterns, the culture, and a defensive mind-set, society often attacks those who think differently. Yet that sudden burst of advanced knowledge in the person who is about to break through pierces people's defenses and resistance. As a result, that champion pushes the barrier forward, often greatly increasing human knowledge. Soon afterward, that barrier is no longer an issue, and that environment is changed forever.

The Bubonic Plague

To illustrate how advanced knowledge breaks through barriers forever, consider the bubonic plague, one of the most devastating diseases ever to afflict mankind. Before the world understood what caused it, this widespread epidemic claimed staggering numbers of lives: More than one hundred million people died! From 1347 to 1351 alone, tens of millions of Europeans fell to the disease—a quarter or more of the continent's entire population at the time.[1]

Especially two factors stopped these massive death tolls. One was the use of quarantines. Inspired by God, this idea literally changed the world. *The New Bible Dictionary* explains:

The origin of the word *quarantine* is the Jewish use of the period of 40 days of segregation from patients with certain diseases (Leviticus 12:1–4) adopted by the Italians in the 14th century because of the relative immunity of Jews from certain plagues.[2]

In other words, a fourteenth-century European had the inspiration to implement Old Testament quarantines—God's prescribed procedure for plagues! Because of this action, and also because someone discovered the second factor—that fleas spread this disease from infected rats—the bubonic plague is not a significant problem for the world today. Quarantines and a worldwide substantial campaign to exterminate rodents—especially in the international shipping industry—have virtually wiped out the disease. This simple, but important, advanced knowledge from God broke through and eradicated that life-and-death barrier.

Similarly, HIV (human immunodeficiency virus), which causes the dreaded condition known as AIDS (acquired immune deficiency syndrome), is prevalent today. AIDS itself is not a disease but a syndrome that makes the body susceptible to "opportunistic infections" and diseases, such as malignancies and neurological disorders.[3] In the near future, someone could break through the barrier of HIV, thus effectively putting an end to AIDS. For if we can stop the virus (HIV), there would be no syndrome (AIDS), which causes the susceptibility to other terminal diseases. AIDS would be history—never to be known among humanity again. The application of advanced, specific knowledge in this area would destroy HIV and AIDS from the world. In an important sense, this breakthrough is only a thought away.

Christopher Columbus

Another example of how advanced knowledge breaks through barriers forever is Christopher Columbus, the great discoverer, whom we discussed earlier. Until the fifteenth century, most people believed that the earth was flat instead of a globe. Columbus, an Italian explorer, believed that the earth was round and that he could sail west in order to reach the Far East. While on an expedition for Spain, he sailed west and discovered America (1492). Although he failed to reach his intended destination of Asia, Columbus discovered the New World, a great land with peoples unknown to the Europeans and Asians. In the process, Columbus also proved that the earth was not flat.

It took only one person to change the world's view in this area. One man broke through the incorrect geographical mind-set, and Columbus was that one. The application of this advanced knowledge forever changed how the world operates. As history records: "The arrival of his ships in the Western Hemisphere was one of the pivotal events in world history."[4]

Alfred Bernhard Nobel

The advanced knowledge of Alfred Bernhard Nobel (1833–1896) also forever transformed the world. A Swedish chemist and engineer, Nobel invented dynamite (1866) and later established the Nobel Prizes (1896) in an effort to ensure that his discovery would not be misused. These prizes include "any of the six international prizes awarded annually by the Nobel Foundation for outstanding achievements in the fields of physics, chemistry, physiology or medicine, literature, and economics and for the promotion of world peace."[5]

In addition to the barriers Nobel faced in inventing dynamite and other inventions, he overcame other adversities. An explosion in his Swedish factory in 1864 killed five people, including his youngest brother. Consequently, the government refused permission for Nobel to rebuild his factory, forcing him to relocate. After other explosions on ships around the world, many nations forbade their ships to carry his early explosive products.[6]

Finally making explosives safe to handle, Nobel paved the way for mining; weapons development; the engineering of buildings, other structures, and highways; and more. Without this invention, we would not have skyscrapers, highways, bridges, an abundance of jewelry made of precious metals and gemstones, or safe weapons to defend ourselves. This advanced knowledge also changed the world forever.

Champion, realize that God has designed *you* to break through specific barriers. You can be the one to make a difference or to advance the level of the world's knowledge in some way. Will you forever change the course of history? Are you willing to think and move beyond the known limits? Be aware, however, that with this course of action often come hostility and resistance.

CHAMPION THOUGHT:
Champions Must Break through Others' Defensive Mind-Sets

As champions venture into the unknown, they not only encounter barriers within their fields of endeavor, but also face the obstacle of defensive mind-sets of the day.

It is important to recognize that you, too, are very likely to face these obstacles as you step into your divine purpose. Therefore, let's examine some expressions of others' defensive mind-sets, so you will know how to overcome them.

CHAMPION THOUGHT:
Breaking Barriers Causes Fear

Christopher Columbus and Early Sea Explorers

Remember that before the fifteenth century, people believed the common notion that the earth was flat. Therefore, when explorers voyaged "to the ends of the earth" in unknown seas, sailors often feared for their lives. They believed that the devil and his monsters lurked in uncharted waters at the ends of the earth. People feared that those who ventured past this barrier literally would fall into hell as they sailed over the earth's "edge" to their deaths, never to return.

These tales became a controlling fear factor in how Europeans explored the earth. Consequently, for many years, seafarers navigated only within sight of land, refusing to explore beyond these barriers.

Finally, however, a certain daring explorer named Christopher Columbus decided to break free from these fears that had paralyzed progress in his generation. He dared to do what few navigators of his time had the courage to do: sail west into the unknown. Yet he broke through global superstitions to explore new, uncharted routes.

After the successful voyages of Columbus, future explorers no longer feared dropping off the edge of the earth. Because Columbus broke through the enormous fear of his day, it is difficult to find someone today who disbelieves that the earth is a globe.

CHAMPION THOUGHT:
Breaking Barriers Causes Hostility and Resistance

Although the breakthroughs that we have been examining have greatly contributed to society, they posed a problem to some people. Champions who venture to break through accepted barriers cannot explain exactly what will happen. For this reason, their critics often become skeptical.

Because those who anticipate breakthroughs are bent on breaking down accepted defenses, their opponents' skepticism often degenerates into hostility. A polarization occurs. The critics say, "We are right. This is the way it is. If you don't agree with us, you're wrong, period." No one can say anything to change their minds. A mentality of "those who are not *with* me are *against* me" sets in.

Have you ever seen this mind-set erupt? When this happens, people become excessively antagonistic toward you. *What is the problem?* you might wonder. *I am not doing anything to affect their lives directly. Why are they so upset?* The answer is they do not like the fact that a change is taking place. Columbus also endured this kind of opposition.

Christopher Columbus

Before his overwhelming success, Columbus faced the scorn of the people in his day when he tried to sail around the world. He wrote, "All who heard of my project rejected it with laughter, ridiculing me."[7] Anyone who attempted to cross this barrier met hostility from society. Since no one had ever broken through this defense, the critics actually believed it could not be done. Break-throughs always cause uproars in the status quo of their environments. This upheaval causes fear, confusion, disorientation, and misunderstanding, which often lead to hostility and resistance.

Mexican Girl

Another example of this type of hostility involves a little girl, whom I met several years ago. During one of our outreach trips to Mexico, the Spirit of God moved greatly, and I witnessed some of the most dramatic miracles that I have ever seen. However, one pastor had organized a group of denominational pastors to boycott our meetings because their mind-set about God did not allow for miracles! Instead, they held their own meetings, while we continued according to our schedule.

In one of our services, a pastor and an older woman brought a little girl to the altar. Her body was twisted like a snake. The woman asked me, "What can God do for her?"

I responded by asking, "What do you *want* Him to do?"

"I want to run," the girl interjected. She had never even walked in her life.

"Where?" I asked.

"Around the church."

I said, "Well, go ahead," and she did! This little girl had never stood before, but right there, she rose and started running. Watching God's power propel that child around the building was thrilling. God is faithful!

It is interesting to see what happens when people try to suppress or stop God. I was surprised to learn that the father of this little girl was the pastor who had organized the boycott meetings! He did not believe that God could do miracles, so the grandmother and another pastor had brought the girl to our service. There, God healed her. It was awesome!

Now, here is the rest of the story. This little girl was the last person we prayed for that night because the pastor who had brought her was afraid that she actually might be healed! Yes, he feared that God might heal her. This pastor had had an argument (in Spanish, of course) with the grandmother, because she wanted to bring her granddaughter to the front for prayer. It was as if sparks were flying between these two adults!

Clutching the girl in his arms, the pastor objected, saying, in effect, "You cannot take her up there because I don't want her father to be angry with me." Now, this was a serious matter to him. "If she gets healed," he continued, "her father will think that I was in agreement and that I thought his daughter should be healed. He will be upset with me because she received a miracle." This kind of thinking was preventing the girl from being able to come for prayer!

The grandmother was very irate with that pastor. "These people are getting healed," she argued. "Are you going to stand in the way to stop my granddaughter from receiving a miracle?"

Although this precious girl had every right to be healed, there was a barrier. Her parents and their friends had erected this wall because of their religion. They had agreed that God does not heal. In their eyes, this child, whose extremities were so misshapened, should not have come to our meeting. Her family was determined to have a crippled person in it. No one except a lone grandmother was willing to break through that barrier of hostility and resistance, so God could heal this child. All it took for a little girl's healing was the faith of one woman with the courage to break through a barrier.

When you get close to your breakthrough, you are likely to meet resistance from others. Do not worry. Remember that to receive your miracle, it only takes one—that one person can be you! Not many will invest even a prayer to believe that you can go beyond the defense that is blocking your way. They have not seen beyond the barrier, so they do not understand what lies on the other side—or even believe there is another side. Champion, if you want to break through, you must choose to penetrate all barriers—and you might have to do it alone with God! That's what this Mexican grandmother and Columbus did. That's what I did in my marriage. You can do it, too.

CHAMPION THOUGHT:
Many Break Down instead of Through

Because of their limited perspective, most people cannot think past barriers. This is all they have ever known and experienced. Therefore, they allow obstacles to restrict them. When average individuals meet a point of resistance, many have a *breakdown* instead of a *breakthrough*. Although they might be in the correct place at the correct time, they do not have the capacity to go all the way through the wall of defense. Consequently, whenever they reach barriers, they stop in their tracks, going no further.

Regardless of anyone else's defensive mind-set, you can choose to break through your barriers instead of breaking down in the midst of trials. Know that God's plan is not merely for you to survive. Remember that you are more than a conqueror; yes, you are an overcomer! Champion, you *can* persist to victory in the midst of hostility and resistance. How can you overcome others' defensive mind-sets? I have discovered several truths that I believe will help you.

CHAMPION THOUGHT:
Do Not Agree with Resistance to Your Breakthrough

You can be sure that others will stand argumentatively and defensively against your attempts to break through. When you face such resistance, you must make a decision. Will you agree or disagree with it? Will you keep moving forward, or will you choose to regress to the accepted norm?

You will be tempted to agree with their resistance, thinking, *It's easier to join them than oppose them.* Don't fall into this trap. Don't surrender. The devil tried to tempt me to do this in my marriage. It certainly would have been easier for me to give Faye a divorce and drop out of her life forever. However, God illuminated a better path. I am happy that I did not give in to resistance.

Don't repeat others' negative words about your vision. Keep your words in agreement with God's Word. Also, don't try to explain why those who resist you should believe in your plan to break through. It will be very difficult and probably impossible to explain to those who do not believe. Instead, let them watch your breakthrough. If anything will convince them, seeing your success will. However, the Bible says that many who doubted Jesus continued in their disbelief even when they saw Him perform signs and wonders. (See John 10:24–26.) Therefore, do not expect to change everyone's preconceived ideas.

CHAMPION THOUGHT:
Do Not Become Bitter against Others Who Are Bitter

When you meet defensive mind-sets, do not judge these people or hold bitterness against them. They do not have the truth that you know. Instead, pray for them to experience the same breakthrough as you.

CHAMPION THOUGHT:
Don't Let the Controversy of Your Faith Stop Your Next Step

Champion, you will always have opposition forces that will try to stop, impede, or divert you. As you launch ahead, the defenses of the masses can cause you to question your sanity as you wonder, *Is something wrong with me? No one else believes there can be a new standard in this area.*

Regardless of the opinions of those who have not heard from God, don't give up on your divine purpose. Break through in faith, as God directs you. Don't let the controversy of your faith stop your next step. Continue going forward in your God-inspired dreams. Remember: it only takes one—not the masses—to change the course of history.

CHAMPION THOUGHT:
Keep Doing What You Are Called to Do and You Will Overcome Adversity

---

How long are you willing to view the same limiting circumstances that are between you and your dream? If you want to achieve your God-ordained purpose, you must break through all the defensive lines. For a moment, let's consider how two ballplay-ers overcame their barriers by persisting in "doing what they do."

Mark McGwire and Sammy Sosa

Not merely baseball fans but millions of people in America and other nations will long remember the summer of 1998 as the Mark McGwire/Sammy Sosa home run chase. Both ball play-ers shattered the 37-year-old record for the most home runs in a season. They did not merely break the record of 61 home runs one time, but over and over and over. Mark McGwire, the St. Louis Cardinals' first baseman, hit number 70! Sammy Sosa, a native of the Dominican Republic who plays for the Chicago Cubs, finished the season with 66 home runs!

Nearly two weeks before McGwire or Sosa broke the record the first time, one reporter wrote:

> This represents the most devastating assault on the major league home run record since Babe Ruth rewrote all the home run standards in the 1920s. It even exceeds the record-setting season of 1961 when Roger Maris broke Babe Ruth's 1927 record of 60 dingers with 61 of his own.[8]

Another reporter recounted the historic moment like this:

> Baseball's new landmark number is 70. Mark McGwire established that threshold today...putting a conclusion to an epic home run chase that captivated the nation. McGwire and Sosa spent the summer chasing Roger Maris'...[record] of 61, the total that the New York Yankees slugger hit in 1961 to break the seemingly unreachable 60 hit by Babe Ruth.[9]

In his 137th game of the season, McGwire shattered Maris' record, who had played in 159 games in 1961, the year he broke

Babe Ruth's number. Babe Ruth had played in 151 games during his record-breaking year in 1927. McGwire "is the only player ever to hit 50 or more home runs in less than 140 games."[10]

The Cardinals team and baseball would never be the same. As one writer expressed it,

> When Mark McGwire launched his 70 home runs...he didn't just shatter the single-season record. He also personified an enormous shift in philosophy for an entire franchise....[This was not] just a superhuman effort by one player. To the Cardinals, it represented a typical total for the entire TEAM.[11]

One man single-handedly changed the face of a team and his sport. This ballplayer overcame many barriers to achieve his breakthrough.

A tangible record of 61 home runs limited both McGwire and Sosa. No one had ever ventured past that mark. However, these two players did not let that boundary limit them. They kept doing what they do, aiming for that mark. Game after game, they pressed on. Finally, one day they made history and broke the record! Now, their names are recorded in the annals of baseball history.

Champion, always continue to press on in the face of adversity. By continuing to step out in obedience to God, you *will* fulfill His calling on your life. The only way you can fail to fulfill your divine purpose is if you stop pursuing your dream or don't ever start.

You might be saying to yourself, *Well, I'm not that athletic. I cannot hit home runs like these men.* Or maybe you are thinking, *I'm not that smart. I cannot invent or discover anything.* Well, neither am I. You don't need to be that smart or athletic, but you *are something*. You have a unique contribution to make to this world. You have attributes, empowerments, and giftings. God has created you with areas of your life that are distinctly different from other people. As you begin to operate in them, you will break through your barriers. Simply keep pressing toward your dream, and one day, you will achieve it! The apostle Paul, while behind the barrier of prison walls, wrote:

> *Brothers, I do not consider myself yet to have taken hold of it. But one thing I do: Forgetting what is behind and straining toward what is ahead, I press on toward the goal to win the prize for which God has called me heavenward in Christ Jesus.* (Philippians 3:13–14 NIV)

CHAMPION THOUGHT:
Hide God's Word in Your Heart to Break Through

A great discovery of godly champions is filling up with the Word of God. Read the Bible regularly—every day, if possible. Hiding God's Word in your heart will help you to have the faith, wisdom, knowledge, and power to break through your barriers. Then, when it seems that everyone is explaining what's *wrong* with your plan to break through, you can focus on what's *right* with it.

I did this during my battle for my marriage. God used His Word to give me revelation, which strengthened me to break through all my obstacles.

Christopher Columbus

Columbus also hid the Word of God in his heart to help him stand against great odds. Through His Word, God gave clear direction and inspiration for his breakthrough. In the *Book of Prophecies,* Columbus wrote:

> It was the Lord who put into my mind—I could feel His hand upon me—the fact that it would be possible to sail from here to the Indies....There is no question that the inspiration was from the Holy Spirit, because he comforted

146

me with rays of marvelous illumination from the Holy
Scriptures....For the execution of the journey to the Indies
I did not make use of intelligence, mathematics, or maps. It
is simply the fulfillment of what Isaiah had prophesied.[12]

Columbus recognized that his inspiration literally came from
God and His Word!

God can do this for you also, if you read His Word. You see, He
frequently gives sudden bursts of advanced knowledge to His people
through daily Bible reading. This can empower you to move beyond
resistance, so you can pierce through every defense standing in your
way. Then, Champion, you can expect to soar through to the other
side of the barrier. No line of defense will be able to stop your breakthrough. That's when you will launch a new standard!

CHAMPION THOUGHT:
Detach from Your Past to Obtain Your Future

To fulfill your divine purpose, you also must break the internal barriers of your past. To gain insight about how to become
free from your past, let's examine the biblical account of the hemorrhaging woman. Some call her the "woman with the issue of
blood."

The Woman with the Issue of Blood

Before beginning this story, it is important to understand the
biblical culture in this context. According to Mosaic Law, bleeding or any kind of discharge—which the King James Version of the
Bible calls an *"issue"*—caused one to become unclean or defiled.
Regardless of what caused the bleeding or discharge, anyone with
this condition remained unclean during the flow and for a specific period of time afterward, depending upon the cause of the
issue.

Those who were unclean for any reason had to separate themselves from the Israelites' camp until they became clean and offered atoning sacrifices. Therefore, anyone who was unclean because of a discharge became an outcast, both socially and religiously. You see, in the Old Testament, since God literally dwelled in Israel's camp, this was not only a separation from the people, but also from God Himself. (See Numbers 5:2–3.)

In light of this understanding, let's begin the story:

Now a certain woman had a flow of blood for twelve years, and had suffered many things from many physicians. She had spent all that she had and was no better, but rather grew worse. (Mark 5:25–26)

Although this woman had tried everything to be healed, still she suffered—and became even worse. However, because she could stand her condition no longer, she was unwilling to give up on her breakthrough.

One day, she heard about an answer. However, it was not an easy solution. This resolution required more than most Israelites were willing to do. She heard people talking about some Man named Jesus, who was walking through town, and God was doing miracles through Him. The Bible continues: *"When she heard about Jesus, she came behind Him in the crowd and touched His garment. For she said, 'If only I may touch His clothes, I shall be made well'"* (vv. 27–28).

Remember, in that day, the Mosaic Law forbade this woman to enter Israel's camp because her issue of blood made her unclean. For this reason, she overcame great resistance just to get near Jesus. Because of the crowds of people around Him, she had to work her way through the physical pressure of others touching her. At any point during this effort, she could have been discovered as being unclean. Then, she would have been declared guilty of defiling all those around her.

With all the boldness she could muster, the woman approached Jesus—but dared only to come from behind and simply touch His clothes. After all, she could have been accused of trying to make Jesus unclean!

Her extraordinary effort, together with her insight about Jesus, was highly unusual. First, she had the advanced knowledge to believe that Jesus could heal her with the simple touch of His clothes! Then, she had to break through the great barrier of being ostracized. Now, she had done that. It was time for her breakthrough! The Bible says, *"Immediately the fountain of her blood was dried up, and she felt in her body that she was healed of the affliction"* (Mark 5:29).

Instead of making Jesus unclean, the power of God emanated from Him to cleanse the sick woman! It was a miracle. This was the breakthrough for which she had waited twelve difficult years.

The Bible explains what happened next:

And Jesus, immediately knowing in Himself that power had gone out of Him, turned around in the crowd and said, "Who touched My clothes?" But His disciples said to Him, "You see the multitude thronging You, and You say, 'Who touched Me?'" (vv. 30–31)

Here, the disciples became a line of defense around Jesus. He wanted to follow up on a miracle that had occurred. However, they attempted to stand in His way. With their natural eyes, the disciples could see only an average crowd and no unique circumstances. Yet Jesus knew differently. The Bible explains:

And He looked around to see her who had done this thing. But the woman, fearing and trembling, knowing what had happened to her, came and fell down before Him and told Him the whole truth. (Mark vv. 32–33)

Imagine her fear. Finally she had received her long-awaited miracle, but the Healer had caught her violating the Mosaic Law! After all this, now what would happen to her? Again, however, this woman made the right decision. Instead of covering her sin, she confessed it.

Jesus did not reprimand her, but responded compassionately, saying, *"Daughter, your faith has made you well. Go in peace, and be healed of your affliction"* (Mark 5:34).

CHAMPION THOUGHT:
Connect to Jesus for Your Breakthrough

This hemorrhaging woman had a tremendous physical challenge that needed the healing power of Jesus. However, *hearing* about Jesus is not the same as *experiencing* His life-changing power. She realized that achieving her dream meant discovering how to connect with Jesus, despite the barriers in her path. The fact that this sickly woman was able to reach Jesus to obtain her breakthrough means that you can, too!

Now, look at your life, Champion. Are you satisfied with what you see? Are barriers from your past and present blocking your way? If you want to go beyond the barrier of your experience, you must detach from your past and present. Break away from all your experiences, excuses, complaints, desires for comfort, and anything else that prevents your escape through the barrier. Only then can you obtain a better future. The following truths will help you to detach from your past.

CHAMPION THOUGHT:
Do Not Line up New Knowledge from God with Your Past Failures

---

Realize that *how* this woman heard about Jesus determined *what* she heard. If she had heard the news about Jesus and filtered it through her extensive suffering, she might have discounted the new information. This is an important key. She had to separate the new information about Jesus' healing power from her past experiences of debilitating sickness. Only then could faith rise in her heart to touch Him. You must never compare the knowledge of God with the defeats of your past.

Most people compare new information with their past experiences. It makes sense to do this, because they can learn from their past. However, when they discover new knowledge from God, this tendency can be dangerous. If new hopeful information from God contradicts their past experiences, they discard it. For example, if people read something in the Bible that they have never seen before, they compare it with their experiences. If nothing in their history has solved their problems, they will be tempted to say, "What I just read can't work either." They have already determined that nothing will work.

You must not do this. It is a major hindrance to your future. Stop taking what you hear from God and comparing it with your past failures. The Bible instructs us to keep our thoughts subject to God, not vice versa:

> *Casting down imaginations, and every high thing that exalt-eth itself against the knowledge of God, and bringing into captivity every thought to the obedience of Christ.*
>
> (2 Corinthians 10:5 KJV)

Begin now by carefully reading the words and verses in this book, which reveal biblical knowledge that may be new to you. Read the Bible and meditate on His Word. Let His truth sink into your spirit, and allow God to speak to you about what you are reading. I believe that you have never heard what He will share with you afterward. You may have heard *about* it, but you have never *really heard* it.

CHAMPION THOUGHT:
The Voice of Your History Cries to Dominate Your Future

You must realize that you are in a spiritual battle. God's Word explains that your enemy, the devil, wants to defeat you: *"Be sober, be vigilant; because your adversary the devil walks about like a roaring lion, seeking whom he may devour"* (1 Peter 5:8).

An easy way for Satan to defeat you is to make your negative past loom so large in your life that you do not consider any encouraging new options for your future. You see, the voice of your history cries to dominate your future. The devil strongly desires to influence and control you. If he can prevent you from penetrating the barrier of your past, he can sabotage your future. It's time to stop the voice of your history from dominating your future.

The woman with the issue of blood had to sever the voice of her painful past, so it would not dominate her hope for healing. This champion successfully broke through that wall of defense, which continually screamed about her twelve-year history. She loosed herself from a lifestyle of condemnation, rejection, and accusation. She did not focus on all the lost money and the wasted time on false cures. She stood strong against bitterness and resentment, which threatened to overtake her, as she heard about others' healings while she was still sick. This woman loosed herself from the past. She let it go, so she could have an exciting future. She recognized that there is no benefit in focusing on the past. Instead, she looked to Jesus to change her future. What she heard about Him separated her from the voice of her past. That's the only way it would not control her future.

Do you need to break the voice of your past, so it will not speak to dominate your future? If you do not make this break, your past will limit your future. You will become bitter very quickly unless you stop focusing on your past failures and pain. This negative attitude will jeopardize the future that God has planned for you.

CHAMPION THOUGHT:
Use Your Misery Factor to Motivate You

Many people enjoy wallowing in bitterness, self-pity, and the pain of their pasts. Thank God, however, there is a limit to the misery that most of us are willing to endure! When we have exerted our greatest human effort and experienced enough pain, most of us will do all we can to stop the turmoil. We will allow misery to push us only so far. Then, we become serious about climbing from our pits! I call this the misery factor. The level of our misery factor determines the level of our commitment. In other words, the more misery we have, the more commitment we have to escape it. Pain motivates many people this way.

The woman with the issue of blood had a high misery factor. Now, after these twelve agonizing years of suffering and spending all her worldly wealth, how was she? Worse. She was at the end of her rope. She wanted to do whatever it took to become free—even if it meant violating the religious laws of her day.

If you have some areas in your life with a high misery factor, don't become defeated. Use your pain to motivate yourself to become free!

Champion Thought:
Attach to God's Promises for Your Future

After you detach yourself from the past, you must attach yourself to something new. That is God. Breaking free from the influence of your past allows you to follow God. You can begin this journey by finding and meditating on passages in the Bible that promise a future of hope in place of your hopeless past. Allow faith to rise in your heart to believe that these promises are yours personally. Focus on the future that God's Word promises you. Use His process, which we discussed earlier, to change your course: Meditation, Revelation, Motivation, Action, Fruit. You cannot attach to the future until you detach from the past.

Champion, Jesus wants to set you free. Will you let Him? He loves you more than you can imagine and wants to remove the pain and sorrow of your past. Not only that, but He also has an exciting and fulfilling future planned uniquely for you!

CHAMPION THOUGHT:
Resistance Persists Even after Your Breakthrough

When you finally pierce through every line of defense to achieve your breakthrough, you will see differently. Your dream will then be a reality, and you will experience the thrill of walking in it. However, the resistance that you faced from others' defensive mind-sets before is likely to persist. You have evidence—factual proof—that negates their opposition. Therefore, their deceptions need not influence you any longer. You have demonstrated truth that is contrary to their perspectives.

CHAMPION THOUGHT:
Your Breakthrough Requires Others to Evaluate Their Limiting Mind-Sets

Recall the pastor in Mexico who refused to attend our miracle services or bring his daughter. After she was healed, the girl's miracle presented a big problem to this father. Suddenly his daughter was walking and running. He probably argued with the grandmother and pastor who had brought the girl to our service. Yet how could the father explain his doctrine? His daughter's miraculous healing forced him to evaluate his apparently error-ridden mind-set about God. Was he willing to change to break through that barrier in his mind?

Are people criticizing the breakthrough that you have already experienced? Often, others will accuse and attack you because they do not have breakthroughs like yours. They cannot leave you alone. You see, if they do not attack and ridicule *your* breakthrough, then they will have to evaluate why *they* are not experiencing the same powerful results as you. Your miracle causes them to face the need to change. In their way of thinking, the unknown is nonexistent or is impossible, and your proof of their wrong thinking makes them uncomfortable. Understanding this will help you to overcome their backbiting.

Others might even judge you, thinking that you did something wrong to arrive on the other side of the barrier. They might begin to believe that God loves you more than them. Instead of rejoicing when you break through barriers, they might become bitter against you. God wants to liberate them also, but will they let Him? They will have to be ready to let go of their limiting mind-sets.

CHAMPION THOUGHT:
Do Not Apologize for Your Breakthrough

Always remember that your breakthrough is yours. You do not have to make excuses for it. Do not apologize to people who are offended because of your breakthrough. Arguing with those who doubt you is futile because they do not live on the same level with you anymore. After you achieve your breakthrough, you live in an entirely new realm, which you do not have to explain to anyone else. If they do not want to follow in your path, it is not your responsibility to force them to come. However, if people sincerely want to know how to breakthrough as you did, be the one to help them. Keep the door to truth open for them.

Identify Your Barriers

Remember that God has destined you for victory. God has purposed humanity to achieve multitudes of breakthroughs, and some of them are yours! Maybe you are to break through in your family, or in another area of life, such as medicine, science, industry, technology, government, sports, or the spiritual realm.

After discovering what God plans as your breakthrough—your contribution to this generation, your purpose—identify your barriers. You need to know what your barriers are, so you can deal with them properly.

Right now as you read this book, before God ask yourself, *Am I happy where I am? How long will I stay here?* It is quite sobering to realize that you must break through to the other side of the barriers in your life.

Ask God to reveal to you the following:

- What prevents me from advancing toward the fulfillment of His purpose for me?
- What hindrances stand in the way of my breaking through every line of defense?
- Are some defensive lines standing against me, speaking volumes of information to keep me from penetrating all resistance?
- Are the mind-sets of others resisting the divine truth that I perceive?

Begin the process of Meditation, Revelation, Motivation, Action, Fruit to identify your barriers and discover how to break through. As the Lord reveals them to you, list the barriers, hindrances, and limiting forces that keep you from experiencing the full dreams and visions that God has placed in your heart. Your list might contain economic challenges, family conflicts, mechanical problems such as your car breaking down, or any number of other challenges.

Be sure that what you believe are barriers are also seen in the Bible as such. You don't want to fight against something that you think is a barrier when it's God's boundary in your life. Believe me, you will get nowhere in that struggle, and you will waste a lot of time and resources.

CHAMPION THOUGHT:
Get Rid of Excuses and Turn Them into God's Uses

As you consider your dreams and visions, you might be thinking, *Well, I don't have enough money.* Then, meditate on God's Word in the area of finances. Maybe you are wondering, *How can I even think of pursuing my dreams until my family challenges are resolved?* Then, meditate on God's Word regarding the family. Perhaps you are physically sick and you think, *I cannot do anything. I'm too weak. I don't feel well. I can't think about anything else right now.* Then, meditate on God's Word on healing.

Don't turn your barriers into excuses for failing to pursue God's purpose. If you have already done this, then it's time to get rid of your excuses and turn them into God's uses. You see, as you meditate on His Word in the areas of your barriers, He will give you divine revelation. When God gives you revelation, you can be sure that He has done this to manifest changes in those areas of your life. Then, as He motivates you and you act on those revelations, you will see the godly fruit that He desires for your life. Remember that God has said it, and *He* will do it. If you follow this process, you will turn your excuses into God's uses.

Evaluate Your God-Given Assets

Discover what God is giving to advance you beyond these defenses that seem to hinder you. Remember that He does not call you to do a work without equipping you and providing the necessary power and resources. His Word promises, *"My God shall supply all your need according to His riches in glory by Christ Jesus"* (Philippians 4:19). As you spend time meditating on God's Word, He will reveal answers to you and give you plans to succeed.

When I did this during the challenge with my marriage, God blessed and strengthened me beyond my expectations. He gave me a champion thought—supernatural wisdom—that helped me to stand in faith for my breakthrough.

Ask the Lord:

- What sudden burst of advanced knowledge will cause me to break through all my barriers?
- What will penetrate every defensive mind-set in the way of my divine purpose?

Evaluate Your Commitment to Penetrate Barriers

Now, you have a decision to make. How long are you willing to stand in confrontation at the line of defense? How long are you willing to listen to the continual rhetoric and never-ending drone of other people's reasons why your vision will not work? How long are you willing to continue struggling against the same negative circumstance, wondering when it will stop?

The truth is that it will never stop on its own. It won't stop until someone breaks through it to get on the other side. It will become a standard operating procedure. It will become normal, until someone breaks through that barrier. Isn't it time to be free of that limitation? Don't you want to walk in the power of dominion and authority in that area of your life?

You can, but it will take commitment. You see, Champion, all the inspiration and ability in the world will not be enough for you to become free if you lack commitment and conviction to break through all your barriers. After you discover your God-given purpose, you must commit yourself to pressing past all the defenses that block your way.

Ask yourself these questions to help evaluate your commitment to achieve your breakthrough:

- Do I have the conviction to penetrate the line of defense?
- Am I willing to do whatever it takes to get through the barriers to fulfill the plan God has shown to me?
- Can I press on to discover what waits on the other side of that limit?
- Will I speak out when the ominous status quo or the majority are in agreement to attempt to mute my voice?

All these questions boil down to one: How committed are you? You must be willing to dig deeply to reach the foundation of truth, so you can destroy the wall of lies that looms before you. You must press through these barriers to receive your breakthrough. However, you do not have to rely on your own strength or will-power. Remember that after you meditate on the Word, God will give you revelation. Revelation then produces motivation, which means that He will help you commit to your breakthrough.

You can walk in the power of His Holy Spirit. The Bible promises breakthroughs *"not by might nor by power, but by My Spirit,' says the LORD of hosts"* (Zechariah 4:6). In other words, your breakthrough will not come through your own strength and power, but through His Spirit. The Spirit of God is in you, giving to you the ability and direction to go beyond every defensive resistance that stands against you.

CHAMPION THOUGHT:
Count the Cost before You Break Through

Many people are not willing to pay the price to break through. They do not want to exert the effort necessary to shatter the surrounding negative mind-sets and barriers. Yet, in reality, the price *not* to break through is greater than that to break through. The price of disobedience to your destiny has eternal *and* temporal consequences.

For example, what if I had not committed to breakthrough in my marriage? What if I had not believed God's Word to restore my family? I would have lost the priceless joy and blessing of beautiful, close relationships with my wife, children, their spouses, and now grandchildren! Also, I believe that I would not be a pastor or in the ministry today, working with God in touching hundreds of thousands of lives for His glory. Financial and emotional destruction probably would have overcome me. The one action that I might have succeeded in was ending my life. Does this all sound like a big price to pay? Yes, in fact, it was too big for me. Instead, I chose to obey God and stand on His Word to break through. While this was not at all easy, it was well worth the price I paid.

Champion, do you need a breakthrough? What will it cost you? Count the cost before venturing to break through. Jesus asked, *"For which of you, intending to build a tower, does not sit down first and count the cost, whether he has enough to finish it"* (Luke 14:28)?

Your breakthrough will take dedication, commitment, and diligence on your part. Are you willing to press on through every adversity? Your breakthrough will mean that you must release yourself from the grip of your past pain and suffering. Are you willing to let it go? Your breakthrough could cost you your relationships with those who resist your divine purpose. Can you endure misunderstandings and possible hostility from others, or is this too much to handle? Be the one who is willing to pay the price. Remember, it only takes one to make a difference—and that's you.

As your first priority, Champion, obey God and persist in faith no matter how high the cost. Only then can you break through every barrier to achieve your divine purpose. Breaking through is your reward for obedience to Him and persistence in faith. It is worth any price. You see, if you don't move forward to the future, you will stagnate in the present and retreat to your past. We will discuss this point in the next chapter.

7
Make Resistance Work for You

C *hange*. Does that word scare you? To many people, change is one of the most frightening experiences they can imagine. In this chapter, you will discover the reason the fear of change has such a stranglehold on people and how to break free from it. You will learn how to discern when it's time to advance and how to avoid the pitfalls of retreating. Also, you will see how to maintain your breakthrough after you have overcome your obstacles.

Henry Ford

Henry Ford (1863–1947), the American industrialist and pioneer automobile manufacturer, formed the Ford Motor Company in 1903; mass-produced the Model T, the first generally affordable and widely available automobile; and developed a gasoline-powered automobile in 1893. Ford's revolution of the automobile industry changed the world. Can you imagine life without cars, trucks, vans, or sports utility vehicles?

CHAMPION THOUGHT:
Recognize the Paradigm Shift

In Henry Ford's era, a paradigm shift—an entirely new model—in transportation occurred. In the United States, we moved from horses and buggies to a new invention called the automobile.

Unwilling to change, many people at first resisted progress, refusing to see the advantages of this new kind of vehicle.

Resistance to positive change can become a great barrier in any area of life. It is easy to fall into the trap of resistance. Listening to the voice of man instead of God can pit you against divine changes. For example, if Abraham had asked for man's opinions, he never would have become the *"father of all those who believe"* (Romans 4:11).

If Noah had taken a vote or an opinion poll, he never would have built the ark to save the earth and mankind. If I had heeded my wife's and friends' advice, my family would have remained in shambles. You must restrict your communications, keep your eyes on your heavenly calling, and make the necessary changes to stay on God's path for your future.

I have seen firsthand the devastating results of being unwilling to move forward when God is ready to create change in one's life. While I was in college as a part-time student, my father was the superintendent of the welding department at a nearby automotive manufacturer. At nineteen years old, after working at the plant for a short time, I became a foreman in my father's department. A statement was ingrained in each employee: "There is the right way, the wrong way, and the company way." Of course, we all were instructed to work according to "the company way."

As I began to take university courses in industrial engineering, new information opened my eyes to another world. I quickly realized that there was the right way, the wrong way, the company way, and the *college* way. I learned how startling discoveries in the use of machines, specifically robotic arms, were revolutionizing the Japanese auto-manufacturing industry. The advantages of this automation were phenomenal. First, it created a safe environment for the employees. Next, time and motion studies revealed that these machines were much more efficient than their human counterparts. Additionally, these robotic arms precisely placed spot-welds at the correct times and temperature. As a result, the welds were very solid, causing the cars to be more dependable. The end product was far superior to those created by the hands of man.

This was a paradigm shift for manufacturing automobiles, similar to the change that occurred in Henry Ford's era. I knew that it was only a matter of time before this new form of automation would reach the United States, revolutionizing our industry also. I saw that robotics would replace the human element in the welding world.

As our corporate leaders began to speak of this industrial change, and it filtered down through the ranks, the response was astounding. This concept was met with the greatest level of resistance that I had ever seen. Most of the employees—such as the 55-year-old welder, who had been welding for 30 years and had only a few years until retirement—were not impressed. To them, the way they had always done their jobs was the *only* way. Unwilling to adapt, they fearfully clung to their old standard: there is the right way, the wrong way, and the company way. They refused to acknowledge that now there was the robotic way.

Because these employees failed to recognize the paradigm shift, they chose not to advance toward the future. Consequently, they were left behind.

It didn't have to be that way. God had a better plan for the people affected by automation. Similar to me, Dick DeVos understood this concept while helping in his father's business. Jay Van Andel and Dick's father, Rich DeVos, who were the cofounders of the Amway Corporation in 1959, planned for their grown children to succeed them in their prospering international business. The younger DeVos, who became the president, wrote about his college and early management training in Amway, saying,

> I became aware of the increasing role that technology would play in the future of our expanding company. I learned that automation didn't replace people; it set them

free to concentrate on tasks that were less repetitive and more intellectually stimulating and productive. In fact, by remaining competitive through automation, the business grew so much that Amway had to hire even more people to keep up with demand.[1]

You see, when you trust God throughout the transitions in your life, He will bring you to a better place.

CHAMPION THOUGHT:
Recognize the Signposts of Retreat

When our manufacturing facility switched to robotics, the engineering employees received intensive industrial psychological training. The fact that machine arms were taking over people's jobs caused frustration, anger, and hostility. When management finally instituted the new way, a sense of hopelessness, purposelessness, and obsolescence permeated our department. Many of the employees became bitter at these hunks of metal! The responses were clear indications that employees were rejecting the paradigm shift and retreating.

This issue brought tragedy into the lives of many people whom I supervised and for whom I was responsible. Frustrated at their inability to stop progress, many chose destructive escape routes, such as alcoholism or drug abuse.

Today, Champion, do you work in an industry in which your particular job classification has changed because of automation? Is your company downsizing with your position in jeopardy of being eliminated? Are you heading toward retirement? On a personal level, are your children growing up and leaving home? Have you recently lost a close family member? Are your friends or spouse looking to others for help or companionship? Are you beginning to feel unneeded in any area of your life?

Do you feel that you are in the process of being made obsolete? In a way, you will be, if you don't wake up to realize that breakthroughs are at hand. In other words, if you don't advance when God desires to make changes in your life or move you into a new role, then you will be left behind. If you don't step into God's paradigm shift for your life, you will miss your breakthroughs. The consequences are devastating. Don't make the mistake that countless others have. When God's change comes, embrace it; don't reject it.

CHAMPION THOUGHT:
The New Guard Need Not Replace the Old

It is *not* true that if you are part of the old establishment, you must be removed to give way to the new. The new guard does *not* have to replace the *entire* old guard. For example, in business, the employees of the new guard—who are often younger and new on the job—can offer the dynamic of fresh perspectives. Frequently, they have knowledge of new advancements in their industry. Bringing in this type of staff may cause fear and resentment in the old guard—who often are aging and advancing toward retirement. However, instead of completely replacing the old with the new guard, wouldn't it be better to have the benefits of both? Consider the advantages of combining the years of experience, strength, and stability of the old guard, who have made great accomplishments until that point, with the innovations and freshness of the new guard. This combination would be a great asset to any company.

However, if this is such a good idea, why don't we see the old and new guards merged very often? It is usually because the old guard will not accept new thoughts to become part of the new solution. (This is what happened in our auto plant.) When change is presented to the old establishment, they refuse to take the necessary steps. Also, sometimes the people of the new guard think they know everything and don't need the old guard. Thus, an irreparable gap forms between the old and new. In this scenario, one group must leave, and it's usually the old guard.

Jesus taught:

No one sews a piece of unshrunk cloth on an old garment; or else the new piece pulls away from the old, and the tear is made worse. And no one puts new wine into old wineskins; or else the new wine bursts the wineskins, the wine is spilled, and the wineskins are ruined. But new wine must be put into new wineskins. (Mark 2:21–22)

When God does a new work in your life, you should not hold on to the past. As He turns a chapter for you, He is moving you to a new level. You need to make that leap and move into your new breakthrough. Otherwise, you will be left behind.

CHAMPION THOUGHT:
Destroy Your Old-Guard "Crabology Mentality"

In Ghana one year, Bishop Nicholas Duncan-Williams delivered a message that I will never forget. Before he was to speak, he told me about his sermon.

The bishop explained, "The church is like a group of people who have 'crabology.'"

"What is crabology? Is it something in Ghana that we don't have in the United States?" I asked, thinking it might be a disease, against which I needed to be inoculated. Although I did not know what crabology was, I was fairly certain that I did not want it.

"No! No!" Bishop Duncan-Williams answered. Then, he asked, "You have seen a basket of crabs, haven't you?"

"Yes."

"When one crab tries to climb out, what do the others do?" he asked.

"They go after that one crab to pull him back down," I replied, "because they hate to see one guy get out. They would rather all boil together."

In other words, crabology is the mind-set that keeps people preferring to die the same death together, instead of helping anyone to escape. This way, no one ever gains freedom or experiences joy from helping someone else break through.

Do you have "crabology mentality"? This is the attitude or belief system that says, "That's the way it has always been. Nothing will ever change it. We're not getting out, and we won't let you out either."

The new guard—whether in a business setting or a new move of God—is often met with crabology mentality from the old guard. Because the people in the old establishment do not want to change, they retreat into negativity. Their limiting mind-sets become a perverted comfort zone, which they do not desire to escape—even if it will result in physical death or the demise of their dreams. Not only that, but they also resist and work against those who will not retreat with them.

Champion, you cannot afford to develop a crabology mentality. It is detrimental to God's purposes not only in your life but in the lives of those around you.

CHAMPION THOUGHT:
Beware of the Root of Bitterness

Today, at our ministry, we had a staff meeting. I taught on the effects of change, objections to change, and then leadership. My goal was to see that any resistance to change would not turn into bitterness, which is a very common reaction.

The Bible instructs:

Follow peace with all men, and holiness, without which no man shall see the Lord: Looking diligently lest any man fail of the

167

grace of God; lest any root of bitterness springing up trouble you, and thereby many be defiled. (Hebrews 12:14–15 KJV)

Notice here, God's warning against bitterness troubling first one person, and then spreading to contaminate others.

Have you ever enthusiastically joined a group of people at your job, in church, with your family, or in another environment? Then, after spending five minutes with them, did you find that your attitude had changed? Hearing their trouble, did you internalize their struggle? Did their resentment become yours? Did your excitement quickly turn into frustration? If so, someone else's root of bitterness defiled you!

CHAMPION THOUGHT:
You Are Not a Garbage Dump

It is important to guard against picking up others' negative attitudes. If you find yourself in a bitter environment, you have a choice to make. Will you listen to evil reports, curses, bitter words, and resentment? Or will you find a way to escape the negativity? You cannot afford to be the garbage dump of someone else's caustic attitude. It will affect you too much. Before long you will become defiled with their bitterness.

Either you must fix the environment or move from it. It's that simple. You might be thinking, *Well, that's where I work. I cannot change this situation, and I'm stuck here because I need the job.* Then, transfer to another department or office. You see, if you cannot change the environment, it's far better to move away from it. Staying there will only pollute you, giving you a poisoned outlook that will then contaminate your family and friends.

Maybe you are thinking, *But I am standing for my marriage. I can't leave.* Then, find a way to avoid mental oppression and bitterness. You don't have to settle for negative rhetoric affecting you.

Do not allow the enemy's voice through others to berate, condemn, ridicule, or accuse you continually. The Bible says, *"We have the mind of Christ"* (1 Corinthians 2:16). Think God's thoughts, not the other person's bitterness and negativity.

CHAMPION THOUGHT:
You Run Your Environment

If you find yourself in a negative setting that you cannot escape, then learn how to run that environment according to God's ways. Raise up your shield of faith by speaking His Word into that place. In a business setting, one of the best locations to do this is in an elevator. It really is. If you step onto an elevator where people are spouting negativity, and you do nothing, thinking, *I can't believe how bad these people's attitudes are,* what have you done? You've picked up their bitterness, haven't you? You stepped off in negativity instead of with a testimony that silenced it. Champion, it's *your* environment. If you don't run it, who will? The enemy.

CHAMPION THOUGHT:
Cut out the Root of Bitterness to Receive Good Fruit

Do you need to remove volumes of negative information from your thought life right now? Has bitterness affected you, whether you originated it or received it from others? Remember that earlier we discussed the need to remove a root if you desire different fruit. This is also true of the root of bitterness. You need to take time to cut it from your life now.

Realize that it only takes one to resolve your situation. Let that person be you. Regardless of others' responses, God can wipe your slate clean so you can move on to receive His breakthroughs and fulfill your divine purpose. You are not responsible for other people's actions, but you are accountable before God for yours. Therefore, I encourage you to remove the root of bitterness immediately by doing the following:

1. Ask God to forgive you for allowing the poisonous root of bitterness to spring up in your life and defile others. Release all bitterness now, and do not pick it up again. Receive God's forgiveness for giving the enemy access through you to bring a destructive force into any area of your life, whether it is your job, church, family, or other setting.

2. Next, think about the people you have contaminated with your bitterness. If possible, go to them to ask for forgiveness. Either way, through prayer in Jesus' name, release those whom you have negatively influenced. Ask God to minister healing to them.

3. If you have become bitter as a direct result of others' actions against you, forgive these people now. Release them to God so that He can deal justly with them, and you can be free of the tie to their sins.

4. If you have picked up others' bitterness, forgive them. Release them. Through prayer, cut them free. Ask God to restore them.

It is critical for you to cut out the root of bitterness from your life. Otherwise, you will jeopardize your divine purpose and block the breakthroughs that God has planned for you. When His change comes your way again, don't resist it and fall into bitterness.

CHAMPION THOUGHT:
Change Is Inevitable

You might find yourself continually resisting change. This is a common challenge for humanity. In traveling around the world to minister, I have seen vast differences in the standards of living. Some regions lack knowledge of entire sections of the Word of God, such as healing. In these places, the people do not realize that the Bible even addresses particular issues. Therefore, the population lives in bondage.

In some areas and villages that are under authoritarian reign, the people are like abused sheep, who keep quiet and waddle along, minding their own business. Because it has been this way for hundreds of years, there is no advancement of civilization in these areas.

Yet, when we traveled only fifty or one hundred miles from villages like this, we discovered other places that were like oases. These areas had incredible road systems, communications, restaurants, and other modern conveniences. Then, a hundred miles away in another sector, again we found no roads, cars, or any sign of modernization. People still cooked with open flames inside their huts, each with only one pot.

How can one hundred miles make such a big difference? It is simple. No one within that one-hundred-mile distance had pierced the barrier to reach the other group. No one had decided to explore beyond the known. For some reason, these people did not have the desire or willingness to change. In fact, they resisted it.

Especially within certain geographic areas in the United States, we can find other examples of people who resist change and have like mind-sets. All across the nation, pockets of people have similar incomes and attitudes within many neighborhoods and rural communities.

Generally, the reason for this is that our socioeconomic environments greatly influence us. When we associate with others, we become accustomed to their lifestyles both socially and economically. A mentality of an expected economic level for people in our neighborhood sets in. A certain way of life and atmosphere becomes familiar. We become comfortable with the hours of work required to earn a certain income and the amount of education necessary to achieve it. Many people in neighborhoods settle into these kinds of molds, and few ever leave. To break out economically, most people must move away.

If you want breakthroughs in your life, you must commit yourself to change as God leads you. If you desire to contribute significantly to your generation, then change is inevitable. Do not resist it. In fact, I encourage you to desire and be willing to change regardless of what it is as long as it aligns with God's will for you.

CHAMPION THOUGHT:
The Way You Perceive Is the Way You Receive

Now, let's get personal. After all, your future is at stake here! Is change difficult for you? When a new direction is presented to you, what influences your decision regarding whether to accept or reject it? It is important to explore the issue of why you think and act as you do regarding change. The reason for this is because the way you perceive is the way you receive. In other words, how you understand change is related to how you will accept it.

CHAMPION THOUGHT:
How You React to Your History Determines Your Future

Much of the way in which you approach change depends upon the many influences in your life from childhood until today. These influences have forged more than a thought. They have created a lifestyle, perhaps causing you to build walls around yourself to form a comfort zone. Unfortunately, living in this safety zone insulates you from a vast area of life experience that God has planned for you.

172

Thoroughly and honestly examine your life now. Did something negative happen in your past, which is so entrenched in your mind that it is now an integral part of you? If so, you probably learned to cope with it, and you might even think that it's not affecting you now. You modified your life to get along with it and continue living. Burying it, you learned to live like the proverbial three "wise" monkeys, whose hands covered their eyes, ears, and mouth. Today, you "see no evil, hear no evil, and speak no evil" that would reveal your difficult past. Instead, you have locked the painful memories in your heart and try to ignore them.

You probably do not realize how much effort this has required. You created what many call a "work-around," which is a temporary solution to a problem. It allows you to continue working, although not as intended. Often work-arounds are not as efficient, but they *do* allow you to complete certain tasks. Therefore, you can "get by." However, the underlying problems remain unsolved and often grow worse with time. You might have experienced this with your computer. Perhaps you have seen that if you use too many cumbersome work-arounds for too long, they can cause valuable data loss from a computer crash. This kind of major breakdown can happen in life, too.

God does not want you simply to get by, settling for second best. He does not desire that you design your future by working around your past problems. No, He has a much better plan that will not jeopardize His purpose for you.

Hey! This is how it is for me, you might be thinking. *It's fine for you, Gary, but I cannot change. I'm glad you're blessed, thank God, but I can't do anything different in my life.*

Do you know why many people resist the necessary change for their breakthroughs? It is because they have built their future on their negative history. For them to become free of their past, they must discard their current mind-sets and lifestyles. Remember, we discussed earlier that you must detach from your past.

173

This is difficult, because living with work-arounds means that people have come into agreement with them. New information, such as this book contains, contradicts the way they have been existing sometimes for decades. To implement the new information requires extensive change, which many find unbearable.

Is this what you are feeling now as you read this book? If so, I want to encourage you. God has a fulfilling future planned for you. Yet today you are living below His best. To reach that bright future, you must commit to change. However, you will not be alone. God will walk with you the entire way to show you the path. Start today by submitting your entire life to Him—including your past. You must open to Him even the protected places in your heart, where you have locked away your difficult, painful, or wounded past experiences. Surrendering it *all* to Him is the *only* way to destroy the evil effects of your past and receive God's healing. Then, you can find the hopeful future that He has destined for you.

Before you can be effective in your environment and positively influence others, you must see what has caused you to be the way you are. Then, find the path to bring God's change into your life. This path involves discovering His truth, which brings the power and freedom to change your thoughts, attitude, perspective, and behavior.

CHAMPION THOUGHT:
Do Not Take the Path of Least Resistance

Another reason for building internal resistance to change is the desire to avoid conflict. People want to create a comfortable environment without conflict, so they search for the path of least resistance. However, as we discussed earlier, conflict is the norm for Christians. You and I live in conflict with this world. The enemy uses people, who walk according to the world's wisdom—which is void of God—to try to influence and control us. Thus, many Christians' lives are fashioned by someone else's leadership other than the Spirit of God. This is one result of following the path of least resistance.

As Christians, we must not follow the world's wisdom, but God's. Doing this will require us to change from any worldly ways that we have acquired. We will need to take stands against ungodly principles because we do not belong to this world, but to God. If we do this with all our hearts, it will be the path of *most* resistance, not the least. However, God will enable us every step of the way.

Do you have any worldly areas of your life that must change? If so, without change, will destruction result? For example, if you have problems with harmful thoughts and you continue to think this way, it could destroy your family, health, mental well-being, livelihood, ethical and moral standing, or integrity. This problem could affect you so severely that you could lose everything valuable to you. Is it worth it? I encourage you to take a stand. Be the one to stop the toll of disaster in your family. That's what I did for my family by the power of the Holy Spirit.

Maybe you are having problems in your business, finances, church, personal relationships, or another area. Be willing to stand up for godly principles in every area of life. Don't resist *His* changes. Listen to God for direction on how to proceed. Be an instrument of God's will in your environment.

CHAMPION THOUGHT:
Do Not Be Conformed to This World

The majority of people are not willing to step out to be different. It is easier to conform to the world and others' attitudes. Remember that the apostle Paul taught us, *"Do not be conformed to this world"* (Romans 12:2). The word *"conformed,"* here, means to "fashion [yourself] according to" or "conform to the same pattern."[2] Of course, this means that we are not to walk in sin. However, I believe that we can also look at this verse as instruction not

175

to conform to others' ungodly attitudes and viewpoints. We are not to allow ourselves to be fashioned and molded into the way this world operates—the world's system as it appears.

Think about this: Everything that you are involved in has a system. Each system has its own policies, procedures, and protocol. This is true, for example, for your job, the stores you shop at, and even the world at large both spiritually and physically. You have the choice of either conforming to each of these systems or not.

Most people do not think outside the system because they are conformed to it. Only those who venture away from it can see a different course. When a system dictates that you cannot do what God is leading you to do, you might be tempted to walk away defeated, agreeing, "It won't work!" The truth is that it does not matter what the system says. You are not to be fashioned in your thought processes after this world. Whose opinion will you accept: man's or God's?

Don't base your decisions and actions solely on the way things look. Instead, view what appears to be impossible as something that God will enable you to accomplish. Yes, you will face obstacles that may influence you to believe that God's vision in your life cannot be fulfilled. However, you must decide if you want to live beyond the barriers. God is the One you are to follow. Remember that if *He* said it, *He* will do it.

Those who break through have decided not to sit idle or accept the consensus—the group's agreement—as the standard of truth. As Christians, you and I have a different standard. To capture the truth of God's Word, we must pierce through man's thoughts. The sudden burst of God's advanced knowledge will take us beyond every line of defense and attitude that stands against us.

You see, there is a difference between the way in which champions and the rest of the world approach life. For example, you can watch two people face the same obstacle. One will listen to the counsel of the system and conclude, "It won't work." The other person will receive a champion thought to break through the barrier.

Wright Brothers

In December 1903, American aviation pioneers Orville (1871–1948) and Wilbur (1867–1912) Wright successfully completed the first controlled, powered flight in a heavier-than-air craft. Even though the current thought at the time was that man could not fly, the Wright brothers broke through that barrier. Their invention of the airplane totally revolutionized the world. "Today, record distances set while traveling in the air are measured in hours rather than in miles. Jet airliners, for example, have made a continent only a few hours wide. Aviation has shrunk the globe and enlarged people's horizons by bringing nations closer."[3] Thanks to this invention, I personally am able to minister the Gospel of Jesus Christ across the world.

Mexico Trip

One of my trips, as I recall, required thinking outside the system. I was scheduled to do a six-day whirlwind ministry tour across the country of Mexico. The plan was to meet with seven different groups of five hundred pastors each, a total of 3,500 pastors.

We began to work on my itinerary so that I could minister in all seven locations during those six days. However, we quickly discovered that there was not enough time to travel from one place to the next. We couldn't drive a car in time. The airline schedules were not meeting our time frames. I was told that no other modes of transportation would work either. The system said that physically there was no way this could be done.

Determined to find a way to fulfill God's plan, I called one of the pastors in Mexico, saying, "If nothing else will work, then I want to rent a private airplane."

After checking the prices, he called me back. "That will cost $17,000!" he explained.

"Well, get one for $6,000," I replied.

"No, you can't rent a plane here for six. It's impossible."

"Yes," I persisted, "there's one for $6,000. Watch; you'll find it!"

"What do you want to fly in?" the pastor asked.

Not willing to forgo safety, I explained, "Well, make sure that all the plane's records are updated within the last three months. I want to see the mechanical records. Make sure that it meets FAA standards. I want to interview the pilot to make sure that he knows what he's doing. I want a pressurized cabin. We have to be able to fly at an altitude of at least twenty thousand feet, and I want a twin engine."

"Why do you need a twin engine?" the pastor asked.

"It's so that if one goes out," I answered, "the other engine can guide us safely into what would become a crash site, and I don't want to spend any more than $6,000," I reiterated.

"There's no way you can get all that, but we'll see what we can do."

Later, I received a call back from that pastor, saying, "I can't believe it, but I found what you asked for."

After listening to the specs and information about the plane, I replied, "That's what I wanted."

"Oh, yeah," he added, "and they came down from $17,000 to $6,900!"

"Why are you amazed?" I asked.

"Well, we never had to try to change somebody's mind like that before."

"Oh, you haven't been around me long enough," I said. "That's what I do. My whole life is changing people's minds!"

You see, I continually encourage people to think outside the system that says, "What God wants to do cannot be done." Champion, do you change people's minds? You should. You need to change the way they think and perceive things. Why? It is because you bring a completely different perspective and approach to life. After all, you and I are champions of God!

Now, when I finally arrived in Mexico and it was time to fly in the rented plane, another obstacle popped up. We were on the runway and the pilot said, "Gary, this is the worst week to fly. Turbulent air, which is coming through the mountains at fifty to seventy miles an hour, is hitting the areas where you want to fly."

"Well, fly over it," I instructed.

He explained, "We only have a small window of time to avoid it because this is one of the worst times of turbulence between the west coast and the Gulf of Mexico."

Handing him a map, I said, "Now, I want you to look at this and tell me the time frames that we can get up and down without difficulties."

He did, and we took off and landed every day exactly in those periods. We had no challenges except once. I commanded some rain clouds to change one time, and they moved. I did not want to sit in the city because of rain, when I was expected to minister to five hundred pastors. Everything else worked perfectly.

"I have never had a week like this in my life!" the pilot told me. "I have been flying for twenty-five years," he continued. "You haven't flown a plane ever, but you were able to tell me what to do, and we made it everywhere we planned to go."

"You probably have never flown with a guy who prayed either, did you?" I asked.

"No, I haven't," he said. "Do you realize that we would have been grounded for three days this week," the pilot continued, "if anything had gone wrong?"

"I can't afford for anything to go wrong," I explained. "I don't have enough days to live to have a day that's not going right."

Have you ever realized that you do not have enough time to live to have something go wrong? Think about it.

All the offerings given toward the ministry that week in Mexico totaled approximately $6,980. The airplane cost $6,900.

It worked with a little extra to spare—all because I had heard from God and rejected the system that said that I could not obey

Him. Champion, do you reject the system that stands in the way of your divine purpose?

Following popular opinions and world systems instead of your God-given purpose causes you to fall to an average or less-than-average standard. Instead of making the difference that God designed for you to make in your environment, you blend in and become part of the normal fabric of society. You lose your God-directed distinction to be a champion for Him.

Dare to be different. When you encounter an attitude, viewpoint, or belief system that is not of God, yet other people agree to accept, turn from it. Do not allow this line of defense to trap you into jeopardizing your God-given purpose. Keep yourself in tune with God. Listen for His champion thoughts to show you how to overcome all negative systems, and then follow His direction.

CHAMPION THOUGHT:
Continually Rejecting the Voice of God Eventually Causes You Never to Hear Him Again

---

Do you realize that you can resist the Word of God and grieve the Holy Spirit? By pushing His Word and convictions away, it is not long before His voice becomes muted. It becomes quieter and quieter and quieter until eventually you cannot even hear God's voice any more. When this happens, your conscience becomes so hardened or seared that you are no longer sensitive to God's leading.

The Bible teaches that two causes exist for a hardened conscience. One is the repetition of sin:

> *So I tell you this, and insist on it in the Lord, that you must no longer live as the Gentiles do, in the futility of their thinking. They are darkened in their understanding and separated from the life of God because of the ignorance that is in them due to the hardening of their hearts. Having lost all sensitivity,*

they have given themselves over to sensuality so as to indulge
in every kind of impurity, with a continual lust for more.
(Ephesians 4:17–19 NIV)

According to the Bible, the other reason for a hardened conscience is deception:

But the Spirit explicitly says that in later times some will
fall away from the faith, paying attention to deceitful spirits
and doctrines of demons, by means of the hypocrisy of liars
seared in their own conscience as with a branding iron.
(1 Timothy 4:1–2 NAS)

Therefore, if you reject God's voice of truth, and you believe something that is false, your conscience will become calloused. Also, if you refuse to obey God, and you continually repeat a particular sin, eventually you will not sense any conviction at all from the Holy Spirit. In that area, you will not change. Instead, you will create excuses and live according to a defense mechanism that you will have built. The end result is that your heart will no longer be open to hear from God in that area, and you will be unable to be renewed according to His plan.

CHAMPION THOUGHT:
Receive and Keep Your Breakthrough by Renewing Your Mind

The way to prevent your conscience from becoming hardened also helps you to receive and keep your breakthrough. You keep your conscience sensitive to Him and maintain your freedom through personal fellowship with God and reading His Word. The Bible says,

That He [Christ] might sanctify and cleanse her [the church,
us] with the washing of water by the word, that He might

present her to Himself a glorious church, not having spot or wrinkle or any such thing, but that she should be holy and without blemish. (Ephesians 5:26-27)

In this way, you refuse to conform to this world and its ways. You fashion yourself after God and consistently renew your mind to His Word and His ways. This also helps you to know God's will.

We briefly studied this earlier in Romans 12:1-2. Now, let's read these verses in another translation:

Therefore, I urge you, brothers, in view of God's mercy, to offer your bodies as living sacrifices, holy and pleasing to God—this is your spiritual act of worship. Do not conform any longer to the pattern of this world, but be transformed by the renewing of your mind. Then you will be able to test and approve what God's will is—his good, pleasing and perfect will. (Romans 12:1-2 NIV)

What does the phrase *"be transformed by the renewing of your mind"* mean? The word *"transformed"* in the Greek means "change, transfigure,"[4] and *"renewing"* means "renovation."[5] We are to remake our minds—our belief systems, thoughts, judgments, decisions, opinions, viewpoints, outlooks, and attitudes—from worldly patterns to God's will. *"Be transformed by the renewing of your mind"* means to be changed or transfigured by the renovation of our minds. In other words, as we renew our minds to God's Word and His ways, we are transfigured into His original plan for us.

An example will help illustrate how the renewing of your mind works. Today, many people hunt for garage sales and auctions where they can purchase painted antique furniture. To the eye, this type of furniture does not appear to be worth much. However, when one continually strips off the paint, layer after layer, the original wood progressively surfaces. Finally, a piece of furniture is restored to the original condition its maker created and intended it to be. Now, the item is a very valuable antique. In a similar way, you are to transform your mind.

Think of your mind as an antique piece of furniture. The world's system continually adds layers of "paint," covering its fine original surface. As you continually read, hear, say, and pray—meditate on—God's Word, your mind becomes stripped of its former views, opinions, and judgments. You begin to *"have the mind of Christ"* (1 Corinthians 2:16).

Therefore, by the Word of God—that is, His promises—you progressively receive more of God's nature manifested in areas of your life. The Bible explains this in 2 Peter 1:4, which says, *"He has granted to us His precious and magnificent promises, so that by them you may become partakers of the divine nature"* (NAS).

The truth in this verse is very powerful because it explains that you partake of God's divine nature through His promises. In other words, meditating on the promises in the Word of God actually gives you His nature! This is how the renewing or renovation of your mind occurs.

Champion, have you renovated your mind? Have you stripped the world's layers from it? Have you been washing your mind so that your thinking aligns with the Word of God? Are you sustaining a moral, ethical standard and balance in your thoughts as God intends? Are you being changed and transformed by the Word of God? As you renew your mind, you maintain a motivation for forward momentum with God instead of retreating to destruction. If you want to accomplish and walk in the God-given dreams of your heart, then you must renew your mind. Otherwise, you run the risk of regressing to your former state and losing the ground you gained!

CHAMPION THOUGHT:
Don't Look Back

Jonas Salk

In the field of medicine, history records Jonas Salk (1914–1995) as the American microbiologist who developed the first safe and effective killed-virus vaccine against polio. His breakthrough in the early 1950s nearly eradicated the dreaded debilitating disease of polio in the United States and other modernized countries.

Now, however, polio is coming back in some areas because doctors have stopped vaccinating their patients. We must never lose the ground that we or our forerunners have gained.

You see, after someone penetrates a barrier once, he or she becomes a pathfinder. That breakthrough becomes an access door for others to experience freedom. However, as that new path becomes accepted and more people experience it, they eventually forget the lead person who broke through. This pattern is very common and may produce no adverse results. However, a potentially dangerous effect of forgetting our history is that we often repeat it.

When a champion forgets the barriers that he has overcome, he is likely to regress, lose his breakthroughs, and fall into former bondages. This is true for us both individually and corporately.

Regarding the heroes of the faith recounted in Hebrews 11, the Bible states: *"If they had been thinking of the country they had left, they would have had opportunity to return. Instead, they were longing for a better country—a heavenly one"* (Hebrews 11:15–16 NIV).

Champion, after your breakthrough, if you look back, you could go back. If you "think back," you are back. If you "act back," you are reproducing fruit from a former nature, of which you are now free.

An example of regressing to a former state is the Crusades. From 64 to 313 A.D. Rome persecuted Christians, killing them because of their faith. However, in 392 A.D. Christianity became the Roman Empire's official religion. Christianity became the standard. Then, in 1095 A.D. the Council of Clermont launched the

Crusades. In these wars, Christians—because of their faith—killed Muslims.

What happened? The Christians' breakthrough became a new defensive wall. Thus, they regressed to the mind-set of killing because of differences in faith. They gave up the ground that they had gained in tearing down that former religious barrier. Thus, they lost their breakthrough. How could they have gone from such a breakthrough to the former status quo? That's why we need to evaluate ourselves continually to see how we line up according to God's standards.

Sadly, as individuals, we also can regress to former bondages. For example, when God delivers a person from an addiction to alcohol, that individual should continually thank Him and remember that God rescued him from a horrible life. He must avoid all remnants of his old lifestyle. If he fails to do this, he is in danger of falling back into his old habits. Most former alcoholics will not take even one drink because they do not want to regress.

In my life, I continually thank God for restoring my marriage. I refuse to treat Faye in ungodly ways as I did before I became a Christian. Now, we express our love to each other often, and we share our miraculous testimony with others. You see, we know that our enemy, the devil, once infiltrated our marriage, and we will not allow him access again. Instead, we daily walk in our breakthrough from God. I keep my mind renewed to God's Word regarding how to be a godly husband, father, and grandfather.

CHAMPION THOUGHT:
Set Your Marker and Don't Go Backward

Don't allow yourself to become susceptible to anything that will drive you lower than God's intentions for you. As we learned in an earlier chapter, this is your *base acceptable bottom,* the lowest point to which you will go. See how far you have come in the course of your life, and put a marker where you are today. Refuse to go below this limit.

For example, do you have a financial marker, stating that you will not go below that income level? I hope you do. You might be thinking, *Well, I just have to settle for whatever somebody will pay me.*

No, you don't! You can go out to make money for yourself—more than anyone will ever pay you. The highest-paid people I know earn money for themselves. They don't wait to see what someone else decides to pay them. Instead, they determine their own income.

In fact, I believe that one of the highest-paying jobs is selling on commission. You might be thinking, *No, I don't have that kind of confidence.*

Well, build it. Why live at your current wages when you could sell something and determine your own income level?

But I just don't know if I could do it.

Do it. See how well it works. Have you ever done something that turned out better than you expected? Or maybe you failed to try because you were afraid that it would not work. That's what happens when the voice of fear cries out. You become repulsed at the thought of change and stepping out with God into His paradigm shift for your life.

The next chapter will reveal the authority of your God-given dream to drive creation to fulfill it. You don't have to struggle with how to do it. God already has a plan in motion to manifest the vision that He has given to you. You simply have to get into *His* boat!

8
The Driving Force of a Dreamer

*I*mpossible—Is that what you have thought or people have said about your dream? Are you trying to line up everything so that you can step into the manifestation of your vision? I have good news for you. There is an easier path. God has established His dream within you to create its own provision for fulfillment! You just need to tap into what He has already set into motion. In this chapter, you will discover how to launch out so you can experience the power of the dream to draw in everything necessary to accomplish it.

Let's begin with the story of my "impossible" dream.

CHAMPION THOUGHT:
Two Can Become One...Again

"I don't love you anymore, Gary."

I could not escape those words. They reverberated inside my consciousness as if some incessant broadcast signal had been implanted in my brain. Each time I heard my wife's voice repeat this thought, the loneliness and rejection weighed heavier. *Why did I let this happen?* I asked myself, straining to shut out the bad memories. *Why didn't I try to fix things when there was still a chance? Why did I drive myself so hard at work and forget about Faye and my children?*

"I don't care about you anymore, Gary."

No form of physical abuse could have devastated me more than the impact of Faye's words. I felt as if I were hemorrhaging emotionally. I had failed as a husband *and* father. At times, a chorus of negative voices from the past joined Faye's bitter indictments: "The first marriage always ends in divorce, Gary. All your relatives go through divorce. It's the second marriage that usually lasts."

Divorce. As hard as I had tried to avoid the word, the bitter reality of divorce now stared me in the face. The curse of failure, which I had feared most of my life, seemed to be closing in on all sides. I had crossed the line once too often, destroying my wife's trust and wrecking our relationship. At last, Faye had reached her breaking point. Now, with the stroke of a pen, my marriage was over on a miserable day in 1976.

Let me share how all this came about. I had a history of mental illness as a teen, and my unpleasant experience with marijuana at a party one summer night had given her plenty of reason to believe that I might once again lose my mental competence. One look at my eerie, wild-eyed expression, and Faye determined that she would not subject herself or our two toddlers to my unpredictable behavior. She threw me out of the house and even secured a court order to keep me away from her and our children, Eric and Laurie.

Faye's resentment evolved into cruelty over the ensuing months. Not only was she deliberate about her lack of affection for me, but she flaunted the fact that other men were sleeping in the bed that I once had called my own. She even attacked my very manhood, telling me that I had no longer satisfied her.

Wrong Side of the Tracks

This was not supposed to happen to me. I had given my life to the Lord back in 1972 and was baptized in the Holy Spirit during the most difficult days of our separation in 1975 and 1976. However, becoming right with Jesus certainly did not make all my problems disappear.

I felt trapped in a complex web of mistakes, which both Faye and I had made, and all I wanted was the easiest escape route. Suicide began to appeal to me as a realistic option. I was willing to do anything to exit my nightmare. Even born-again people can commit suicide. I know, because I tried it. Satan will deceive and confuse anyone he can, and although I was a Christian in 1975, I was a prime target.

Faye's animosity overwhelmed me, and I was too immature in the knowledge of spiritual matters to resist the devil's strategy. Therefore, in the fall of that year, while I was wallowing in depression one night, I drove my Volkswagen onto a railway crossing in Newark, Delaware, and shut off the engine. I planned to wait there until a train would come to end my troubles forever.

However, as I waited, nervously straining to hear the faint trill of an approaching train, I heard a voice within me say, "Gary, you will *'not die, but live, and declare the works of the LORD.'*" Although I did not realize it at the time, I now know these words are from Psalm 118:17. I had only begun to recognize the voice that had reassuringly spoken to me that night. In the stillness of that moment, I knew the Lord was with me.

When I heard the clacking and rumbling of the train approaching in the darkness, I braced myself against the steering wheel and cried out in anguish, "God, only You can deliver me!"

The thunderous vibrations of the train came toward me. Yet, to my surprise, nothing happened to me! The huge locomotive sped past my car on another set of tracks, only a few feet from where I was parked. Later, I learned that the train had been rerouted temporarily due to repairs!

That night signaled the beginning of my deliverance. Over the course of the next two weeks, which included time in a private mental clinic, I met with a local charismatic pastor who told me that demonic spirits tormented me. Learning about the work of demons was new to me, but in my hopeless condition, I was willing to try anything. The pastor arranged for another Spirit-filled believer to join him in casting out the spirits that had been driving me to self-destruction. God miraculously set me free![1]

My deliverance seemed too simple at first. However, during the next week I realized that the haze clouding my mind was gone. I could think clearly, and I began to see how Satan had been working to destroy me—and my family. Now that I was delivered, I began to fast, pray, and claim God's Word for my marriage to be restored.

My despair began to subside, and in its place came an inner fortitude that I had never known. Strengthened with a new conviction and resolve, I began to sense the joy of the Lord. I did not know it at the time, but God was preparing me for one of the most tumultuous spiritual battles I would ever experience.

The Real Fight Begins

My situation looked hopeless from the outside. All Faye wanted was a divorce, and she reminded me of that every time I visited our children. Yet an unusual grace rested on my life that seemed to shield me from her boisterous berating. She did everything she could to make me angry, but I was too intent on seeing our relationship healed to react to her emotional outbursts.

It was during the intensity of those days that I learned about spiritual warfare. The Holy Spirit taught me how to pray for Faye. He constantly encouraged me that the love of God, which was dwelling in me, would overcome my wife's bitterness. I researched the Word of God high and low to discover how God could move in these circumstances to bring transformation on my behalf, and thus fulfill the covenant He had made with us in our marriage. As I continued to pray and meditate on various scriptural promises of victory, an overcoming faith began to grow inside me. Even when my circumstances looked irreversible, I refused to accept defeat, knowing that the Lord would change Faye's heart!

During this time of crisis, God gave His life-sustaining revelation to help me. Especially one Scripture—merely one short sentence from the Bible—sent me on a journey that has brought triumph after triumph and changed me *"from glory to glory"* (2 Corinthians 3:18). I believe it will do the same for you. It is 1 Corinthians 7:11. Read it with your heart wide open and realize, as I did, that it only takes one. Let me begin with the previous verse, so you can see the context:

> *And unto the married I command, yet not I, but the Lord, Let not the wife depart from her husband: but and if she depart, let her remain unmarried, or be reconciled to her husband: and let not the husband put away his wife.*
>
> (1 Corinthians 7:10–11 KJV)

When I studied this single sentence in verse eleven, I suddenly understood the answer. I received God's revelation and saw my victory in the spiritual realm. It was as if a light had been turned on; bells and whistles started sounding in my brain. *Who lets the wife remain unmarried, or lets her be reconciled?* The answer is her husband! That is me. I learned that I had the authority to *let* Faye be reconciled to me. (Later in this chapter, I will share more with you about the power of this little three-letter word, *let*.) This was a promise I could stand on!

Now, at that point in our stormy relationship, Faye was as obstinate in her determination to shove me out of her life as I was bent on saving our marriage. On several occasions, she made it very clear that one of her boyfriends would be coming over to the trailer to spend the evening.

On one such occasion, I left her home but secretly returned minutes later while the man was there, so I could stand outside the modest mobile home to pray. Laying my hands on the outside walls of the trailer, in Jesus' name I commanded the bond between Faye and her partner to be broken.

Surprisingly, I felt no resentment toward my wife during those awkward moments. Some men might have stormed into the trailer with a shotgun, but there was no sense of vengeance in my heart. Instead, I thought about God's broken heart over wayward Israel, and how He compared His love for His people with the love of a man for his adulterous wife. It gave me insight into the depth of forgiveness that Jesus offers each of us, and how He had forgiven me for my own immoral behavior.

Soon, Faye began to acknowledge an interest in spiritual things. She even started going to church and eventually made a commitment to Christ, though she still did not want to go to church functions with me. She would not consider making the marriage work. Divorce was still her goal.

Outside Pressure

In fact, divorce seemed to be everyone's goal for Faye and me. My Christian friends were convinced that I should pursue the dissolution of my marriage, and they always had Scriptures to bolster their opinions. Even church leaders usually counseled me to let Faye go. "After all," they said, "she's the one who wants out."

Still, I remained undaunted. I knew it could work. I had to remind myself constantly that my God was the God of the impossible. I knew that He was the Restorer of the breach. What He had joined together, no man or woman could separate, despite what either of us had done to destroy our marriage.

In 1976, Faye began attending a charismatic prayer group—another clear sign to me that the Holy Spirit was working in her life. The prayer gathering itself, however, was not the healthiest environment for her because six people involved in the group also were divorcing. They were leaning on one another for emotional support—and praying that the legal details in each divorce case would be worked out!

I did not understand why Christians failed to stand on God's Word and believe for reconciliation. Again, I found myself praying against the negative spiritual forces that were driving Faye to accept divorce as the only option.

At times, it seemed that Faye and I were engaged in a fierce battle of willpower. However, as I continued to love her, the emotional walls she had erected during our years of pain began to crack. Then, just when her heart would soften a bit, she would react again in her typically boisterous manner, constructing another defense. When I naively promised her in early 1976 that I would give her anything she wanted, she coldly informed me that all she wanted was "a divorce, thank you"—and she wanted me to pay for it!

"Faye, I love you, and God is going to put our marriage back together," I responded gently.

Infuriated, she shot back, "You're weird, Gary. I'm never going back to you. I don't love you anymore!"

Divorce but Not Defeat

During an intense time of prayer and fasting for Faye, the Spirit of God spoke to me, saying, "Give her everything she asks for." I began to wrestle with the overwhelming thoughts of obeying this command. At that time, my two children were three and four years old, and I reasoned, *What if this divorce is never reconciled? If I give Faye everything she asks for, I will have to pay more than the maximum child support for the next 14 and 15 years for two children. How can I afford this?* Nevertheless, I obeyed the Lord. I gave Faye exactly what she wanted—an all-expense-paid divorce, which included ownership of all our possessions and custody of our two children.

At the divorce proceedings, the judge asked us if we had any statements regarding our divorce decree or the final dissolution of our marriage. "Mrs. Whetstone, you already have listed the reasons for the divorce as incompatibility and so forth. Do you have anything further to say for the record?"

"No," Faye answered, eager to close the door on our marriage.

Then, the judge turned to ask me, "Mr. Whetstone, do you have anything else that you want to say?"

"Yes," I answered. "I would like to approach the bench." Pointing to the Bible near the witness box, I said, "You have that little Book up there. I want to read something from it!"

He replied, "We do not *open* the Book. People only *lay their hands on* the Book."

"If you don't mind," I pleaded, "I will open the Book *and* lay my hand on it. Is that okay?"

"Fine. Just do it," the judge urged. "We have other cases after this. We do not need any lengthy dissertation here. You two are going to divorce, and that's the end of it. Your marriage is over."

"Yes, Your Honor," I answered, "but before it's the end, I want to read this." That day in the courtroom before the judge, I quoted the Scripture that had been the watchword for me throughout this spiritual battle:

> *And unto the married I command, yet not I, but the Lord, Let not the wife depart from her husband: but and if she depart, let her remain unmarried, or be reconciled to her husband: and let not the husband put away his wife.*
>
> (1 Corinthians 7:10–11 KJV)

After I confidently quoted the passage, I declared, "Let it be on the court record that I will permit my wife to remarry *only me*. I will *let* her be reconciled *only to me*, and I will *not* allow her to remarry anyone else."

The judge immediately turned to Faye, saying with disdain, "I do not blame you for wanting a divorce from this man."

He probably thought I was a fanatic. Why? What was so different? Was it wrong that conviction rose in my heart to see the full restoration of my relationship? Is it God's best that countless couples surrender their marriages in disgust and frustration, only to face new lives with other partners from similar battlegrounds as their previous spouses? No, I knew that God had a better plan for me.

You see, I did not quote those words from the Bible in the courtroom that day for the judge's benefit. Instead, it was a declaration of my faith. It was my announcement to the spiritual powers around me that I would not tolerate Satan's designs for my marriage. Although the papers were signed and the state of Delaware now considered my marriage terminated, I refused to accept man's law on divorce. I knew God was in control.

The Power of Love

As we strolled out of the courtroom that day, I asked Faye to go to lunch with me. "After all," I told her, "we're not married now. We are free to date."

Faye was actually bewildered by the way I treated her. As hard as she tried to resist, the love of God continued to melt her heart and short-circuit all her excuses. Although I had been through much pain with her, I sent flowers and showered Faye with sincere affectionate remarks. By the way, after court that day, we did go out for lunch!

You see, I had forgiven her, and I was praying that she would forgive me, too. I knew that I deserved all Faye's mistreatment. During the first years of our marriage, when my drive for a promotion at the auto-manufacturing plant was so consuming, I had neglected her and our children. Yet, now, I wanted her only to see that Jesus had changed me.

I visited Faye and the children as often as possible after the divorce, always offering to vacuum, fold laundry, or baby-sit. Soon, I could tell that she was beginning to warm up to my deliberate advances. That spring, Faye began a period of deep soul-searching. God's love finally was touching the most sensitive places of her broken heart, and she no longer rejected me as quickly or reacted as harshly.

In time, remarriage actually became a clear option for Faye—finally! However, as she considered the decision, she realized that it meant more than forgiving me and recommitting herself to me. It was a spiritual decision that involved her relationship with the Lord.

Faye was scared. Yet she knew that the spiritual breakthrough she needed could not occur unless she decided to trust God and marry me again. As we both chose to forgive and restore each other, the blood of Jesus erased the effects of our sin, disappointment, and pain. That was the most beautiful part of our "second chance." This time, Jesus is the foundation of our marriage.

When Faye and I remarried in July 1976, it was not all romantic bliss. We still had our rough times. We had to spend long, laborious hours talking through our differences, and we had to learn to trust each other all over again. However, this time we knew it was different. We considered our marriage commitment irrevocable, and we would not allow the word *divorce* to be spoken in our home.

Reunited in God's Purpose

Much has transpired since God reunited Faye and me more than two-and-a-half decades ago. Several years later, after sensing a call into the ministry, we sold our business, loaded the children into the car, and moved to Tulsa, Oklahoma, to attend Rhema Bible Training Center. Our training there prepared us to return to Wilmington to establish a church. Today, as the Holy Spirit has touched the lives of many hurting people, Victory Christian Fellowship has grown to be the largest nondenominational church in the state of Delaware.

Many marriages have been restored as a result of our testimony. People have heard about our story, and couples who were in the midst of marital turmoil have come to our church altar to seek God's intervention. Faye and I do not stand on any legalistic formula about divorce and remarriage because we realize that everyone's situation is unique. Instead, we pray for couples, instruct them in God's Word, and impart the Holy Spirit to their lives.

Even so, when people hear how God healed our marriage, they must face the fact that God's forgiveness can reverse any situation totally, no matter how insurmountable the odds may appear. I know this is true because the same woman who used to scream at me, "I don't love you anymore, Gary," is now by my side again, proclaiming her love for me. What God put together, man could not put asunder. Today she is my devoted wife and our congregation's beloved "Mama Faye." Our past of disappointment, neglect, and adultery has been washed away—and the power of God's love has made all the difference.

Now, I know firsthand that *it only takes one* to stand in prayer and faith for God to restore a marriage—or to create any miracle, for that matter. In fact, it only takes one in agreement with God to do anything!

Champion, what challenge do you need to resolve, or what dream do you need to fulfill? It only takes one to stand and believe for your breakthrough. *You* can be that one. Alone, you can change *your* world or even the *entire* world because you are God's champion for such a time as this.

CHAMPION THOUGHT:
The Responsibility of Establishing Stable Relationships Has Shifted

---

Are you seeing rocky relationships in your life or the lives of friends and family? If so, it's time for a breakthrough. As humans, we need stable relationships. However, today, it is very common for relationships to be broken in every area of life. For example, in the corporate world, we are seeing more evidence that management does not always watch out for their employees. In families, divorce is rampant. Also, many double-income parents send their children to day care at the age of two or even younger. In the church world, members of congregations often sit isolated by race, culture, age group, or economic status.

In the midst of a world of eroding relationships, where can people find the stability of love and care? All too frequently now, the responsibility of establishing that security has been neglected by corporations, spouses, parents, and churches. What can individuals do when they find themselves in the turmoil of unraveling relationships? They need to learn that with God, one person can rise in the authority of truth to experience a breakthrough. It does not matter who or where they are, all Christians have that ability in God. If I can learn how to do this, *anyone* can!

CHAMPION THOUGHT:
To Engage the Purposes of God, Exercise Your Authority to "Let"

As I mentioned, the life-changing passage that the Lord enlightened for me during my divorce was 1 Corinthians 7:11 (KJV). Remember that regarding the wife, it says, *"If she depart, let her remain unmarried, or be reconciled to her husband: and let not the husband put away his wife."* When I meditated on this single sentence, God revealed to me how to bring restoration and transformation to my marriage. The key is in the power of the word *let*. From this one truth, I discovered that it only takes one to initiate all God has purposed for an individual. When one person accepts that God-given responsibility and authority, that one can bring everything back into alignment with God's will for his or her life.

You must understand the word *let* because the Bible uses it often. This word has at least two distinct meanings. One definition of *let* is "to allow or permit" as in "to let him escape." Another is "to cause to; make" as in "to let one know the truth."[2] To *permit* something, you passively yield without resistance, and it happens by default. You allow it to take place. On the other hand, to *cause* something, you initiate an action, which therefore produces a result. You make it happen. Both are meanings of *let*. For example, think of a ball. If you *cause* it to roll, you actively push it to create the effect of rolling. Alternatively, if you *permit* it to roll, you passively sit by without becoming involved with the rolling ball. It is already in motion, and you do not intervene.

In both definitions of *let*, we see that the person who either permits or causes has authority to act or not. Every Scripture that says you should "let" means that you are accountable and responsible for the outcome of the sentence. The "ball" is in your court. You can either use or fail to use that important authority to make certain events happen or prevent them. Champion, it is critical to realize that what you let—permit or cause to—happen will either enable or disable destruction. It will either engage or disengage the purpose of God.

You see, you are responsible for the outcomes in your life because the effects are traceable back to the cause. Whether you have positive or negative fruit in any area of your life, ask yourself, *What did I do either to allow this result or to make it happen?* If it is negative, you need to find the information, do the research, and discover the details, so you can determine if you are *allowing* destruction to occur because of inactivity or *causing* it.

In the case of the destruction of my marriage, I understood who had the authority in that word *let*. I did! One day, God showed me that I could let the conflict in my marriage end in one of two ways: Either I could allow it to take its natural course and end in divorce, or I could cause a course change, so that my wife and I could remarry. Obviously, I chose to walk in my God-given authority to change our circumstances, and the two of us became one...again!

The important question is what will *you* let in your life? I am not asking simply what do you *want* to happen? No, I mean what are you empowered by God's authority to *permit* or *cause* to take place? Now, you have a choice. You can either permit the system as it exists to rule—it will dictate to you what it can and cannot do—or you can cause a change.

Think about it. When you face a challenge in your finances, your health, a relationship, an area of communication, or another area, how much authority do you have to change it? You, as only one person, can exercise all the necessary authority to change that situation. The reason is that you are resting not on an opinion but on God's Word, which He backs. The Bible explains:

> *For this reason we also thank God without ceasing, because when you received the word of God which you heard from us, you welcomed it not as the word of men, but as it is in truth, the word of God, which also effectively works in you who believe.* (1 Thessalonians 2:13)

Remember that the Word of God—truth—effectually works in you who believe. If you know this truth, you can cause a change to occur in any area of challenge.

CHAMPION THOUGHT:
Nothing Is Hopeless—Everything Can Change

If you are facing a challenge now, you might have to deal with frustration, disappointment, disillusionment, hopelessness, and a sense that nothing will ever change. This is not true. Nothing is beyond the reach of God's authority to change. Everything is subject to hope. Creation is waiting for someone to declare the Word. You see, in the spiritual arena, Champion, you have absolute dominion through God's authority in you because of your God-given spiritual position. It's time to release

His Word into your natural environment to change your circumstances.

CHAMPION THOUGHT:
You Are Authorized to Act; Nothing Will Change unless You Do

You need to understand that when someone is authorized to act on behalf of another, that authority goes into effect. However, unless that one acts, there is no effective authority. The same is true of you. God has authorized you to fulfill His purpose and will on this earth. But unless you know that you have His authority, nothing changes. Unless you speak His Word, nothing alters. Unless you initiate a change, no transformation occurs. In other words, as you move in your divine purpose, changes will occur.

CHAMPION THOUGHT:
Not Walking in God's Authority Causes You to Defer to the Devil

We discussed in another chapter that the enemy's goal is to abort your purpose. The devil was out to steal not only my marriage and family but also my life and future ministry. If I had not stood against him, I would have surrendered my divine purpose to Satan.

Realize that spiritual opponents continually try to restrict the realm of authority that God has delegated to you. They don't want you to know about your authority or to operate in it. The Bible teaches:

For our struggle is not against flesh and blood, but against the rulers, against the authorities, against the powers of this dark world and against the spiritual forces of evil in the heavenly realms.   (Ephesians 6:12 NIV)

God has given you His authority to carry out His will on the earth. However, you must use it. If you don't use your God-given authority, Satan will usurp it to enslave you and abort your purpose. In other words, if you don't walk in the authority that God has given you, you defer to the devil. You open the door for him to abuse you and throw you off God's course. Do you realize that many of us actually *let* the enemy rule in our lives, not because we invited him but because we *permitted* him—often unknowingly?

CHAMPION THOUGHT:

Sleeping or Inattentiveness Creates an Open Door for the Enemy

---

The Bible explains:

Jesus told them another parable: "The kingdom of heaven is like a man who sowed good seed in his field. But while everyone was sleeping, his enemy came and sowed weeds among the wheat, and went away."   (Matthew 13:24–25 NIV)

These sleeping workers were unable to stop the enemy from accessing their master's field. You see, being asleep or inattentive causes an open door for the enemy. It creates vulnerability.

The same is true of your life. God has given a purpose to you. If you are not alert in protecting it, Satan will try to come in to destroy you and God's plan for your life.

CHAMPION THOUGHT:

The Voices of Limitation Work in Concert, so that You Will Believe Only Them

---

Gulliver's Travels

Do you remember Jonathan Swift's (1667–1745) book *Gulliver's Travels*? Although it is considered a children's classic today, Swift originally wrote this book as a satire about the political and social events of his day and humanity in general. His goal was for adults to reexamine their perspectives.

Recall in the book that after a shipwreck at sea, the English surgeon Lemuel Gulliver exhausts himself swimming to the closest land in sight. Finally reaching the island of Lilliput, he falls into a very deep sleep for more than nine hours.

Upon awaking, Gulliver discovers that tiny people called Lilliputians, who are no more than six inches tall, have tied him to the ground with strings and pegs. (Notice that *while he slept*, his enemy came to bind him!) As Gulliver breaks his left arm free and loosens some of the cords on his hair, the Lilliputians launch minuscule arrows. Like needles, they prick his hand, causing him pain. Yet he cannot feel the tiny arrows and spears upon his body because they are unable to pierce his clothes.

Although Gulliver realizes that he can easily free himself and is likely able to fight the Lilliputians' greatest armies, he decides to lie still due to the threat of more minute arrows. Because the Lilliputians feed him and give him drink, he begins to embrace their "hospitality," as he calls it. In reality, Gulliver *allows* or *permits* the small creatures to enslave him. Eventually, at his request, he is granted some freedom, but Gulliver agrees to several restrictions, including never leaving the miniature kingdom.

One interpretation of *Gulliver's Travels* is especially insightful regarding what Gulliver's relationship should have been with those who bound him:

Swift makes the Lilliputians seem ridiculous by having Gulliver compare them to dolls. The little doll-like men strut and posture like full-sized men. Yet we cannot take them seriously. They are too tiny to be considered as majestic as they think they are. But "we" are not Gulliver and he takes them seriously. Especially the emperor.[3]

Are *you* like Gulliver? Do you *allow* the enemy to bind you, when you have the great power of God within you to break free? You see, like many of us, the fictional Gulliver is a champion, but he *permits* himself to be tethered by insignificant opponents. He is a giant in comparison with his minute captors, yet he does not rise to overpower them.

Similarly, until we know the truth of who we are in Christ, we do not break free from everything that binds us. Our enemy, who keeps us bound, does not have the authority or power to do so. Yet he deceives us into thinking that he is powerful. The voices of limitation work in concert to convince us to believe them. If we do, then we surrender to the devil. In other words, the only time that Satan can have power over us is when we give it to him. Champion, the truth is that, through Christ, we are greater than all obstacles, and we have the authority to defeat them in Jesus' name! We must use it.

CHAMPION THOUGHT:
Creation Is Waiting at Your Beck and Call

Remember that you have an identity in Christ Jesus, and that God designed and fashioned your very person for His purpose. Both knowing that your position will never change and understanding your divine purpose cause forward momentum, like a ball beginning to roll. As you step into your purpose, be sure to permit that momentum to continue as you break barriers, defend your purpose against all enemies, and cause any course changes as God directs.

Don't think that your God-given dreams and visions, which stir within you, and your heart's desires that honor and glorify the Lord have a small effect. No, Champion. They have a most profound and authoritative effect on creation. Remember we studied earlier that purpose literally drives creation! Your divine dreams have authority to move creation. All resources follow the power of that purpose.

You don't need luck. You don't need an opportunity. You don't need a handout. You don't need a lift up. You don't need someone to give you a break. You don't need a special favor. Your greatest need, besides meeting the person of Jesus as your personal Savior and Lord, is the unveiling of the reason that you exist. If you know that purpose, Champion, you will automatically have God's limitless power to fulfill it. When only one person hooks up to his or her divine purpose, all creation will move to serve that purpose!

God's Word promises:

> For the earnest expectation of the creation eagerly waits for the revealing of the sons of God. For the creation was subjected to futility, not willingly, but because of Him who subjected it in hope; because the creation itself also will be delivered from the bondage of corruption into the glorious liberty of the children of God....And we know that all things work together for good to those who love God, to those who are the called according to His purpose. (Romans 8:19–21, 28)

This passage reveals the power of your divine dream's driving force. You see, everything in creation is sitting bound in futility, frustration, and vanity. Yet it waits expectantly for you—a child of God—to command it to move. Until then, creation is staged and poised, ready to cooperate to be the provision of your divine vision. It's waiting at your beck and call, prepared and standing in readiness for your vision to move it. Creation has already been notified. You move; then, it moves.

CHAMPION THOUGHT:
Once Vision Is Known, Provision Comes

Another way of looking at this is to realize that once you know your purpose—the reason or cause for your existence; your divine dreams and visions—then *provision* comes for it. *Pro-* is a prefix "having especially a meaning of advancing or projecting forward or outward."[4] Provision comes to serve and manifest the vision. It brings to bear that purpose.

You might be thinking that too many details must work together in order for your dreams, visions, and purpose to become a reality. The truth is that nothing needs to be resolved. Your dream is already reality. As you move the vision, provision will happen.

CHAMPION THOUGHT:
Your Dream Is like a Ship, Drawing In Provision

My family and I live on a large bay, where we see many kinds of boats and even very large ships. It is well known that when a large ocean-going vessel, such as a tanker or cargo ship, moves through the water, it creates after it a tremendous draw. The ship's motion causes a vacuum behind it, and because nature abhors a vacuum, it draws water into itself. If a small vessel is following too closely, it also can be pulled into the ship's propeller.

Similarly, your life is like a ship. God gives you forward momentum from knowing your championship position in Him and your divine purpose—the dream within your heart. As you step out to move according to that vision, creation is literally drawn into and follows the momentum of your dream. It then becomes the provision. Everything—knowledge, education, finances, materials, relationships, political power, social influence, and whatever you need physically, mentally, and spiritually—now comes to serve your divine purpose as God's champion!

In 1959, when they were in their thirties, Jay Van Andel and Rich DeVos, friends since high school, launched Amway. From the meager beginnings as a soap-and-vitamin business based in their homes, Amway has grown to a 390-acre complex with "more than 3.6 million independent business owners...in more than 80 countries and territories."[5] Pioneers in direct sales, Van Andel and DeVos developed an innovative company that is based on person-to-person marketing.

What was their secret? How did they build upon the dreams of their hearts from nothing? Both men openly and enthusiastically admit that the answer lies in the power of God. In a section entitled, "Zero in God's Hands Is the Beginning of a Whole New World!" Rich DeVos wrote in his book:

> When Jay and I began our business, we had nothing. Our other business schemes...had left us with a zero balance. But we went on believing in ourselves and trusting God....For Jay and me it was never enough to believe in ourselves. We also believed in a loving Creator whose dreams for us were far greater than any dreams we could have on our own. Now look at what we—God and all of us—have done together.
>
> I wish I had more ways to thank the millions of people who have made our company a success, but all of us would be ashamed to take credit for what God has done. All the natural resources that we use in this business are God's creation, not ours. All the human energy spent...is God's gift to every one of us. And the tools of capitalism and the goods and services that have been produced are a direct result of God's invitation to each of us to subdue the earth and to use the products of our hands and hearts to honor our Creator....
>
> Often at the bottom of a new composition, Bach would scribble these words: *Deo Gloria.* "To God be the glory!" If I

had a flow pen big enough, I would write these words across the face of our factories, warehouses, and our offices everywhere, "To God be the glory. Great things He has done."

If you have a zero balance in your financial, spiritual, or psychological bank, don't be afraid. Trust what you have into the hands of God and watch with amazement what will happen. In 1939, with the Axis powers under Adolf Hitler threatening all the world with tyranny, King George VI read this story in his Christmas radio address to the people of England.

"And I said to the man who stood at the gate of the year: 'Give me a light that I may tread safely into the unknown.' And he replied, 'Go out into the darkness and put your hand into the hand of God. That shall be to you better than light and safer than a known way.'"[6]

Writing about Amway's beginnings, Van Andel said,

Rich and I sought to run our sales organization according to biblical principles....Knowing that we were dependent upon God for the ability to do what was right, we bathed our activities in private prayer. All of our corporate meetings were opened with prayer, and Rich and I were quietly breathing prayers all the time. We believe it was effective. Without God's grace, Amway would never have been successful.[7]

Champion, as you depend upon God and step out in His dream for your life, everything you need will be drawn toward you to help you fulfill His plan!

CHAMPION THOUGHT:
Command from Your Position of Royalty

The New Testament declares that, as Christians, we are a "*royal priesthood*" and "*a peculiar people*":

> But ye are a chosen generation, a royal priesthood, an holy
> nation, a peculiar people; that ye should show forth the praises
> of him who hath called you out of darkness into his marvellous
> light.   (1 Peter 2:9 KJV)

The Bible also teaches that Jesus "*is Lord of lords and King of kings; and those who are with Him are called, chosen, and faithful*" (Revelation 17:14). Therefore, you are a king and lord under the kingship and lordship of Jesus. Remember that, as we studied earlier, you "*who receive abundance of grace and of the gift of righteousness will reign in life through the One, Jesus Christ*" (Romans 5:17).

As a royal priest, king, and lord for God, you reign over and move creation to fulfill the divine dreams within you. Under God's authority, you are a driving influence in this world of chaos and confusion, giving it order, direction, and purpose.

The Bible describes Jesus as the "*captain*" of your salvation (Hebrews 2:10) and "*the author and finisher*" (Hebrews 12:2) of your faith:

> Looking unto Jesus, the author and finisher of our faith, who
> for the joy that was set before Him endured the cross, despising
> the shame, and has sat down at the right hand of the throne
> of God.   (Hebrews 12:2)

Here, we see that despite all His suffering, Jesus moved forward. He carried out God's will because He saw "*the joy that was set before Him.*" Do you realize that this joy includes you? After all, you—and your fellow Christians—are the reason Jesus went to the cross.

Think about it. Jesus, the Captain of your salvation, saw the joy of *you* living in His royalty, reigning in His authority, moving in His name, and operating with the Holy Spirit to fulfill His will on the earth. Remember that Jesus, through whom "*all things were made"* (John 1:3), is *"upholding all things by the word of His power"* (Hebrews 1:3). In all His power and authority, *you* are the joy of His heart!

You must understand that you are the one whom God will use. He has created you for a specific purpose, and in Christ, you have all that is necessary to accomplish God's will. You then are to inaugurate everything to serve the royalty of His life within you. Under Jesus, you are to move creation as a king and lord—one who commands that which is under his influence.

As you step out, knowing your royal position and authority, the world recognizes that you are different. Necks turn, eyes pop out, mouths drop open, heads are scratched, and questions are asked. What makes you so unusual? The answer is that you are identified with the King of kings and Lord of lords. You are not a mere human being. You walk in all God's royal power and authority.

This is how Joseph, the dreamer, rose from a prisoner to the royal position of running Egypt, second only to Pharaoh himself. (See Genesis 41.) This is how the three Hebrew children Shadrach, Meshach, and Abed-Nego, who were not intimidated by the fire, moved from the furnace into prosperity and promotion in Nebuchadnezzar's kingdom. (See Daniel 3.) This is how Daniel survived the lions' den, prospered, and received promotion. (See Daniel 6.) This is how the Jewish orphan Esther, as we studied earlier, was selected as queen in Persia.

The Bible, church history, and our lives today witness to the fact that God's *"peculiar people"* (1 Peter 2:9) have the power and authority to rule creation. Because of this, you can be certain that against all odds, you as a dreamer will also be successful in fulfilling your divine purpose.

CHAMPION THOUGHT:
Have the Passion for Discovery, Not Recovery

When you finally recognize all that God has set in place for you to achieve His divine dreams in your heart, you will have a great passion for discovery and not *recovery*. In other words, when you realize that your future is far greater than the losses of your past, you will never again give attention to that which has caused you pain. Instead, you will focus on the exciting fulfillment of your future, which God has set before you to discover and walk in.

CHAMPION THOUGHT:
Don't Wait—You Make It Move

Get rid of the thought that until other people or circumstances are ready to move, you cannot move. This way of thinking is a thing of the past! God has breathed a new day, a fresh revelation, a solid position, and a clear objective. The divine dreams and the visions of your life are now drawing creation to follow them. All provision necessary to bring your vision to manifestation is now on notice because you are ready to move it. The Spirit and the Word of God agree. It's time to go for it!

In the next chapter, you will see how God has designed you to focus on the finish and to move *"from glory to glory"* (2 Corinthians 3:18). This is an awesome revelation!

9
Focus on the Finish

Fulfilling your divine purpose should not be an oppressive struggle. This chapter will help you walk in God's wisdom so you may step over the threshold of your natural perception into seeing the supernatural finished works in Christ Jesus. Operating in His completed works is a place of rest and power as you move *"from glory to glory"* (2 Corinthians 3:18). You will discover how to focus on the finish, avoid distractions, and never let go of your divine dreams. These are important keys that will lead to fulfillment.

Sammy Sosa

Sammy Sosa understands how to focus on the finish. As a ballplayer for the Chicago Cubs, he shattered the home-run record in 1998, even though his life was full of distractions, disappointments, and impossibilities. He never let go of his dream and went on to break through several lines of defense.

Growing up poor, Sosa "sold oranges and shined shoes as a child in the Dominican Republic to help his family have food to eat."[1] Yet he had a dream that some day he would play professional baseball. His focus and tenacity finally paid off. Not only did he play, but he excelled, and the world took notice. He accomplished fantastic feats in his sport: "Sammy Sosa was voted the National League Most Valuable Player in a landslide over home run king Mark McGwire"[2] and had "the most RBIs...runs...and total bases...in the majors"[3] in 1998.

Focusing on his divine dream, Sammy, along with his mother, gives the glory to God. Before his home-run competition with Mark McGwire was over that season, Sosa's mother declared, "What I know is that my son will get as many home runs as God wants, not one more or one less." She continued, "What is happening this year to Samuel is because of the prayers that I say every day."[4]

However, baseball was only a part of Sammy Sosa's divine dream. Now he helps others not to let go of their dreams. "Mr. Sosa...donates hundreds of thousands of dollars to charities that support schools and medical facilities in Chicago and in his homeland: 'God gave me so much opportunity,' he says."[5] Sammy Sosa's vision of playing baseball and helping people became a reality.

CHAMPION THOUGHT:
God Designed You to See the Glory of Completion

God sees everything in the glory of completion, and that's the way He designed you. He fashioned you to see things in the state of completion—not in fragments, but as finished pictures. The complete picture is called the glory. For example, a flower in its full bloom is considered as being in its glory.

When you go to a store to buy seeds for flowers, the packets do not display the size, look, or color of the seeds. No, they picture the flowers in full bloom. You don't see the seeds, because how the seeds look is irrelevant. You want to see the flowers in the glory of their finished state.

Before someone builds a house or building, he examines an artist's rendition of the architect's design to see what the completed building will look like. Fashion designers show sketches of their completed outfits—not merely swatches of cloth or individual pieces of the pattern. Why? It's because we are designed to see completion, wholeness, and the glory.

CHAMPION THOUGHT:
Focus on the Finished Picture

To fulfill your divine purpose, you need a perspective of where you are headed. As humans, we require the complete picture of something in order to pursue it. We lose all motivation, hope, and perspective if we focus only on the individual parts.

For example, when you buy a puzzle, the outside of the box does not show a multitude of pieces all in a pile. No, you see a picture of the puzzle put together. As you assemble the pieces of that puzzle, you focus on the picture that reveals the end product. This helps you to gain the proper perspective and motivation to complete the task. What would it be like to put that puzzle together without a picture of its finished state? It would probably be so difficult that you would give up before you completed the puzzle. Similarly, fixing your eyes on the finish that God has set before you enables you to fulfill your divine dream.

CHAMPION THOUGHT:
Human Hands Mar God's Glorious Workmanship

Have you seen a child assemble a model, such as an airplane or car? After looking at the completed model on the front of the box, he is excited to start the adventure. However, after opening the package and seeing the multitude of pieces, glue, and decals, he becomes discouraged. Then, with some adult encouragement, he attempts to begin the project.

What happens if that child does not closely focus on the finished picture of that model? He will be very disappointed with the outcome because his final project will not even resemble the completed image on the box. Frustrated, he will point to the picture

214

and cry out to the adult, "It's supposed to look like that! What's wrong?"

This is a valuable lesson for us as Christians. You see, when we look at God's vision for our lives, it is perfect in its glory. However, when human hands touch anything in its glory, it becomes marred. Remember, as we studied earlier: *"We are His workmanship, created in Christ Jesus for good works, which God prepared beforehand that we should walk in them"* (Ephesians 2:10).

The vision that God has for you is a glorious finished masterpiece of good works, which He has already prepared for you to walk in. You don't have to create anything. You simply are to move into the glory of what Jesus has already done. If, however, you don't focus on His finished works, you will attempt to do them on your own. The outcome will not resemble God's image for your life. Frustrated and disappointed with the result, you will cry out, like the child, *What's wrong?* The answer is that your human hands have marred God's glorious workmanship because you did not focus on Jesus' finished works.

CHAMPION THOUGHT:
Build Only as God Directs

As the child should build his model only according to the finished picture on the box, so you are to build your life and God's kingdom only in alignment with Jesus, the Cornerstone. The Bible explains:

> *Jesus Christ Himself being the chief corner stone, in whom the whole building, being joined together, grows into a holy temple in the Lord, in whom you also are being built together for a dwelling place of God in the Spirit.* (Ephesians 2:20–22)

Champion, you are not building for the short term or temporary fulfillment. No, you are building an eternal dwelling place for

God! The divine imagery that God has given to you has eternal ramifications.

Jesus needs to be the foundation of all that you build, and you must use only His materials. As the apostle Paul wrote:

> No other foundation can anyone lay than that which is laid, which is Jesus Christ. Now if anyone builds on this foundation with gold, silver, precious stones, wood, hay, straw, each one's work will become clear; for the Day will declare it, because it will be revealed by fire; and the fire will test each one's work, of what sort it is. If anyone's work which he has built on it endures, he will receive a reward. If anyone's work is burned, he will suffer loss; but he himself will be saved, yet so as through fire. Do you not know that you are the temple of God and that the Spirit of God dwells in you? If anyone defiles the temple of God, God will destroy him. For the temple of God is holy, which temple you are.　　　　　(1 Corinthians 3:11–17)

If you build with your own materials or on a foundation other than Jesus, you mar the glory of God's finished works. If you have done this, when God tests your work, your investment will burn up very quickly like wood, hay, and straw. Don't make this mistake. Get the blueprint of God's finished works before you step out.

CHAMPION THOUGHT:
Enter into His Rest and Receive It "Done"

God has a glorious future planned for you. He has already won the victory and prepared the pathway for you to follow. You just need to step into His finished works. These are not beginnings or attempts but His *finished* works—the completion of the very work of God. If you do this, you will receive your heavenly reward, as God says, "Well done, good and faithful servant" (Matthew 25:23). It will not be, "Well begun, good and faithful servant."

As you focus on God's purpose for your life, you operate in His nature of seeing it *"done, as in heaven"* (Luke 11:2 KJV). In the Lord's Prayer, Jesus instructed us to pray: *"Our Father which art in heaven, Hallowed be thy name. Thy kingdom come. Thy will be done, as in heaven, so in earth"* (v. 2 KJV).

This verse says, *"Thy will be done"*—not begun—on earth as it is in heaven. God doesn't want us simply to begin. He wants us to see His will and, therefore, bring it into manifestation on earth. God always gives us the "done" picture, and we then work with Him to bring it into being on the earth. This is a place of rest because God has already done the works.

Children of Israel

When God revealed His plan to bring the Israelites into their Promised Land, He showed them a glorious vision of their future. However, the writer of Hebrews explained that the children of Israel did not enter into God's rest. They failed to mix that Word with faith, *"although the works were finished from the foundation of the world"* (Hebrews 4:3). The Israelites simply had to walk into the Promised Land, resting in the power and truth of God's Word. His works were finished. He had already won the victory for them. However, they did their own works, not God's. Consequently, they lost their promise and wandered in the wilderness for forty years.

Hebrews teaches that we also are to stop doing our own works and enter into God's rest: *"There remains therefore a rest for the people of God. For he who has entered His rest has himself also ceased from his works as God did from His"* (vv. 9–10).

Realize that you are to step out in faith to do the works that God has ordained. Rest in the knowledge that these acts are the finished will of God, not man's acts to finish the will of God. In other words, receive them as already done.

You see, when you are doing the works in your own power, the best you can do is to begin. Without God's truth and vision, you cannot see the finish. The only way you can cross God's finish line is through the revelation of the gift of righteousness. The work that you do without this gift and God's truth simply establishes your *own* righteousness. By doing the works through your flesh, you are demonstrating your belief that God answers based upon *your* actions. No, God answers because He said that He will answer.

Remember that God already sees the finished product of your life. You are simply to lay claim to your divine destiny and walk in His finished works. Therefore, you need to release your purpose, visions, dreams, and gifts to God and rest in Him. He has the plan for your life.

CHAMPION THOUGHT:
God's Dreams and Visions in Your Heart Are His Spiritual Imagery

---

God has designed us as a people of imagery. When we receive communications that consist of words, we develop images as perceptions of the meaning of those words. These perceptions involve many factors, but look at what the prophet Habakkuk wrote: *"I will stand my watch and set myself on the rampart, and watch to see what He will say to me"* (Habakkuk 2:1).

Here, the prophet said, in effect, "I will watch to see the complete imagery of what God says to me."

Imagery is a supernatural ability of your human spirit. Jesus explained: *"It is the Spirit who gives life; the flesh profits nothing. The words that I speak to you are spirit, and they are life"* (John 6:63).

Notice that Jesus' words are *"spirit"* and *"life."* His Word impregnates your spirit with dreams and visions; it becomes spiritual imagery that depicts His will for your life.

On the other hand, your mind also has the power to create imagery from your flesh, which the verse here says, *"profits nothing."* This is why the images of your mind can be taunting, fear-driven, and confusing. Therefore, you need to recognize that the imagery of your mind and the imagery of your spirit can potentially have two different origins.

If you are a believer who is capturing the Word of God in your spirit, then the mental image of that communication will agree with the spiritual image. God not only speaks into your spirit, but also into your thinking. You receive the mental imagery of the spiritual imagery. Speaking about His *"new covenant"* (Hebrews 8:8), God declared: *"I will put My laws in their mind and write them on their hearts"* (v. 10). When you are hearing from God and keeping your mind renewed, as we studied earlier, your spirit and mind will see the same images from God.

When you consider that God speaks to you in concepts that produce images, you then can begin to understand the dreams and visions of your heart in a far greater way. They are *"spirit"* and *"life."*

CHAMPION THOUGHT:
The Enemy Can Create Imagery and Speak through Scripture

Do you know that the devil also speaks to you in images? He will even use the Word of God to try to draw you into a perspective that God never intended. Therefore, don't allow what you see to dominate you until you have confirmed it. Examine *every* image, dream, vision, and what you believe is a Word from God regarding your purpose. Align it with the character, nature, and Word of God. If it does not match any one of these three areas, then it is not from God.

You might say, "But this is from the Bible!"

It doesn't matter what the image is. See who is behind it, because the devil can use the Scriptures to mislead you.

Jesus in the Wilderness

For example, when Jesus was fasting in the wilderness for forty days, Satan used the Scriptures to tempt Him. (See Luke 4.) Why did the devil use the Bible? He was trying to manipulate God's Word to serve himself. Satan repeatedly brought to Jesus images—even from the Scriptures—to tempt Jesus to fulfill his demonic will. The enemy knows the power of imagery. One of these temptations was for Jesus to curb His hunger by commanding a stone to turn into bread. Satan knew that the power of the image of bread would cause that stone to become what Jesus said.

Champion, can you imagine the enemy trying to harness God's power by bringing to *you* the image of what *he* wants you to see from the Word? Ugh! This is serious. You must get it right the first time because the wrong image by the wrong spirit—even using Scripture—can produce a deception.

Deborah, Judge of Israel

Let's examine Deborah in the book of Judges. She was a prophetess and judge of Israel in the days of the Canaanite King Jabin's oppression of Israel. After hearing a Word from God about how to defeat their enemies, Deborah commanded the armies of Israel to battle the Canaanite captain of the army, Sisera. She explained to Barak, the Israelite captain of the army, that God said He would defeat the enemy.

Although Deborah had a clear image of God's will, Barak hesitated. Regarding entering into battle, Barak said to Deborah,

> *"If you go with me, I will go; but if you don't go with me, I won't go." "Very well," Deborah said, "I will go with you. But because of the way you are going about this, the honor will not be yours, for the LORD will hand Sisera over to a woman." So Deborah went with Barak to Kedesh.* (Judges 4:8–9 NIV)

As Deborah had predicted, God led a woman named Jael to slay Sisera, and the Israelites went on to defeat the Canaanites. Deborah continually gave the glory to God, so no man ever would take the glory from the Holy One.

In this biblical account, Deborah had an image of victory. She focused on the finish and assembled God's champions to defeat their enemies. A song about the battle became a memorial throughout all Israel. It declared that Deborah awoke, decreed the Word of God, and mobilized the armies. That Word created an image of victory, which was strong enough to deliver a nation through one woman's command.

CHAMPION THOUGHT:
You Must Not Require Evidence before You Know the Outcome

This story of Deborah reveals another important truth. Because God's people can see beyond the physical appearance, we do not require evidence before we know the outcome. If you are walking in God's authority to rule your environment, you must realize that the finished image in your spirit never comes from the physical evidence. This is why you must focus on the spiritual image of the finish and not on what you see with your physical eyes. Yes, it takes faith to live as God's champion!

CHAMPION THOUGHT:
Go from Glory to Glory

The apostle Paul wrote, as we briefly discussed earlier,

Where the Spirit of the Lord is, there is liberty. But we all, with unveiled face, beholding as in a mirror the glory of the Lord, are being transformed into the same image from glory to glory, just as by the Spirit of the Lord. (2 Corinthians 3:17–18)

Notice, Paul said that the very presence of the Spirit of God produces liberty. That's the truth from God's initiative before the human element enters the scene.

In the next sentence, Paul explained how the liberty of the Spirit occurs when humanity is involved. He said that "*where the Spirit of the Lord is, there is liberty*," but when we are engaged, here's how that liberty functions: "*We all*" step into this environment "*with unveiled face*," or openly with complete candidness, looking or "*beholding as in a mirror the glory of the Lord.*" Some might say, "Oh, this is the shekinah glory or the haze of God's manifested presence." (See 2 Chronicles 7 NAS.) No, that's not it, because this glory is defined in the next sentence.

Paul said, "*We...are being transformed into the same image*" of the glory of the Lord. That word "*image*" is critical. This is not an image of our human faith. It is the divine imagery of liberation in the Holy Spirit. This gives you a vision of the *complete* manifestation of all that Jesus died for.

As a side note, remember that you see this imagery fashioned and formed in you through the Word of God. Do you recall that in our discussion about renewing your mind, I explained that, according to 2 Peter 1:4 (NAS), meditating on the promises in the Word of God actually gives you His nature? This is the process of fashioning you into God's image.

You are being molded into God's image as you look "*with unveiled face*" at "*the glory of the Lord*," which is the complete manifestation—or finished picture—that Jesus died to purchase. Paul said that when you look at this glory, you "*are being transformed into the same image from glory to glory, just as by the Spirit of the Lord.*" In other words, you see God's completed work in its glory—you focus on the finish—and the power of His Spirit changes you into that image, causing you to experience His completion in your life. You go "*from glory to glory.*" You move from experiencing *one* picture of completion to a *greater* picture of completion to an *even greater* picture of completion. Going "*from glory to glory*" is progressively receiving and walking in greater spiritual freedom, revelation from God, and His power.

In short, focusing on the finish engages the Spirit of God, who then brings you into living His completed vision for your life. This is the glory of your life. Thus, you fulfill your divine purpose.

CHAMPION THOUGHT:
Are You in the Bucket Brigade?

Champion, are you going from glory to glory, or is your life an ordeal of emergency and crisis management? Many people's lives are like bucket brigades. They continually pass out "buckets of water," putting out "fires" in their lives. They wait for the next miserable calamity, hoping to extinguish it with prayer. Are you going from tragedy to breakthrough and then back again, instead of going from glory to glory?

CHAMPION THOUGHT:
Set Value-Driven Priorities

If you live in the "bucket brigade," then you must make some changes. Your priorities need realignment. Examine and adjust your judgments about the things of value in your life. For example, be sure that you have what I call value-driven priorities. In other words, make certain that what you spend the majority of your time on is contributing to your values and divine purpose, not simply crisis management or catering to other people's demands.[6]

God wants you to continue from glory to glory. Therefore, you must remove the distractions and obstacles in your life that monopolize your time, thus preventing you from focusing on God's finish for your life. If you will make these adjustments, then every day you will find greater and greater freedom and fulfillment. Every place you go, the very glory of God will radiate and penetrate. You will not be average in anything that you do, but you will walk in the purposes of God with excellence.

CHAMPION THOUGHT:
Go from Glory to Glory in Your Micro and Macro Visions

In every area of your life, make sure that you properly set your priorities and goals. You see, your life consists of multiple small visions. For example, I have visions of my mental health, motivation, and ability to accomplish personal goals. Also, I have visions regarding my family, such as their health and provision. I have visions concerning the areas over which I have leadership, and so forth. All these contribute to my overall vision of my divine purpose.

As in the field of economics, you need to look at the overall broad picture of your life's purpose—the macro view. Then, you must also examine all the small parts that work together to create the overall dream—the micro view. Every one of those small desires of your heart also needs to be met, so you can fulfill your life's purpose. Remember we studied earlier that your vision moves creation to become the provision. The same is true for every one of the micro visions in your life. In fact, as each of these smaller dreams is fulfilled, you go from glory to glory.

CHAMPION THOUGHT:
The Power of Change Is Released in the Supernatural Imagery of Glory

I shared in an earlier chapter that I didn't know God's purpose for a man, a husband, and a father. The Scriptures painted a picture. It was an image of kindness, love, gentleness, appreciation of loved ones, recognizing others' significance, protecting other people's interests, and seeking the betterment of others. These were not mere words, framed in sentences and structured in paragraphs. No, they painted an image of me. This was not a picture of an incomplete, frustrated male, who was unable to keep his family together. This was a vision of a man whom God created and Jesus brought into right relationship with the Father. This was a portrait of a male serving God in a home. It was a picture of a husband who does love his wife as Christ loved the church and has unlimited ability to give.

Upon capturing that image, I consequently focused on the finish, and the Spirit of God was free to change me into that image from glory to glory. It was not a picture of going from destruction to reconstruction or from chaos to completion. No, no, no! It was an image of going from the *first* image of completion to a *greater* image of completion to an *overwhelming* image of completion to an *absolutely unlimited* image of completion. You see, as you go from glory to glory to glory to glory to glory, you experience unlimited growth in the life of God. His power to change you never ends.

It is critical for you to recognize that you possess the supernatural enablement from God to see the completion of His purposes. When you see the finished picture—imagery from the Spirit of God within you—firmly lay hold of that picture, being fixed and immovable. The Spirit of God will then move to bring that vision into manifestation. The changes will happen by grace, through God, by His Spirit. Then, human handprints and man's fabricated designs cannot mar God's glory in that area.

For example, if you are married or considering marriage, you need to know what God's image of a marriage is. Is your or a loved one's marriage the *wrong* image of a marriage? If so, compare it with the picture that God painted in His Word about the joining together of a man and woman. Focus on God's intended vision. When you do this, your marriage is changed into that same image from glory to glory to glory. You will no longer see the incompleteness of your spouse. You will not see your mate's limitations or lack of knowledge. You will not see the inability to bring about change.

Instead, you will see your marriage and spouse as God does. As the supernatural imagery of glory is uncovered and revealed, the power of change will be released in your marriage.

CHAMPION THOUGHT:
Yoke Yourself with the Holy Spirit and the Word, Letting Them Bring You to the Finish Line

---

As you focus on the finished image from God, the Holy Spirit begins to break the yoke and lift the burden of bringing it into being. The Bible declares:

> And it shall come to pass in that day, that his burden shall be taken away from off thy shoulder, and his yoke from off thy neck, and the yoke shall be destroyed because of the anointing.
> (Isaiah 10:27 KJV)

Why does the Spirit break the yoke and lift the burden? It is because you are not designed to carry the weight of life or be the only one who can do the work! Only God can do this for you.

Jesus wants you to take *His* yoke upon you, for His yoke is easy and His burden is light. He invites you:

> Come to me, all you who are weary and burdened, and I will give you rest. Take my yoke upon you and learn from me, for I am gentle and humble in heart, and you will find rest for your souls. For my yoke is easy and my burden is light.
> (Matthew 11:28–30 NIV)

Think about it. You are to be yoked to the Spirit of God and the Word of God (Jesus). It is time to let them carry the full responsibility of bringing you into the completed vision. You are to be along simply for the ride, while they carry the load. I hope you get the picture. This yoke is not difficult. This burden is not heavy. It is not oppressive and ominous. It's not disturbing and full of distress or frustration. You don't have to question or be concerned about whether the vision will manifest. The responsibility of crossing the finish line is on the Holy Spirit and the Word. It's on their shoulders, not yours.

You see, *"the weapons of our warfare are not carnal but mighty in God for pulling down strongholds"* (2 Corinthians 10:4). Champion, you are not battling your intellect against a demonic spirit. Jesus Himself has already rendered the kingdom of darkness void—without authority and power. Now, Jesus has all authority and power over heaven and earth, and He has delegated it to you. Oh, what a light burden and easy yoke this is!

Picture yourself with the Word (Jesus) on one side and the Spirit of God on the other. One defeated the enemy; One raised Jesus from hell and is here to manifest the living Word of God. You are yoked between them, and the Father is leading you with His ever-loving, gentle cords and bands of love. He is drawing you into security, establishing you with significance, and causing you to live in fulfillment. Oh, this is awesome! The joy, strength, and life that come from being yoked together with Him is glorious!

CHAMPION THOUGHT:
His Imagery Is Proof That He Is Doing It!

Champion, don't ever become distracted from what Jesus has purchased you for. He died and rose again to bring you into completion. His imagery in your spirit is proof that He is carrying you to the finish line. In other words, if you can see His imagery for your life, then you have it. Why? Faith brings it from that which is unseen.

Remember, *"Faith is the substance of things hoped for"* (Hebrews 11:1). We don't hope for something incomplete. We have expectancy for completion. Also, *"Faith is...the evidence of things not seen"* (v. 1). What you see in the natural realm is not as it is in the Spirit. However, when you perceive in your spirit God's completed image, that is the evidence of what you cannot see. His picture proves to you that the Spirit of God is moving, changing, and bringing everything together for you to break through the ribbon, cross the finish line, win the race, and walk in the manifestation of the completed image. Champion, don't ever give up; God has called you to live in the glory of His finished works.

CHAMPION THOUGHT:
After You Do the Will of God, You Receive the Promise

The finish line, which Jesus has for you, is not one that puts you back three steps after you have gone forward four. No, when you cross that line, it is finished, and you will receive a reward. Yes! The Bible says, *"Do not throw away your confidence; it will be richly rewarded. You need to persevere so that when you have done the will of God, you will receive what he has promised"* (Hebrews 10:35–36 NIV).

This confidence has anchored you in knowing, seeing, and doing the will of God. Don't cast it aside because *"it will be richly rewarded."* You need unwavering patience to endure and persist. Then, after you do God's will, you will receive the promise.

CHAMPION THOUGHT:
Don't Draw Back, or Another Will Receive Your Prize

Realize that God Himself orchestrates this earth. You do what He says. You speak what He declares. You have the divine imagery. Then, you are changed into that finished image from glory to glory, but you must not lose your perspective. You must stay focused because the book of Hebrews continues: *"For yet a little while, and He who is coming will come and will not tarry. Now the just shall live by faith; but if anyone draws back, My soul has no pleasure in him"* (Hebrews 10:37–38).

If you withdraw or step back from God's revealed image of completion, then you no longer participate in what He has been releasing in the earth on behalf of that vision. You remove yourself from that picture. Someone else will step into your glory because God will find another who is obedient to Him. Oh! Can you imagine yourself doing the will of God, quitting, and then discovering that someone else on the way to the finish line picked up all that you had done? Champion, don't draw back from your finish line.

CHAMPION THOUGHT:
Focus on Your Own Finish Line, Not Another's

As you focus on your finish line, remember that it is *yours*, not someone else's. A common snare that the enemy often sets for Christians and non-Christians alike is looking back to see where other people are. Simply changing focus can easily cause a runner to trip and fall. Likewise, if you compete or compare, you have already lost your focus on the Lord, and you are looking at other people. You are to run the race set before you, and they are to run theirs. For this reason, it is pointless to compare yourself with others.

Joshua

In the Old Testament, when Moses died, his assistant, Joshua, had great opportunity to compare himself with his predecessor. Can you imagine thinking that you must fill the shoes of the great leader Moses?

In the first chapter of the book of Joshua, God commanded Joshua, saying,

Moses My servant is dead. Now therefore, arise, go over this Jordan, you and all this people, to the land which I am giving

to them; the children of Israel. Every place that the sole of your foot will tread upon I have given you, as I said to Moses....No man shall be able to stand before you all the days of your life; as I was with Moses, so I will be with you. I will not leave you nor forsake you. (Joshua 1:2–3, 5)

Here, God first explained that Moses' race was complete. He then announced Joshua's finish line and instructed him to get going on his own race! Notice that God said, *"I have given you."* It was already finished. Joshua simply had to lead the Israelites in God's finished works and move into the Promised Land.

Now, why did God mention Moses first? I believe it was because He did not want Joshua to look back, wondering, *How did Moses do it?* No, God wanted the new leader to focus on his own finish line, asking, "How has God already done this?" You see, we must not look at someone else's divine vision or wonder how God operated with another—even if that person is or was a great man or woman of God. No, it is crucial for us to recognize that God is speaking a *current, fresh Word* in our spirits today. That which was in the past is dead.

Champion, God has a unique course designed for you to run today, and the only way you can see it is by hearing from Him for yourself. You do this by sustaining radical communion—a high level of fellowship—with Him. Then, you can understand what God is speaking to you because nothing hinders your connection with Him.

Now, in Joshua's day, the Promised Land was a physical, geographical territory, which he first had to conquer before possessing. Today, we, too, must conquer a territory before we can possess it, but ours is in the spiritual realm. In both eras, God's champions enter their Promised Land by walking in His finished works. The victories have already been won. Radical communion with and obedience to Him empower God's champions to use His authority to break through all barriers, change every circumstance that is out of His will, and seize His promises.

Champion, are you beginning to see that when God speaks a vision to you, the picture is already painted, the race is finished, and the victory is yours? There is no question. It is "a done deal"! You simply walk into your Promised Land.

CHAMPION THOUGHT:
Don't Sink with What Remains Unsilenced

Peter

We examined in an earlier chapter how Peter walked on the water to Jesus. Many people focus on the fact that he also eventually sank. To me, it is more important that he actually did walk on water! However, we should briefly examine why Peter sank, so we can learn from his mistake.

Let's read what happened to Peter just after he stepped out on the water:

> But when he saw that the wind was boisterous, he was afraid; and beginning to sink he cried out, saying, "Lord, save me!" And immediately Jesus stretched out His hand and caught him, and said to him, "O you of little faith, why did you doubt?" And when they got into the boat, the wind ceased.
>
> (Matthew 14:30–32)

Peter did not finish the walk on the water because he shifted his focus. You see, when he stepped from the ship, he anchored his faith in the finished imagery that Jesus' word "Come" (v. 29) had created and the physical sight of Jesus walking on the water. Peter actually walked on the water for a bit. Then, however, he turned to look at the boisterous wind, shifting his faith from Jesus to the stormy circumstances. Fear consequently gripped him as he looked at the storm, which had not been silenced, and he began to sink!

Have you ever stopped to think that for the period during which Peter *did* walk on the water, the storm remained unsilenced? He began to sink only when he happened to notice the raging storm. You see, it did not matter whether or not the storm was silenced. The spiritual imagery of that word *"Come"* and Jesus walking on the water was more powerful than any circumstances Peter faced. When Jesus spoke this command and walked on the water, it was finished. Peter simply had to step from the boat, not fall into fear, and continue walking until he crossed his finish line.

Champion, don't sink with what remains unsilenced. Instead, soar with God, who says, "It is finished."

CHAMPION THOUGHT:
Don't Allow the Enemy's Seeds and Weeds to Distract You

Parable of the Tares among the Wheat

Earlier, we briefly discussed Jesus' parable of the enemy sowing tares or weeds in the wheat field. Now, let's reexamine this story from another perspective.

When the laborers noticed the weeds sprouting, they said to the landowner, "We thought you planted wheat. What are all these weeds doing here? Should we pull them up?" What was the owner's response in Jesus' story?

> *But he said, "No, lest while you gather up the tares you also uproot the wheat with them. Let both grow together until the harvest, and at the time of harvest I will say to the reapers, 'First gather together the tares and bind them in bundles to burn them, but gather the wheat into my barn.'"*
> (Matthew 13:29–30)

Why did Jesus say not to pull up the weeds, which would also uproot the wheat? The answer is simple. God calls us to focus on the completion of *His* work, not what the enemy does. The devil attempts to distract us. Of course, we have the responsibility to fight in spiritual warfare. However, our focus is to be on the completion of God's Word, not the choking effects of the enemy.

In other words, Jesus said, "Keep your eyes on the harvest, which is coming up, and leave the weeds alone." Champion, don't allow the enemy's seeds and weeds to distract you and take you off course. You will never run out of weeds if you look at them. Likewise, you will never run out of harvest if you will simply look at it.

CHAMPION THOUGHT:
Keep Your Eyes on the Finish Line

Mark McGwire

In the summer of 1998, after Mark McGwire first broke the home-run record, he had another goal in mind. "When I got to 62 so early in September," McGwire explained, "everybody said to shoot for 70. I come into the clubhouse after I was taken out and they already had a hat (with the No. 70 on it) made."[7] He had an image of another finish line, focused on it, and finished at 70 home runs for the season.

A runner also must keep himself focused toward the future of going across the finish line. He cannot look down at every step, because if he does, he will trip and fall. Likewise, remember, we are to fix our eyes upon Jesus, *"the author and finisher of our faith"* (Hebrews 12:2). He authored our unseen dreams, finished them, and manifests them. Don't lose sight, for the divine visions, which are not here on earth yet, are already there in heaven, and He brings them here. Fixing your eyes on the finish line gives you confidence that your dream will manifest.

CHAMPION THOUGHT:
Lay Hold of Your Vision, Never Letting Go

We have learned that when you connect with your purpose, God impels you and creation waits for the command to fulfill your divine purpose. Your responsibility is to lay hold of that vision, capturing the image of it and keeping it before your eyes. Never let go of your divine purpose and vision.

Let me give you an example of how I laid hold of a vision when I was in my early twenties. In 1975, when my wife, Faye, and I went through great marital difficulties, I could not see any way for our marriage to be reconciled. At that time, we were going through our divorce. Faye had a restraining order against me so that I could not see her. This court order also restricted my visiting rights with my own children.

One day I was reading the Bible, and I saw 1 Timothy 3:5, which says, *"For if a man does not know how to rule his own house, how will he take care of the church of God?"* As a young believer, I understood that no possibility existed for God to use me because of the condition of my family life. I had an image of failure.

Feeling sorry for myself, I began to pray. This might sound unusual, but I had an experience again with the Lord. I began to envision tens of thousands of people streaming into the kingdom of God. As I watched that vision unfold within me, I heard God speaking that He would use me to bring about a great awakening, a revival, which would turn God's people to Him and open the floodgates of the world for salvations to pour into the kingdom of God.

This was spiritual imagery from God Himself. I thought, *Oh, that's a wonderful dream,* but it saddened me.

I recall asking God, "Why are You showing me these people coming into Your kingdom? I just read Your Scripture that says if I cannot lead my own family, how can You possibly—according to Your own Word—use me in Your church?"

And the Spirit of God spoke to me something that changed my life then and continues to change my life today. He said that if I would keep my eyes on the vision—the very purpose for which

He had created and placed me on this earth—God Himself would orchestrate everything around me. He would arrange my family, finances, knowledge, influence, relationships, and whatever was necessary to accomplish that vision. He would cause resources to stream into that purpose, working *"all things...together for good to those who love God, to those who are the called according to His purpose"* (Romans 8:28). My job was to keep my eyes on the vision, or focus on the finish line, and God would turn the impossibilities into realities.

At that time, of course, I loved God, but I had been missing the knowledge of my call according to His purpose. Once I saw this vision, it was clear, and that was all I needed. The God who revealed my divine purpose also gave me this vision. I realized that He showed this image to me because it was His will, and He would fulfill it. God said, *"I have purposed it; I will also do it"* (Isaiah 46:11). After all, only He could do it. I was in no position to do it myself. Yes, I had great questions and many uncertainties, but the vision and the purpose were clear.

During all these years following this encounter with God, He has been faithful and will continue to be. I have seen the continued manifestation of that vision from glory to glory. Not only were my marriage and family restored, but I also have seen multitudes of people across the world saved and turned toward God. It has been an awesome journey.

What about you? Are you laying hold of your vision? Maybe you don't know what that vision is yet. Remember that before the foundation of the earth, God fashioned your destiny and purpose. He already sees the finished product. You are merely to lay claim to what is rightfully yours in the spirit realm! He has spoken His Word into your life and is watching over it to perform it. His Word gives you the imagery of purpose in your life. Once you see that imagery or dream, you can identify your divine purpose, and your reason for being on the earth becomes clear. As you walk in that purpose, then you go from glory to glory.

CHAMPION THOUGHT:
Don't Finish Alone!

Now, my friend, you are running your race as God's champion. You have everything you need to finish the course. You have the Holy Spirit, the Word of God, and His vision. You have the necessary knowledge, enablement, and truth set before you. Creation is following your dream, and barriers are breaking. Nothing stands in your way.

God has promised you: *"Every good gift and every perfect gift is from above, and comes down from the Father of lights, with whom there is no variation or shadow of turning"* (James 1:17).

God doesn't change. He is not fickle. He doesn't go back on His Word. His promises to you are not "yes and no," but "yes and amen": *"For all the promises of God in Him are Yes, and in Him Amen, to the glory of God through us"* (2 Corinthians 1:20).

You have everything that you need. Jesus completed it all and has made you complete in Him. You are going from glory to glory. You know that you will finish your race. As the apostle Paul declared:

> I have fought the good fight, I have finished the race, I have kept the faith. Finally, there is laid up for me the crown of righteousness, which the Lord, the righteous Judge, will give to me on that Day, and not to me only but also to all who have loved His appearing.　　　　(2 Timothy 4:7–8)

You, too, will have *"the crown of righteousness"* waiting for you when you cross the finish line.

Now, there's one more thing. Champion, don't finish alone. God has called you to break through the barriers, pave the pathway, break the ribbon, and cross the finish line so that those behind you can do likewise. Let me show you how.

10
The Master Multiplier

hroughout these pages, you have read the stories of many
champions. What do all these people have in common
with you? Think about it. They broke through barriers and
became extraordinary in their ordinary lives. However, their breakthroughs did not solely affect themselves. They paved the way for
others' lives to be transformed. In this last chapter, we will discuss
how to multiply your breakthroughs in others. That is the next
level to which God is calling you.

CHAMPION THOUGHT:
Success without a Successor
Is Only Delayed Failure

I have heard it said, "Success without a successor is only
delayed failure." Champion, I have good news for you! Delayed failure does not have to be part of *your* life because you have the power
of multiplication. You don't have to be the one and only. Let me
explain.

CHAMPION THOUGHT:
With You in It, It's a Wonderful Life

George Bailey

Have you seen the classic movie *It's a Wonderful Life* with Jimmy Stewart? After facing apparently impossible circumstances, the lead character, George Bailey, gives up on life and attempts suicide. However, his guardian angel rescues him and gives George the unique ability to see what life would be like if he had never been born. George is horrified at the abounding evil events and influences that result from his absence on the earth. This insight gives him a new lease on life, and he goes on to break through his barriers, paving the way for others to succeed also.

Although this is just a movie, it illustrates the ripple effect that our lives have on others. Often, we don't realize the significance of our impact. You see, if we quit before breaking through our barriers, we create huge gaps in others' lives.

What would have happened if Noah had not built the ark? What if Alexander Graham Bell had not invented the telephone? What if Henry Ford had given up before he had mass-produced affordable automobiles? Imagine life on planet Earth without the enormous impact of individuals like these and a multitude of others like them. Personally, what if I had not pressed on, standing on the Word of God for my family? Or, most importantly, what if Jesus Christ had not come to earth as a Man to save us?

Now, think about what would happen if *you* quit before you accomplish all that God has planned for you? It would be a great tragedy. God has designed your life to create a chain reaction of breakthroughs in the world around you. Life would not be the same if you fail to fulfill your divine purpose. Not only would you miss achieving your dreams and visions, but countless other people would stay limited, hindered, and bound because you would not be in the position to help them.

Never doubt that a single person can change the course of a city, nation, world—or a home. Yes, it only takes one to make a difference!

CHAMPION THOUGHT:
Your Breakthrough Paves the Way for Other People

In this book, we have discussed numerous examples of individuals who revolutionized history. When people break through in areas such as communications, sports, medicine, race, gender, family, and other barriers, they carve new paths for others to follow.

I believe this principle is God's desire for all humanity. The changes that He wants to effect in our lives should not end merely with ourselves. They are to commence the beginnings for many others. Likewise, your breakthrough will launch a new lifestyle, but God does not want it to be only for you. When you cut through a line of defense, your success and freedom form the basis for how you and those around you begin to live, think, and operate. In short, it becomes no longer a breakthrough for you alone but a pathway for others to find new lives as well. You must hold the door open in that barrier—not only for yourself but also to facilitate and help others to follow you. This is what champions do.

CHAMPION THOUGHT:
Live to Give

Amway

Rich DeVos, the Amway cofounder, explains that since God created us all in His image, we are to help others' dreams come true. "It isn't enough," he wrote, "to believe that I am created by a loving Creator to dream great dreams. I must also believe that you are created in the very same way to the very same end."[1]

Serving others and giving has helped many people not only to fulfill their own dreams but also to help others achieve theirs. In his book, Rich DeVos included a story about an Amway distributor who recalled the advice of a renowned leader in Amway, Dexter Yager. The distributor said, "From the beginning Dex told [my wife] and me that learning to serve is the key to success. 'The purpose of living,' Dex told us over and over again, 'is giving.' Once we discovered the truth of that little saying," the distributor explained, "our lives changed and our business prospered."[2] When this distributor and his wife began monthly tithing (giving 10%) to their church and charities, they saw a big difference. "Try it. Find a need and meet it," Rich DeVos encouraged. "See what it does for you, for your family, and for your business to help others whose needs are greater than your own."[3]

For years, I have challenged others to "live to give." God has called us to help people whether it is to pave the way for their breakthroughs or to sow into their lives in other ways. Be sensitive to the Lord's direction as He leads you to those who need His help through you.

CHAMPION THOUGHT:
Identify the Path to Manifest God's Purpose

God's purpose encompasses much more than your individual life. The dynamic of the Holy Spirit does not simply sit in the face of resistance but breaks through all barriers so that multitudes can be set free. You must press in to connect with the Spirit of God to find the path, not only for yourself but also for the others who will follow you.

It is likely that there are numerous ways through your barriers. For example, in the Bible, some people received healing when Jesus spoke or touched them. Others were healed when they touched the hem of His garment. The best way to your breakthrough is God's way for you. Discover His route, and then follow it by faith.

To achieve God's plan for your life and pave the path for others, be aware that you might need to:

- Forge a new path, doing what you have not seen anyone else do.
- Follow someone who already has broken through the same barrier that you face.
- Build on another's unfinished work.
- Restore a forgotten path.

CHAMPION THOUGHT:
Forge a New Path

Often, one person single-handedly discovers a paradigm shift that completely changes the world forever. When this happens, humanity can soon forget the forerunner, who set the new standard and cut the trail for all to follow. Clear examples of this exist in many fields, especially in the areas of transportation and communication.

Henry Ford

Think about Henry Ford's era again. Before his work, the accepted standard for private transportation was the horse or mule. Then, Ford entered the scene and created the automobile. Suddenly, the previous constant standard faltered, and nothing was the same ever again. It would not have mattered if Ford's first car had cost a million dollars. Neither would it have been important if it had cost a lifetime's earnings for that first car to roll off the assembly line. It was the beginning of a new era. One day, a car would be affordable and become the standard means of private transportation in many nations across the world. Henry Ford's breakthrough created a pathway for the world to follow.

Bill Gates

In modern times, consider Bill Gates, the American entrepreneur who, at age 20, founded the Microsoft Corporation (1975), which became the "world's most prosperous computer software firm."[4] By age 31, Gates' work had made him a billionaire. Having started computer programming as a teenager, he launched his first software company while still in high school.

Gates has paved the way for nearly every home in the United States to have a personal computer. It could be said that what Ford did for the American highways, Bill Gates did for the information highway.

CHAMPION THOUGHT:

Follow Someone Who Already Has Broken through the Same Barrier That You Face

---

Review others' breakthroughs. Has someone already cleared a path that you can follow? Look for what can help you to break through your specific barriers. If others have cut a path in your particular area, learn how they did it. I often say, "R. & D. is definitely the way to go." The world's system calls this "research and development," but I say that "research and *duplicate*" is better. For example, because someone has invented the wheel, don't waste your time reinventing it. That person's discovery can roll you a lot farther down the road than you can go on your own.

Now, you might not be able to travel entirely in that person's "vehicle" and follow everything he has done. However, at least look into assimilating the discoveries and methods that he employed to achieve his success. This will add great insight into breaking through your barriers to achieve your dream.

In short, you do it; or find someone who has done it, and then do what he did. You see, once a pathway from God is already forged, you don't necessarily have to find another way.

Roger Bannister

Earlier, we discussed Roger Bannister, the medical student from England who was the first person to run the mile in less than four minutes. When he broke the record in 1954, it had been nearly a century since anyone had run the mile in less than five minutes! Yet Bannister broke that four-minute barrier with a record of 3 minutes 59.4 seconds.[5] Then, suddenly, within two months, others began breaking this new record. Bannister's miraculous feat seemed to pave the way for many others.

A year after his breakthrough, Bannister wrote *The Four-Minute Mile.* The first chapter begins with these words from the book of Habakkuk: *"Write the vision and make it plain upon tables, that he may run that readeth it"* (Habakkuk 2:2 KJV). Bannister's book became a great source of inspiration and motivation for those who have followed him.

Mark McGwire and Sammy Sosa

Similarly, in 1998 Mark McGwire and Sammy Sosa faced a nearly forty-year-old standard for the most home runs in a baseball season. For decades, no one could touch that record. Then, both players broke through that old standard in the same season. Game after game that year, they each broke through that barrier time and again. Then, only three years later, in 2001, Barry Bonds of the San Francisco Giants broke the record by hitting 73 home runs that season![6]

My Marriage

When God restored my marriage to Faye, our miracle created a pathway for others to follow. As we have shared our marital breakthrough, we have seen faith rise in other couples, and, as a result, God has mended many marriages. Divorced couples have even remarried each other. Our testimony blazed a trail for others to follow—not because we are more special than other people. It is simply how God works. We experienced a breakthrough. Now, it's our turn to help others through the barrier of divorce.

If you need your marriage restored, ask God if our path can help you achieve *your* breakthrough. Your success will also be creating a path for those around you to follow.

The Woman with the Issue of Blood

Jesus healed people in many different ways. Here's how it happened on one occasion:

> *When they* [Jesus and His disciples] *had crossed over, they came to the land of Gennesaret. And when the men of that place recognized Him, they sent out into all that surrounding region, brought to Him all who were sick, and begged Him that they might only touch the hem of His garment. And as many as touched it were made perfectly well.*   (Matthew 14:34–36)

These people touched the hem of Jesus' garment! Where do you think they heard about simply reaching out for the bottom of His clothes? When they touched the material, what happened? All *"were made perfectly well."* Now, I do not believe that all these people simultaneously had this idea on their own.

This event in Gennesaret occurred after someone else had touched the hem of Jesus' garment. Do you remember the woman with the issue of blood? She touched Jesus' hem and received her healing, breaking through giant barriers in her social, economic, and physical world. We have no record of anyone else before this time doing such a thing! It was unheard of—an unclean person pressing the multitudes who thronged Jesus, believing that merely a touch from His clothes would bring healing. I believe that this woman told everyone she saw, "If you touch the hem of Jesus' garment, you will be healed!"

Picture the people in this passage. They did not go through what this woman had. No, they probably lined up on the street with their hands out as Jesus walked by. Miracles abounded. Why? These people were following the example of one woman. When she penetrated the barrier of her disease and its devastating effects, she came to the other side, healed.

In my lifetime, with my own eyes, I have seen Jesus heal thousands of people. If you need healing, He can do it for you, too. He paved the path for all to follow. Many people have broken through serious diseases, such as cancer and other life-threatening illnesses. Each one of these individuals becomes a champion, instilling in others faith and hope that they, too, can overcome through Jesus.

CHAMPION THOUGHT:
Build on Another's Unfinished Work

When God gives you a dream, you might need to look into the option of building on another person's unfinished work. There is no need to reinvent what someone else has already discovered. You see, often, one person creates the initial difference and others follow in that paradigm shift, building upon and perfecting that breakthrough. Then, humanity steps into that transformation to enjoy new benefits and freedoms. Eventually, the novelty wears away, leaving a wide path for all to follow. The significant then becomes the routine. This happened with Christopher Columbus.

Early Sea Explorers and Christopher Columbus

Inspired by Columbus' success, other Europeans later sailed westward into uncharted waters. These included:

- John Cabot (1450–1498), the first European to discover the mainland of North America
- Vasco Núñez de Balboa (1475–1519) the first European to discover, with the help of native peoples, a shortcut through Panama to what would later be called the Pacific Ocean
- Ferdinand Magellan (born circa 1480–1521), the first person to sail completely around the world (He reached Asia by sailing

west from Europe, thus fulfilling Columbus' original dream and proving that the earth is round.)

Space Explorers and John Glenn, Jr.

In 1961, the Soviet Union launched the first man into space, Cosmonaut Yuri Gagarin (1934-1968); he orbited the earth once. Less than a month later, Alan Shephard, Jr., (1923-1998) became the first American in space, but he did not orbit our planet. Then, in 1962, U.S. Marine test pilot and astronaut John Glenn, Jr., made history as the first American to orbit the earth.

Glenn also dreamed of becoming a U.S. senator and eventually did so in 1974, after overcoming physical setbacks. However, the ambitious senator from Ohio had yet another dream. Former astronaut John Glenn desired to return to space one day. In 1998, 36 years after his first historic flight, his vision became reality. At age 77—well past the age of any previous space traveler—Senator John Glenn made history, this time as the oldest person to orbit the earth. Breaking the age barrier for astronauts, he paved the way for older people to travel to space. Glenn recalls:

> When I was a boy, like many children before and after me, I looked at the night sky and wondered what was out there and whether we could get there. Nobody at that time could have predicted, or even imagined, where we would be today. Yet we've achieved so much because people believed, experimented and persisted. They never took "it can't be done" for an answer.[7]

It has been said that John Glenn also blazed the trail to put a man on the moon. As we discussed earlier, astronaut Neil Armstrong fulfilled this dream in 1969 when he stepped onto the desolate lunar surface. Today, more than thirty years later, 16 countries and over 100,000 people are working together to build the International Space Station. Humanity has come a long way since Glenn's first flight into space. Each step of that way, the space program has built upon previous discoveries and breakthroughs.

CHAMPION THOUGHT:
Restore a Forgotten Path

Charles Parham and William J. Seymour

As we studied earlier, in 1901 Charles Parham, the founder of Pentecostalism in America, restored the ancient, forgotten path to receiving the baptism in the Holy Spirit. His student, William J. Seymour, built upon Parham's teaching, and multitudes followed their path.

During the following decades and centuries, many other Christian leaders have built upon Parham's ministry. The Pentecostal movement paved the way for the charismatic movement, as recorded by the *Dictionary of Pentecostal and Charismatic Movements*:

> Part of the groundwork for charismatic renewal, reflecting its deep roots in the Pentecostal movement, had been laid by the ministries of Oral Roberts [(1918-) healing], David J. du Plessis [(1905-1987) vision of renewal for denominational churches] and Demos Shakarian [(1913-1993)] and the Full Gospel Business Men's Fellowship International ["first organized expression"].[8]

Israelites Crossing the Jordan River

God performed a great miracle for His children when He parted the Jordan River, as we discussed earlier. The Israelites had come against this great barrier as they were about to enter the Promised Land. (See Joshua 3 and 4.) Notice what Joshua told the Israelites afterward:

For the LORD your God dried up the waters of the Jordan before you until you had crossed over, as the LORD your God did to the Red Sea, which He dried up before us until we had crossed over, that all the peoples of the earth may know the hand of the LORD, that it is mighty, that you may fear the LORD your God forever. (Joshua 4:23–24)

Here, Joshua reminded the people that God had parted the Red Sea for them earlier. Apparently, for the children of Israel, parting the waters was a forgotten path, which God used Joshua to restore.

CHAMPION THOUGHT:
Your Breakthrough Is a Landmark

After the Israelites safely crossed the parted Jordan, God commanded Joshua to instruct the people to create a landmark of twelve stones. This was to remind them of what He had done for them both at the Jordan River and the Red Sea. (See Joshua 4:20–24.) This landmark signified God's power to create miracle breakthroughs in the midst of hopelessness and imminent defeat. These twelve stones spoke volumes as a memorial: God did it once, and He will do it again!

The same is true for your and my breakthroughs today. Our miracles serve as modern landmarks to remind ourselves and others of God's power, which is available to all His children. These landmarks pave the way for others to follow in our same miraculous paths.

Champion, you can be the one who makes a difference! You can forge a new pathway, follow another's breakthrough, build on an existing breakthrough, or restore a forgotten path. However God leads you, you can be the one to open a door that allows other people to walk in victory. Then, watch out! Suddenly you might find that everywhere you go, people are following the pathways of your breakthroughs!

CHAMPION THOUGHT:
You Are a Repairer of the Breach and a Restorer of Paths

God's people are not only to restore paths, but the Bible explains that we also are to rebuild the old places from godly former generations and repair the breach. God's Word states:

> *And they that shall be of thee shall build the old waste places:*
> *thou shalt raise up the foundations of many generations; and*
> *thou shalt be called, The repairer of the breach, The restorer*
> *of paths to dwell in.*   (Isaiah 58:12 KJV)

Do you know what a breach in a wall is? It does not mean that the whole wall is down, but there is a gap or an opening in it. A part of the wall is broken down where the enemy has pierced it. When breaches exist in the "walls" of people's defenses, the enemy has access to them in particular areas. Soon, they begin to accept the broken-down walls as normal. Sin and destruction become the common way of life. They then compromise their values and convictions in those areas. This widens the gap even further. It becomes a vicious cycle. The Bible explains that these cycles of defeat and compromise are yokes.

Eventually, these people's lives become so broken down that they have virtually no defense against the enemy. He has access to devour them. Their walls of protection have such gaping holes that destruction runs rampant in their lives. No one is standing guard to stop the enemy. When this happens, God calls on His champions to intervene in the path of history to repair the breach and restore the path. These champions know that the Holy Spirit dwells within them and will break the yokes through them. Remember that we read earlier:

And it shall come to pass in that day, that his burden shall be taken away from off thy shoulder, and his yoke from off thy neck, and the yoke shall be destroyed because of the anointing.

(Isaiah 10:27 KJV)

Adolf Hitler

In World War II (1939–1945), the world desperately needed brave hearts to stand against Adolf Hitler (1889–1945). This man was an evil genius—one of Satan's greatest tools. While a very captivating person, he had a perverted conscience. After overcoming several significant failures in life, Hitler succeeded in mobilizing Nazi Germany as one of the most horrible killing machines recorded in history. He ordered the annihilation of millions of innocent people as his army marched across Europe, conquering nations. Those targeted for genocide included Jews, Russians, Slavs, Poles, and others.

The world leaders of Hitler's era contemplated what to do. At first, most declined to become involved. Some nations believed that this was not their war. Some feared their own inferiority against such militaristic might, while others felt unable to defeat such a knowledgeable foe. The United States tried diplomacy, while Great Britain and France engaged in a policy of appeasement. The Soviet Union signed a nonaggression treaty with Germany and claimed this would protect its people. However, Hitler later betrayed and attacked the Soviet Union. Eventually, Italy, Japan, and other nations supported Germany. Together, they were called the Axis powers. It appeared that no one would stand in their way.

However, when Germany invaded Poland to its east, other nations including Britain and France could remain neutral no longer. Yet Hitler conquered much of Europe. The German dictator then attacked to the west, and France fell. He launched massive air attacks against Great Britain. Hitler's armies also conquered much of Northern Africa.

This death-grasp on the world tightened. Then, Japan, Germany's ally, attacked the United States at Pearl Harbor on December 7, 1941. Finally, the president of the United States, Franklin D. Roosevelt, changed the course of history. A nation with more firepower rose to stop the aggressive Axis powers.

President Roosevelt understood that individuals can change the course of history. Near the beginning of the war in 1939, Roosevelt had written to Hitler and Benito Mussolini (1883–1945), the Italian dictator, pleading with them to stop attacking and conquering other nations. The U.S. president wrote, "Heads of great governments in this hour are literally responsible for the fate of humanity in the coming years....History will hold them accountable for the lives and happiness of all."[9] Indeed, history has held them responsible.

Immediately after the Japanese attacked Pearl Harbor, the United States and Britain declared war on Japan. Several days later, the United States also declared war on Japan's allies, Germany and Italy. Although the war continued for nearly four years, ultimately the United States and her allies defeated Hitler and the Axis powers. Nations had fought together to repair the breach in the world and restore the path of peace.

CHAMPION THOUGHT:
It Only Takes One to Stand in the Gap

Whenever a break exists in the wall of anyone's life—or even in an entire nation—giving access to the evil one, God looks for someone to *"stand in the gap."* This is what we read earlier in the book of Ezekiel:

And I sought for a man among them, that should make up the hedge, and stand in the gap before me for the land, that I should not destroy it: but I found none. (Ezekiel 22:30 KJV)

God seeks for someone to *"make up the hedge."* He searches for the one who will stand in that broken spot to interrupt the assaults of the enemy for hurting people and to rebuild the wall so the enemy has no more access. This happened in World War II, as we just discussed, and it also occurred on September 11, 2001.

Todd Beamer, Fellow Passengers, and Crew

In the midst of the horrendous pain, suffering, and loss of life during the coordinated terrorist attack on September 11, 2001, some very good things happened. Afterward, countless stories unfolded of individual faith and valiance on that day. We heard of many rescuers who heroically entered the burning towers of the World Trade Center to save people but died or were seriously injured in the process.

We learned of the brave crew and passengers, such as Christian businessman Todd Beamer (1969–2001), who were on the fourth hijacked plane that day. Authorities believe that Beamer led a counterattack against the terrorists, after hearing about the three other airliners crashing into U.S. building landmarks.[10] This courageous counterassault took place aboard United Airlines Flight 93, en route from Newark, New Jersey, to San Francisco, California. However, the jet crashed in a rural Pennsylvanian field, killing all aboard but miraculously none on the ground. *World* magazine stated of the passengers' revolt, "Government officials believe their action averted a disastrous attack on Washington."[11] Vice President Dick Cheney concurred.[12]

World reported Todd Beamer's last words during a cell-phone call, which clearly reveal his dependency upon God:

> Mr. Beamer couldn't contact his wife, Lisa; he spoke with GTE supervisor Lisa Jefferson instead, logging on at 9:45....He told her he and several others were going to "jump" their guard.
>
> A teacher and sponsor of his church's high-schoolers, he asked Ms. Jefferson to join him in praying the Lord's

prayer. He ended it with words of his own: "God, help me. Jesus, help me." Then, she heard him say: "Are you guys ready? Let's roll." It was 9:58....

Flight 93 crashed and exploded near Shanksville, Pa., at 10:10. Air Force fighter pilots were under orders to shoot down the airliner if it had come near Washington.[13]

Shortly after the terrorist attack, President Bush addressed Congress and the American people, commending the nation for its valiant response. Singling out "an exceptional man named Todd Beamer,"[14] the President recognized Beamer's young, pregnant widow, Lisa, who was present in the Congressional chamber.

To field the great outpouring of response Lisa received afterward, she began a foundation. "The words of Genesis 50:20 [NIV] have continually come to my mind since September 11th," Lisa Beamer wrote, quoting the Bible, "'You intended to harm me, but God intended it for good to accomplish what is now being done, the saving of many lives.' Todd's sacrifice has already resulted in the saving of many lives. God will use this foundation to continue saving lives," she continued.[15] Do you see the power of one life? Remember, the ripple effect can be so extensive that it reaches beyond one's life span.

Several of the passengers and crew who fought the terrorists aboard United Airlines Flight 93 on September 11, 2001, were originally scheduled to be on different planes. Tom Burnett (1963–2001), Jeremy Glick (1970–2001), and Todd Beamer were among these.[16] Wives Lyz Glick and Lisa Beamer believe their husbands' travel plans changed because they had a higher calling to be on that plane. Regarding this, Lyz Glick explained in a television interview, "I believe that Jeremy was meant for a higher purpose."[17] Although not specifically referring to her husband, Deena Burnett expressed her belief "that God has a plan for each of us."[18]

Believing God had a plan that put her husband on United Flight 93, Lisa Beamer said, "Todd had a more important job to do on that plane than he had to do here....God ultimately has a plan. He takes us where we need to be."[19]

Being in the center of God's will is where you and I need to be—wherever that takes us. No other place is better. Only there can we stand in the gap as God has purposed us. Any cost you must pay to be in His will is well worth it.

All the champions of September 11, 2001, saw a cause worth fighting for. They stood in the gap, physically laying down their lives to save others in the midst of attacks. They paved the way for terrorists to know that America will defend freedom fearlessly and vigorously. We will not allow others to put us into bondage.

This charge is for every one of us today. You and I must champion the cause of freedom, too. However, as Christians, we have an additional dimension to this duty. God has also called us to lay down our lives to save others as spiritual enemies attack them. Maybe you will not have to risk your physical life—or maybe you will—for others' spiritual freedom, but know that God has purposed and equipped you to liberate others from spiritual bondage. You are to stand in the gap for their freedom.

CHAMPION THOUGHT:
"It Takes Only One Bold Individual"

That day, Todd Beamer, the passengers, and crew took a stand that changed the course of history. After interviewing Ervin Staub, who has studied heroism and violence for 30 years, *USA Today* reported:

Unlike on the other three hijacked planes [on September 11, 2001], there is evidence that passengers aboard [Flight] 93 knew that the United States was under attack, not just one plane....Under this scenario, it takes only one bold individual to galvanize others into action, studies by Staub and others show. "One determined person has enormous power here," he says.[20]

Since Todd Beamer is the one who uttered Flight 93's now-famous battle cry, "Let's roll!" he was likely that one.

When Todd Beamer teamed up that day with several individuals, including Jeremy Glick and Tom Burnett, he stood in the gap for a nation and the world. Jeremy's wife, Lyz, summed it up very well when she said, "I think it shows that one person can make a difference, that one person in this country has the opportunity to change this world."[21]

CHAMPION THOUGHT:
In Jesus, You Are the One!

Yes, one person can change the world. By now, you must recognize that this one person is *you*! You might not have the opportunity personally to launch a counterattack against terrorists or leap up the stairwells of a burning building filled with people. However, you can rescue people right where you are and wherever God leads you. Hurting, fearful, bound, and confused people fill this world. They are all around you. Realize that God has given you the power to help them! You can change the world one person at a time.

Remember that God does not require a majority to do exploits. He only needs one to champion His cause. Yes, it really only takes one to make up the hedge and stand in the gap to turn evil into triumph! The greatest example of this is Jesus.

Jesus Christ

When Adam sinned, God sought for One to make up the hedge and stand in the gap for humanity. Remember, Ezekiel said that God could find no one to stand in the gap, so what did He do? The Bible says, *"Therefore He [Jesus] is also able to save to the uttermost those who come to God through Him, since He always lives to make intercession for them"* (Hebrews 7:25).

God sent Jesus as man's Intercessor to stand in the gap and *"once for all"* (Hebrews 10:10) mend the walls of our lives. When Jesus fulfilled His heavenly Father's plan for our salvation, this was the ultimate breakthrough. Now, through Him, all may be saved. The Bible promises:

> *That if you confess with your mouth, "Jesus is Lord," and believe in your heart that God raised him from the dead, you will be saved. For it is with your heart that you believe and are justified, and it is with your mouth that you confess and are saved.* (Romans 10:9–10 NIV)

Because Jesus stood in the gap and paved the way, we can use the above verses to lead multitudes of people to salvation.

Today, we have no excuse; these verses show how anyone can find salvation. Why not make it easy to become saved in your neighborhood and hard to go to hell? Don't make it difficult to go to heaven by expecting people to change *before* they accept Jesus Christ. If you make salvation complicated, you become a gate to keep people out of heaven! Instead, show people that God can save and then change them. You can be the one who brings salvation to your neighborhood. You can be the one to open the door of salvation for your family and others in your sphere of influence.

You see, Jesus uses Christians today to carry out His ministry on the earth. Remember that we are His *"royal priesthood"* (1 Peter 2:9), who intercede for the lost. We are to make up the hedge and stand in the gap for others. God is looking for someone in the human race to take the power of Jesus to the hurting. He has empowered you and every Christian to do the work of His Son on the earth. Jesus said,

> *Most assuredly, I say to you, he who believes in Me, the works that I do he will do also; and greater works than these he will*

do, because I go to My Father. And whatever you ask in My name, that I will do, that the Father may be glorified in the Son. (John 14:12–13)

Champion, are *you* willing to stand in the gap for a lost and dying world? Through the power of Jesus, are you ready to rebuild the wasted places, repair the breach, and restore the lives of the hurting? The world is waiting for you to pave the way! Do not accept a breach.

The Bible declares: *"Some have compassion, making a difference"* (Jude 22). Someone needs to have compassion and make a difference. Someone needs to break through to pave the way for others. Will you do it? Will you press on to break through every line of defense to act as the champion that God created you to be? You can make a difference. Your conviction can change the course of history.

CHAMPION THOUGHT:
Now That You Know the Truth, You Have No More Excuses

Don't say, "I have to figure this out." No, God has given you new champion thoughts about how to do it. His wisdom is always available. You know what to do!

Don't say, "I'll decide what to do." No, you must simply obey God.

Don't say, "I'll do it when my ship comes in." No, all provision will be released when you follow the vision.

Don't say, "Okay, I'll plug myself into God to do this." No, once God's power grabs you, don't let it go!

No longer can you hide behind the lies and excuses of the past. God has shown you His truth. Remember that simply *knowing* the truth sets you free. Therefore, if you have read this book and know God's truths in it, *you are now free!* Walk in Him!

As you therefore have received Christ Jesus the Lord, so walk in Him, having been firmly rooted and now being built up in

Him and established in your faith, just as you were instructed, and overflowing with gratitude. (Colossians 2:6–7 NAS)

CHAMPION THOUGHT:
Release the Gifts That God Has Deposited within You

So what's next? People will come to you with needs and questions. No longer will you be without the answers. You won't have to respond with confusion and doubt. Now, you can give them solutions from God boldly and confidently. Those answers likely will cause you to act in new ways. By faith, you will do things that are unlike anything you have ever done before. You will speak Words from God and incorporate His truths that He has deposited within you.

Remember that God designed you for such a time as this. He has given you gifts that the world needs. One is His nature. You might be unaccustomed to placing a demand on His nature within you, but as you step into your divine purpose, you will need to do this more and more. Remember that God has finished works, which He foreordained for you to walk in. You cannot do these acts in your own strength. These works require you to step out in faith on God's Word, releasing His nature and gifts within you. Only when it is beyond your abilities and strength will God receive all the glory for your breakthroughs. This is how He shows Himself strong.

CHAMPION THOUGHT:
Go with God outside Your Comfort Zone

God sees His deposit within you. Do you see it? What deposit does He want released? Where is it? How does it function? Is it comfortable for you, or is it so far beyond your human abilities that it's outside your comfort zone?

As you release God's deposit from within you, you will find yourself in unfamiliar territory. Living and touching lives as God's champion requires you to move outside your comfort zone. Then, you will not be walking in your own strength. You see, many believers are accustomed to comforts that result from the natural realm and their own strength. They might even think that these are the result of faith. Always remember that if you can do something without God, then it is *you doing it,* not Him! God calls you to act on your faith, knowing that only *He* can do the works. When you operate as God's champion, you will no longer be able to hide in the comfort of your own strength. Instead, you must walk by faith in Him.

When you hear from God and move in Him, you will soar past all negative environments and natural limitations. You see, God is calling you to walk on an entirely different plane of existence, a higher level with greater authority than you have ever known before. Get ready, because you will be living outside your senses—beyond what you can see, taste, hear, touch, and smell. You will be launching out as God enables you by faith—beyond all worldly wisdom. Then, you will break through, paving the way for others' miracles. Thus, you will go from glory to glory.

CHAMPION THOUGHT:
Your Environment Is Ready for an Intervention from God

Realize that God's gifts within you have extraordinary authority and power—beyond the scope of human life. When you encounter other people, look for ways to contribute to their lives by releasing His gifts and truths from within you. Use your faith to step from the natural into the supernatural realm, from the seen into the unseen spiritual arena.

It's time to recognize that your environment is ready for an intervention from God. People need help. Circumstances need to be reversed. The world is looking for answers. What will you do? Will you take that step? Will you speak the Word of God? Will you share His truths? Will you act? Will you respond to God by putting His Word to the test, watching Him perform what He said?

CHAMPION THOUGHT:
Your First Step Engages God's Works

After you take the first step of obedience, it will thrill you to discover that what appeared to be difficult before will be easier than you thought possible. You will be able to speak God's Word in previously intimidating environments. His truths will pour from your mouth as never before. You will find yourself in the midst of breakthroughs and miracles, unsure what you did to get there. You will be stepping into *God's* works. You see, after you take that first step, you engage His finished works. It all hinges on whether you will take that first step, because the works are already finished.

CHAMPION THOUGHT:
Now, It's Your Turn

Personally, I stand with my own testimonies of one breakthrough after another. Now that you have completed *It Only Takes One*, I trust that breakthroughs will also fill your life. As you pave the way for others, God's blessings will overtake you. His Word promises:

> *If you extend your soul to the hungry and satisfy the afflicted soul, then your light shall dawn in the darkness, and your darkness shall be as the noonday. The LORD will guide you continually, and satisfy your soul in drought, and strengthen your bones; you shall be like a watered garden, and like a spring of water, whose waters do not fail.* (Isaiah 58:10–11)

As you grow in the strength of God's nature and character, your individual gifts will come to their full expression. You will begin to fulfill God's purpose for creating you. There is only one you who can fulfill your unique purpose. This is why it only takes one—and that one is you!

God is with you. You already have everything necessary to accomplish your divine purpose. No obstacles can stop you. My life is an example. Multitudes of other individuals have also achieved their divine purpose. Now, it's your turn. The world is waiting for you. Go for it, Champ, in the matchless name of Jesus!

Gary Whetstone Worldwide Ministries

The Great Commission calls us to effect real change, to bring a light to the nations! This light is the message of Jesus Christ and God's love for the world and what motivates us at Gary Whetstone Worldwide Ministries. Below are ways you can become a light to the nations with us!

Prayer Command Centers: These are places and times whereby one or two to any number of people assemble for prayer in houses, at workplaces, in schools, at any place of meeting, or even on the Internet. People spend thirty to forty-five minutes in focused prayer once a week. The purpose is for the people of God to take responsibility in prayer to engage Jesus' authority in the earth. To help you get started, Prayer Command Center Kits are available from your local Christian bookstore.

Churches: Pastor Whetstone invites you to visit the Victory Christian Fellowship churches, based from one of the fastest-growing churches on the U.S. East Coast. You also can watch live on the Internet. Visit today or call for prayer:

Victory Christian Fellowship in Delaware
100 Wilton Blvd., New Castle, DE 19720 U.S.A.
Phone: (302) 324-5400
Victory Christian Fellowship in Baltimore, Maryland
2929 Sollers Point Rd., Dundalk, MD 21222-5355
Phone: (410) 282-6201

Books and the "Life's Answers" Series: Allow the Holy Spirit to educate, liberate, and empower you through Dr. Whetstone's books and "Life's Answers" teaching series! Major topics include empowerment, freedom, family and relationships, finances, and prayer. Many of these materials are available as books, eBooks, audio cassettes, audio CDs, video CD-ROMs, video cassettes, and VCDs.

School of Biblical Studies: The School of Biblical Studies, a video Bible school, is a time-proven program that trains champions to live far above ordinary lives. Whether you take one course or the entire curriculum to pursue your degree, you will walk in greater knowledge of who you are as a child of God.

You may choose to study at home through the audio/video Extension School or attend one of the more than 360 Branch School locations worldwide. Since 1986, more than twenty thousand students have graduated in more than thirty countries. The first three classes of the School of Biblical Studies course *Your Liberty in Christ* is available on a free CD-ROM ($60 value) in the back of Gary V. Whetstone's book *Your Liberty in Christ.*

Internet Ministry: Our web site at www.gwwm.com is a fountain of spiritual wisdom. Wherever you have access to the web, you have access to our ministry, twenty-four hours a day, seven days a week! Put Gary Whetstone Worldwide Ministries at your fingertips!

For more information, visit our web site at www.gwwm.com, E-mail info@gwwm.com, call (302) 324-5400, or (800) 383-4223, fax (302) 324-5448, or write Gary Whetstone Worldwide Ministries, P.O. Box 10050, Wilmington, DE 19850 U.S.A.

About the Author

Gary V. Whetstone is the senior pastor and founder of Victory Christian Fellowship in New Castle, Delaware, and founder of Gary Whetstone Worldwide Ministries. He holds an earned doctorate in Religious Education.

Since personally experiencing God's miraculous deliverance and healing in 1971, Dr. Whetstone has devoted his life to helping others experience freedom through God's Word. Today, he ministers around the world in churches, seminars, and evangelistic crusades. Gifted in teaching, Dr. Whetstone provides practical biblical instruction wherever he ministers and has seen God work powerful signs, wonders, and miracles. Hundreds of thousands have become born-again, Spirit-filled, healed, and set free.

Having a great burden to minister to the local community, Pastor Gary V. Whetstone and his church have launched life-changing outreaches in several areas. These include HIV/AIDS; substance and alcohol abuse; inner-city community outreach centers; Saturday Sidewalk Sunday school; food and clothing outreach programs; and many large evangelistic campaigns, such as the dramatic production "Jesus, Light of the World," which draws over forty-five thousand people annually.

Desiring to spread the truth and good news of the Gospel throughout the world, Dr. Whetstone's passion is to see the Word of God cover the world as the seas cover the earth. This vision is being accomplished through many ministry outreaches. These include sending mission and evangelism teams around the globe;

radio and television broadcasting; ministry through the Internet; and the School of Biblical Studies. An extensive audio and video training program, this school equips Christians to experience God's presence and to understand the Bible. In addition to local church and international branch locations, the School of Biblical Studies is available to individuals by extension in their homes using audio cassettes, videotapes, CDs, CD-ROMs, and VCDs. Currently, this home-study program is in English but soon will be available in Spanish and other languages.

Gary V. Whetstone has appeared on many national and international radio and television programs, and has authored key books, among which are *The Victorious Walk, How to Identify and Remove Curses!, Make Fear Bow, Millionaire Mentality, Your Liberty in Christ*, and his personal testimony of miraculous deliverance and healing in *Conquering Your Unseen Enemies.* The large number of study guides he has produced are testaments to his gifting in practical biblical teaching and are available for use with his numerous video and audio teaching series.

God has gifted Dr. Whetstone with an incredible business sense and ability, enabling him to publish a series of teachings from *Purchasing and Negotiations* to *Success in Business* and *Millionaire Mentality*, which have aired on his radio and television programs, called "Life's Answers."

Dr. Whetstone and Faye, his wife of more than 30 years, have a particularly dynamic testimony of a restored marriage, which achieved national attention and was the cover story in *Charisma* magazine. Gary and Faye now conduct annual Marriage Advance seminars for couples looking to enrich their relationships deeply.

Their two adult children, Eric and Laurie, along with daughter-in-law Rebecca, grandsons Isaiah and Carmine, and son-in-law Feb Idahosa, are involved actively in local and international outreaches for Jesus Christ.

Notes

Chapter 1: Unlock Your Future with One New Thought

[1] *Random House Webster's Unabridged Dictionary*, 2nd ed., s.v. "authority."

Chapter 2: God Awakens You—His Champion

[1] W. E. Vine, *The Expanded Vine's Expository Dictionary of New Testament Words* (Minneapolis: Bethany House Publishers, 1984), s.v. "righteousness."

[2] Ibid.,s.v. "inferior."

[3] *Random House Webster's Unabridged Dictionary*, 2nd ed., s.v. "guilt."

[4] Ibid., s.v. "condemn."

[5] For more in-depth teaching on righteousness, please refer to my book *Your Liberty in Christ*. A course by the same title is available in the School of Biblical Studies.

[6] Trent C. Butler, ed., *Holman Bible Dictionary* (Nashville: Holman Bible Publishers, 1991), s.v. "Abram."

Chapter 3: Behold His Masterpiece in the Mirror

[1] *Compton's Interactive Encyclopedia Deluxe* (The Learning Company, 1998), s.v. "Bell, Alexander Graham."

[2] William J. Federer, ed., *America's God and Country Encyclopedia of Quotations* (Coppell, TX: Fame Publishing, 1996), 131–132.

[3] Catherine Millard, *The Rewriting of America's History* (Camp Hill, PA: Horizon House Publishers, 1991), 2.

[4] Gary De Mar, *God and Government: A Biblical and Historical Study*, vol. 1 (Atlanta: American Vision Press, 1982), 126.

[5] James Strong, *Strong's Hebrew and Greek Dictionaries* (Cedar Rapids: Parsons Technology, 1996), G2564.

[6] Ibid., G2753.

Chapter 4: Forward Momentum

[1] *Compton's Interactive Encyclopedia*, s.v. "Bannister, Roger."

[2] Ibid.

[3] Eddie L. Hyatt, *2000 Years of Charismatic Christianity* (Lake Mary, FL: Charisma House, 2002), 137.

[4] Stanley M. Burgess and Gary B. McGee, eds., *Dictionary of Pentecostal and Charismatic Movements* (Grand Rapids: Zondervan Publishing House, 1988), s.v. "Parham, Charles Fox," 660.

[5] Hyatt, *2000 Years*, 138.

[6] Ibid.

[7] Burgess and McGee, eds., *Dictionary*, s.v. "Parham, Charles Fox," 660.

[8] Hyatt, *2000 Years*, 138–139.

[9] Ibid., 143.

[10] Burgess and McGee, eds., *Dictionary*, s.v. "Azusa Street Revival," 35.

[11] Ibid., s.v. "The Pentecostal and Charismatic Movements," 3.

[12] Ibid., s.v. "Charismatic Movement," 130.

[13] Ibid., s.v. "The Pentecostal and Charismatic Movements," 3.

[14] Hyatt, *2000 Years*, 178.

[15] Ibid., 179.

[16] Burgess and McGee, eds., *Dictionary*, s.v. "The Pentecostal and Charismatic Movements," 3.

Chapter 5: Just Step Out

[1] Charles Osborne, ed., *1969: The Year in Review* (New York: Time-Life Books, 1970), 180–181.

[2] Ibid.

[3] For more information about the authority of the believer, please see my book *Conquering Your Unseen Enemies* and "Life's Answers" tape series entitled *Victory in Spiritual Warfare*, available at bookstores and carried by Whitaker House.

[4] "The 'Ripple Effect' of Mr. Kimball's Sunday School Lesson in 1855," Koenig's International News <http://www.watch.org/articles.html> (5 June 2000). The origin of this story may be from Joseph M. Stowell's *Following Christ: Experiencing Life the Way It Was Meant to Be* (Grand Rapids: Zondervan, 1996), 130–131.

[5] "Biographies: Billy Graham." Billy Graham Evangelistic Association <http://www.billygraham.org/about/billygraham.asp> (30 September 2002).

[6] George W. Bush, *A Charge to Keep* (New York: William Morrow and Company, 1999), 136.

Chapter 6: Break through Every Barrier

[1] *Compton's Interactive Encyclopedia*, s.v. "Plagues and Epidemics."

[2] *The New Bible Dictionary*, (Wheaton, IL: Tyndale House Publishers, 1962), s.v. "quarantine."

[3] *Taber's Cyclopedic Medical Dictionary*, 16th ed., s.v. "AIDS."

[4] *Compton's Interactive Encyclopedia*, s.v. "Columbus, Christopher."

[5] *The American Heritage Dictionary of the English Language*, 3rd ed., s.v. "Nobel Prize."

[6] *Compton's Interactive Encyclopedia*, s.v. "Nobel, Alfred."

[7] DeMar, *God and Government*, 126.

[8] John Dewan, "The Mark McGwire/Sammy Sosa Home Run Chase," STATS, 1998.

[9] "McGwire Hits 70th Homer, Sosa Settles for RBI Crown," JERSEY CITY, New Jersey (Ticker): SportsTicker Enterprises, L.P., 28 September 1998.

[10] Mike Kaiser, "Mark McGwire Central, Run for 70?" *St. Louis Post Dispatch* online, 19 October 1998.

[11] Jim Henzler, "Stats Focus," STATS, 1998.

[12] DeMar, *God and Government*, 126.

Chapter 7: Make Resistance Work for You

[1] Dick DeVos, *Rediscovering American Values* (New York: Dutton, 1997). 7.

[2] Strong, *Strong's Hebrew and Greek Dictionaries*, G4964.

[3] *Compton's Interactive Encyclopedia*, s.v. "Aviation."

[4] Strong, *Strong's Hebrew and Greek Dictionaries*, G3339.

[5] Ibid., G342.

Chapter 8: The Driving Force of a Dreamer

[1] For more information about this part of my life and the topic of spiritual warfare, see my book *Conquering Your Unseen Enemies*, available at bookstores and carried by Whitaker House.

[2] *Random House Webster's Unabridged Dictionary*, 2nd ed., s.v. "let."

[3] *Gulliver's Travels Notes* (Lincoln: Cliff's Notes, 1969), 23.

[4] *Random House Webster's Unabridged Dictionary*, 2nd ed., s.v. "pro-."

[5] <http://www.amway.com/ourstory/o-hist.asp> and <http://www.amway.com/ourstory/o-headaerial.asp> (11 November 2002).

[6] Rich De Vos, *Compassionate Capitalism* (New York: Plume, 1994), 250–251.

[7] Jay Van Andel, *An Enterprising Life* (New York: Harper Business, 1998), 53.

Chapter 9: Focus on the Finish

[1] Marisela Maddox, David Mark, and Andrew Fox, "Nice Guys Finish First: Watching Two Exceptional Characters Rewrite Baseball History: Approaching the Record," *World*, 19 September 1998, 26.

[2] "Sosa Named NL MVP," *Dallas Morning News*, 20 November 1998, 1.

[3] Gerry Fraley, "Sosa Wins MVP by a Long Shot," *Dallas Morning News*, 20 November 1998, 9B.

[4] Maddox, Mark, and Fox, "Nice Guys Finish First," 26.

[5] Ibid.

[6] To learn more about setting goals and value-driven priorities, see my "Life's Answers" teaching series entitled *Success in Business*.

[7] "McGwire Hits 70th Homer, Sosa Settles for RBI Crown," JERSEY CITY, New Jersey (Ticker): SportsTicker Enterprises, L.P., 28 September 1998.

Chapter 10: The Master Multiplier

[1] Rich DeVos, *Compassionate Capitalism* (New York: Plume, 1994), 24.

[2] Ibid., 242.

[3] Ibid., 243.

[4] *Compton's Interactive Encyclopedia*, s.v. "Gates, William III."

[5] Norris and Ross McWhirter, *Guinness Book of Records*, 10th ed. (New York: Sterling Publishing Company, 1971), 549.

[6] Microsoft Encarta Encyclopedia 2002 (Microsoft Corporation, 2001), s.v. "Bonds, Barry Lamar."

[7] John Glenn, "Why We Must Venture into Space," *Dallas Morning News Parade*, 25 October 1998, 7.

[8] Burgess and McGee, *Dictionary*, s.v. "The Pentecostal and Charismatic Movements," 130–131.

[9] *Compton's Interactive Encyclopedia*, s.v. "Franklin Delano Roosevelt."

[10] John Ritter and Tom Kenworthy; Alan Levin, contributor, "Passengers Likely Halted Attack on D.C." *USA Today*, 17 September 2001 <http://www.usatoday.com/news/nation/2001/09/16/flight193.htm#more> (23 August 2002).

[11] Edward E. Plowman, "'Jesus, Help Me': Heroic Passengers May Have Thwarted a 4th Suicide Attack; Last Words Caught on Cell Call," *World* Magazine, 29 September 2001 <http://www.worldmag.com./world/issue/09-29-01/opening_1.asp> (23 August 2002).

[12] Carl Limbacher, "Cheney: Hero Passengers Foiled Terror Attack on Washington," NewsMax.com, 16 September 2001 <http://www.newsmax.com/archives/articles/2001/9/16/120749.shtml> (23 August 2002).

[13] Plowman, "'Jesus, Help Me,'" (23 August 2002).

[14] "President Bush's Address to Congress and the American People," NewsMax.com, 20 September 2001 <http://www.newsmax.com/archives/articles/2001/9/21/02114.shtml> (23 August 2002).

[15] "A Message from Lisa Beamer and Family" <http://www.beamerfoundation.org> (15 April 2002).

[16] The following sources were used to compile the information regarding the changes in flight for the three men mentioned: *Reader's Digest*, September 2002, 160–161; Ritter and Kenworthy; Levin, contributor, "Passengers Likely Halted Attack on D.C." (22 August 2002); Angie Cannon, Janet Rae-Dupree, Suzie Larsen, and Cynthia Salter, "Final Words from Flight 93," *U.S. News & World Report*, 29 October 2001.

[17] "A Heroic Last Stand" Dateline NBC's interview by Jane Pauley, 14 September 2001 <http://www.msnbc.com/news/629077.asp> (23 August 2002).

[18] "Deena Burnett: On a Mission," Dateline NBC's interview by Maria Shriver, 20 August 2002 <http://www.msnbc.com/news/796178.asp> (22 August 2002).

[19] Marilyn Elias, "Widow of Sept. 11 Hero Carries On." *USA Today* (21 November 2001) <http://www.usatoday.com/life/2001-11-21-lisa-beamer.htm> (18 April 2002).

[20] ———, "Sept. 11 showed Americans what we're made of" *USA Today* <http://www.usatoday.com/life/2001-11-21-heros.htm> (23 August 2002).

[21] John Ritter and Tom Kenworthy; Alan Levin, cont., "Passengers likely halted attack on D.C." USA Today 17 Sept. 2001 <http://www.usatoday.com/news/nation/2001/09/16/flight193.htm#more> (22 August 2002).

Other Books and Cassettes by Dr. Gary V. Whetstone
DISTRIBUTED BY WHITAKER HOUSE AND
AVAILABLE THROUGH YOUR LOCAL CHRISTIAN BOOKSTORE

BOOKS

Conquering Your Unseen Enemies
    Trade Paper   ISBN: 0-96644-622-4
    Spanish version   ISBN: 0-96644-626-7
How to Identify and Remove Curses
    Hardcover   ISBN: 0-96644-624-0
    Trade Paper   ISBN: 0-96644-621-6
    Spanish version   ISBN: 0-96644-625-9
Make Fear Bow
    Trade Paper   ISBN: 0-88368-776-3
Millionaire Mentality
    Hardcover   ISBN: 1-92877-406-7
    Trade Paper   ISBN: 1-92877-401-6
    Spanish version   ISBN: 1-92877-402-4
The Victorious Walk
    Trade Paper   ISBN: 0-96644-620-8
    Spanish version   ISBN: 0-96644-629-1
Your Liberty in Christ (book & CD)
    Trade Paper (w/ CD)   ISBN: 1-58866-254-3

LIFE'S ANSWERS TEACHING SERIES
(AUDIO CASSETTES)

Assignment against the Church   ISBN: 0-88368-894-8
Freedom from Insecurity and Inferiority   ISBN: 0-88368-895-6
God's Covenant with Your Family   ISBN: 0-88368-896-4
How to Fight for Your Family   ISBN: 0-88368-897-2
Millionaire Mentality   ISBN: 0-88368-898-0
Mobilizing Believers   ISBN: 0-88368-899-9
Purchasing and Negotiations   ISBN: 0-88368-900-6
The Power of God's Prophetic Purpose   ISBN: 0-88368-901-4
Prayer Command Centers   ISBN: 0-88368-902-2
The Prevailing Power of Prayer   ISBN: 0-88368-903-0
Success in Business   ISBN: 0-88368-904-9
True Success: How to Find the Field
    God Has Planted for You   ISBN: 0-88368-905-7
The Unshakable Foundation   ISBN: 0-88368-906-5
Victory in Spiritual Warfare   ISBN: 0-88368-907-3
What God Has Joined Together   ISBN: 0-88368-908-1

OTHER POWERFUL Books

from Whitaker House

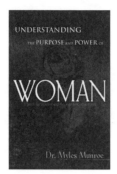

Understanding the Purpose and Power of Woman
Dr. Myles Munroe

To live successfully in the world, women need to know who they are and what role they play today. They need a new awareness of who they are, and new skills to meet today's challenges. Myles Munroe helps women to discover who they are. Whether you are a woman or a man, married or single, this book will help you to understand the woman as she was meant to be.

ISBN: 0-88368-671-6 • Trade • 208 pages

Understanding the Purpose and Power of Men
Dr. Myles Munroe

Today, the world is sending out conflicting signals about what it means to be a man. Many men are questioning who they are and what roles they fulfill in life—as a male, a husband, and a father. Best-selling author Myles Munroe examines cultural attitudes toward men and discusses the purpose God has given them. Discover the destiny and potential of the man as he was meant to be.

ISBN: 0-88368-725-9 • Trade • 224 pages

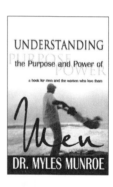

Understanding the Purpose and Power of Prayer
Dr. Myles Munroe

All that God is—and all that God has—may be received through prayer. Everything you need to fulfill your purpose on earth is available to you through prayer. The biblically-based, time-tested principles presented here will ignite and transform the way you pray. Be prepared to enter into a new dimension of faith, a deeper revelation of God's love, and a renewed understanding that your prayers can truly move the finger of God.

ISBN: 0-88368-442-X • Trade • 240 pages